Giuseppe Verdi

# LETTERS

## OF

# GIUSEPPE VERDI

*Selected, translated, and edited by*

CHARLES OSBORNE

HOLT, RINEHART AND WINSTON
New York   Chicago   San Francisco

First published in the United States in 1972

Library of Congress Catalog Card Number: 79-138896

ISBN: 0-03-086007-5

First Edition

Printed in Great Britain

# Contents

# List of Illustrations

# Editor's Note

The main single published source of information about Verdi is the volume called *I copialettere*. (The Italian word means 'letter book' and is the same in singular and plural.) The original *copialettere* (plural) are five large scribbling-books bound in cardboard, in which Verdi used to keep copies of his correspondence. He began the first notebook in 1844, at the age of thirty, immediately after the production of his fifth opera, *Ernani*, and he continued, with gaps, to enter copies of letters in this and the four further books, or to have copies entered by his wife Giuseppina, for nearly sixty years. The last entry is dated a few days prior to his death in January, 1901. These books contain not only drafts of letters by Verdi to his publishers, librettists, opera managements, conductors and agents, but also a good many letters received from his correspondents, as well as notes about accounts, loans and business expenses. Most of these 'copies' of letters are, in fact, first drafts, and contain a certain amount of alteration and addition, some of which is in Giuseppina's hand.

In 1913, twelve years after Verdi's death, these notebooks were published in Italy in one huge volume, as *I copialettere di Giuseppe Verdi*, edited by Gaetano Cesari and Alessandro Luzio. This volume consisted not only of the contents of each original *copialettere* but also of hundreds of supporting documents and letters, quoted in footnotes or contained in an appendix which occupied almost as much space as the letters in the five original *copialettere*.

Since 1913, many more Verdi letters have been published in Italy. Alessandro Luzio, for instance, went on to edit four volumes of *Carteggi Verdiani* containing letters by both Verdi and Giuseppina. But the prime source remains the *Copialettere* publication of 1913, and it is from this volume that I have made my selection. In doing so, however, I have by no means felt obliged to confine myself to the letters in the original five *copialettere*, but have ranged freely through Cesari and Luzio's book, and have chosen many letters from their appendix, and one or two from their footnotes. Thus, I have availed myself fully of their valuable and exhaustive researches. I have not, however, taken over the Italian editors' footnotes: I have rearranged the letters into strict chronological order, and have, where I thought it necessary, added notes of my own on the recipients, the people mentioned, or the general background and circumstances. In the letters, the use of dots [. . .] does not, as is usual, indicate the omission of words. Verdi used dots the way some people use dashes.

I have been greatly helped by Mrs Teresa Du Gard and Mr Kenneth Thomson.

# Introduction

Italy's greatest composer, and one of the three most admired and loved writers of opera in the history of music (the others are Mozart and Wagner), was born into an illiterate inn-keeper's family in a village called Le Roncole in the north of Italy on 10 October, 1813. As a child he revealed unexpected inclinations towards music, so strongly that he was allowed to have lessons from the village organist. By the time he was twelve, Giuseppe Verdi was himself playing the organ in the little church at Le Roncole on Sundays. The weekdays he spent at the nearby town of Busseto where he continued his musical studies as part of his school curriculum. A man named Barezzi, a merchant, leading citizen and amateur musician in Busseto, befriended young Verdi, took him to live in his house and encouraged him to cherish ambitions well beyond the humble class into which he had been born. In his middle teens, Verdi began to compose songs and orchestral pieces for the local Philharmonic Society, music which was impressive enough to convince his benefactor that the lad should be sent to Milan to study for the career of a professional musician. At Barezzi's instigation, Verdi's father applied to a charitable institution for a scholarship for his son. The application was successful, and the amount was added to by Barezzi. Verdi was refused entrance to the Milan Conservatorium on the ground that he was above the age-limit of fourteen, but he studied privately in Milan for some years, returned to Busseto and married Barezzi's daughter Margherita, and wrote his first opera, *Oberto*. (He may have written an earlier one called *Rocester*, but it has not come to light and was in any case never performed.) *Oberto* was produced at Italy's leading opera house, La Scala, Milan, in 1839, a few weeks after Verdi's twenty-sixth birthday.

By the time *Oberto* was staged, Verdi had had his first taste of personal tragedy. His two children had died in infancy. While he was at work on his second opera, his wife died. In a state of despair and nervous exhaustion he completed the work, a comic opera called *Un giorno di regno* which was booed at its first performance and was hastily withdrawn. Embittered by misfortune and failure, Verdi decided to give up music, and was only with great difficulty coaxed by the Scala impresario into embarking upon a third opera. Fortunately *Nabucco* was an enormous success, and from that moment the composer's future was assured. He was, of course, to have his ups and downs, but there was no doubt that Donizetti's successor had been found. The melodic fecundity, dramatic energy and, as it seemed to his audiences, patriotic fervour of Verdi's operas from *Nabucco* onwards, ensured their popularity. *I Lombardi* and *Ernani* were followed by *I due Foscari* and *Giovanna d'Arco*: the subjects came from Tommaso Grossi, Victor Hugo, Lord Byron and Friedrich Schiller. Commissions to compose operas were lavished on Verdi from opera houses throughout Italy and also from abroad. Verdi himself was later to refer to this period of his life as his years in the galleys. A new opera was expected of him every few months. Eight months, for instance, separate *Ernani* and *I due Foscari*. Three months later came *Giovanna d'Arco*, and, six months after that, *Alzira* which Verdi later said was 'really ugly'. The 'galley years' did, in fact, produce some fine operas, among them *Macbeth* (1847) and *Luisa Miller* (1849), but it was not until the three indisputably great works which followed one another between 1851 and 1853, *Rigoletto*, *Il trovatore* and *La traviata*, that Verdi felt able to relax and to work at a less hectic pace. His middle period can properly be said to have begun with *Rigoletto*. By this time he had purchased property at Sant'Agata, near Busseto, and was living with Giuseppina Strepponi who had sung in the first performances of *Nabucco*, and whom he was eventually to marry in 1859.

Verdi's position as the leading Italian composer, Rossini having lapsed into silence and Donizetti having died insane, was consolidated with the operas of his middle-age, in particular *Un ballo in maschera* (1859) and *La forza del destino* (1862). His last and greatest period was ushered in with *Aida* (1871). By this time, Verdi was a wealthy man, and more concerned with philanthropy and farming than with continuing to produce operas. He considered himself retired after *Aida*, yet there were still three masterpieces to come from him: the *Requiem* (1874), *Otello* (1887) and finally, in his eightieth year, *Falstaff* (1893). In these last two operas, he collaborated with his finest librettist, the composer and poet, Arrigo Boito. He was in his eighty-eighth year when he died on January 27, 1901. When his coffin was borne through the streets of Milan to the Musicians' Rest Home which he had endowed, two hundred thousand people lined the black-draped streets to say farewell.

The greatest artists are not always the most admirable characters, nor do the most upright and honourable of men necessarily turn out also to be those with the finest artistic talent. But Verdi was a great man. It was not easy in early nineteenth-century Italy for a child from a poor family to step out of his class, to make the most intelligent use imaginable of the meagre education available to him and to supplement it by his own curiosity about the world, yet he managed to do it. He managed in the process, which is surely even more difficult, to retain his humanity and warmth throughout a long life, and always to act honourably and fairly. True, he was a creature of moods, and he could often be gruff and testy in manner. He was also by temperament inclined to melancholy, a sceptic and a pessimist. But his gift for friendship was real, and survived many trials. His loyalty to his friends and to the standards of behaviour he set himself never faltered. An ardent supporter of the liberal cause in the *risorgimento*, he worshipped human greatness in men. His god was Shakespeare. The only saint in his calendar, he once said, was Manzoni, the great writer and patriot in whose memory he composed the *Requiem*. His enemies were hypocrisy, mediocrity, pretentiousness, and the clergy.

Verdi's character and personality are revealed clearly in his letters; for, although his formal education was not impressive, he read a great deal in Italian and French, his range of reference was extensive, and he expressed himself with directness and ease. To his publishers he could be terse and businesslike, to his librettists frequently blunt and demanding, but to his friends the tone of voice can become more yielding. Always, there is the utmost sincerity in his utterance. 'The word "intrigue" does not exist in my dictionary', he wrote indignantly to a politician who had accused him of having plotted to be nominated as Deputy in the first Italian Parliament. Highly articulate, he wrote as he spoke and acted: with pride, perhaps even with stubbornness, but also with integrity and vigour.

The letters of Verdi have been widely drawn upon by his biographers, and several in this volume are therefore already known in at least partial English translation. Many more, however, appear here in English for the first time. They cover the greater part of the composer's long life, from the age of thirty through more than half a century to within a few days of his death at the age of eighty-seven.

*The Letters*

*To Ignazio Marini, Barcelona*                    *Milan, 11 June, 1843*

[The popular bass, Ignazio Marini, had sung the title rôle in *Oberto*, Verdi's first opera to be produced, at the Teatro alla Scala, Milan, in 1839. The new opera to which Verdi refers, which was first performed at the Teatro la Fenice, Venice, on 9 March, 1844, was his fifth, *Ernani*. The rôle of Silva would have been suitable for Marini, but it was performed by Antonio Selva. Marini's next Verdi première was to be in 1846, when he sang the title rôle in *Attila* at the Fenice.

Although he did not create the rôle of Silva in *Ernani*, Marini did take it into his repertoire. He was the Silva in the first English performances of *Ernani* at Covent Garden in 1847, when the baritone rôle of Don Carlo was sung by a contralto, Marietta Alboni, the baritone originally engaged having found it too high.

At the time of this letter, Marini had been singing abroad, in Barcelona.]

It gives me great pleasure to hear that you are coming back to us, and I am sure the Milanese will greet their favourite bass with rapture. I have lately written two operas, *Nabucco* and *I Lombardi*, with rôles in which I expect you to excel. Both the Prophet in *Nabucco* and Pagano in *I Lombardi* seem as though written for you, and indeed I must say I have the greatest desire to hear you in them. I shall write something for the Carnival season in Venice, because I don't want to take the risk of writing another opera for Milan at the moment, which is why I have had to refuse all the kind offers Merelli[1] has made me. We shall meet in the future, and I shall consider it a rare fortune to be able to write an opera for an artist such as yourself. You may be sure I shall give you a rôle worthy of you.

[1] Bartolomeo Merelli, at that time impresario of La Scala, who had been responsible for presenting Verdi's first four operas: *Oberto*, *Un giorno di regno*, *Nabucco* and *I Lombardi*. *Oberto* had been reasonably successful, *Un giorno di regno* a complete failure. The following two operas had been immense successes, but Verdi evidently did not want to push his recent luck at La Scala too far.

[2]

*To Giuseppe Cavalieri, Ferrara*                    *Venice, 12 December, 1843*

[In Venice to direct rehearsals of *I Lombardi*, which had had its première in Milan in February, 1843, and to produce his new opera, *Ernani*, Verdi experienced considerable difficulties with his prima donna, the German soprano, Sophie Loewe, who was to sing in both operas.

This letter was written by Verdi to an acquaintance in Ferrara at an early stage in the rehearsals of *I Lombardi*.]

Venice is beautiful, it's poetic, it's divine, but . . . . . . . . I wouldn't stay here voluntarily. My *Ernani* is progressing, and the librettist is doing everything that I ask. I am having two rehearsals of *I Lombardi* every day, and all of them are doing the best they can, above all la Loewe.

The first time we encountered each other was at the first rehearsal of *I Lombardi*: we exchanged the fewest possible words of greeting, and that was the end of that: I haven't been to visit her yet, nor do I expect to unless I have to. However, I can only speak well of her, for she works very conscientiously, with not the slightest trace of capriciousness.

Laugh if you want to, but I shall be back in Milan as soon as *Ernani* gets on to the stage.

[3]

*To Giuseppina Appiani, Milan   Venice, 26 December, 1843, an hour after*
*midnight*

[Giuseppina Appiani, born the Countess Strigelli, was the widow of a son of the painter Andrea Appiani. Her husband had committed suicide, leaving her with a family of six children. Her salon in Milan was much frequented by artists and musicians: she had befriended both Bellini and Donizetti. It was in her house that Bellini composed the greater part of *La sonnambula* in 1830, and Donizetti *Lucia di Lammermoor* in 1842. Verdi's friendship with Signora Appiani, who was about forty-five years of age when he first made her acquaintance, continued until 1854 when it was abruptly terminated (see letter No. 85).

This letter was written immediately after the first night of *I Lombardi* in Venice. But, at its première in Milan eleven months earlier, the opera had been immensely successful.]

You are impatient to hear the news of *I Lombardi*, so I hasten to speed it to you: it's not a quarter of an hour since the curtain fell.

*I Lombardi* was a great fiasco: one of the really classic fiascos. Everything was disapproved of, or just tolerated, with the exception of the cabaletta of the vision. That is the simple truth which I relate to you with neither pleasure nor sorrow.

[4]

*To Giuseppina Appiani*　　　　　　　　　　*Venice, 10 March, 1844*

[This letter was written the day after the première of *Ernani* in Venice. During the rehearsal period, the soprano, Sophie Loewe, had made it known that she disapproved of Verdi's ending the opera with a trio. She had already suffered such an ending in *I Lombardi*, but was used to appearing in operas which ended with a brilliant cabaletta for the prima donna, and she actually ordered Piave to provide the words for one, which that compliant librettist did. Verdi, however, was adamant, and ordered Piave to throw the cabaletta away. Madame Loewe gave in unwillingly, and from then on her relations with Verdi were extremely strained.

Verdi and his prima donna made up their quarrel several months later, and in 1846 the composer chose her again to create a new rôle, that of Odabella in *Attila*.]

*Ernani*, performed last night, was a pleasant enough success. If I had had singers who were, I won't say sublime, but at least able to sing in tune, it would have gone as well as *Nabucco* and *I Lombardi* did in Milan. Guasco had no voice at all, and was so hoarse it was frightening. It is impossible to sing more out of tune than la Loewe did last night. Every number, big or small, was applauded with the exception of Guasco's cavatina; but the most effective pieces of all were Loewe's cabaletta, the cabaletta of a duet that ends as a trio, the whole of the first act finale, the whole of the conspiracy act, and the trio of the fourth act. They took three curtain calls after the first act, one after the second, three after the third, and three or four at the end of the opera. That's the true story.

Within the week, I shall be in Milan.

[5]

*To Vincenzo Flauto, Naples*                          *Milan, 21 March, 1844*

[Vincenzo Flauto was the impresario of the Teatro di San Carlo, Naples, and of the Teatro Massimo. Salvatore Cammarano (see note to letter 8) wrote four libretti for Verdi, beginning with *Alzira*, the opera referred to in this letter.]

It's true, the advantage of writing an opera to the words of that famous poet Signor Cammarano, and with those performers, also the boost to the reputation of any good composer of being asked to write for the Teatro Massimo, all add up to ensuring that I lose no time in accepting the offer you make me, on the following conditions:

1. The management will pay me 550 (five hundred and fifty) gold napoleons of 20 francs each, payable in three equal instalments: the first when I arrive on the spot, the second at the first orchestral rehearsal, and the third on the day immediately following the first performance.

2. The management will forward to me in Milan Signor Cammarano's libretto by the end of the present year, 1844.

3. I shall not be obliged to put the opera on the stage before the end of June.

4. The singers will be chosen by me from the resident company, so long as the company includes Tadolini, Fraschini and Coletti.[1]

With sincere respects,

Yours,
Verdi.

[6]

*To Francesco Piave*                                *Milan, 12 April, 1844*

[Francesco Maria Piave's first libretto for Verdi had been *Ernani*. He was to provide nine more, but *Attila*, to which this letter refers, was not one of them. When the time came for the opera to be written, Verdi decided that the gentle Piave was not the right person for the subject, and instead gave it to Cammarano.

[1] *Alzira* had its première at the Teatro di San Carlo on 12 August, 1845, with a cast headed by the three singers Verdi stipulates in Clause 4: Tadolini, Fraschini and Coletti (see *Personalia* for notes on these singers).

Piave (1811–1876) was born in Venice, and originally studied for the law. He became attracted to the theatre, and when Verdi met him he was resident poet and stage manager at the Fenice Theatre, Venice.

Zacharias Werner (1768–1823) was a minor German playwright and disciple of Goethe. His play, *Attila, König der Hunnen*, is a romantic tragedy in five acts.

Mme de Staël (1766–1817) wrote her important treatise on romanticism and German culture, *De l'Allemagne*, in 1810.

*I due Foscari, Giovanna d'Arco* and *Alzira* were to be written and produced by Verdi before *Attila*, which had its première in Venice in March, 1846.]

Here is the synopsis of Werner's tragedy. There are some magnificent things in it, and it is full of good effects. Read Madame de Staël's *De l'Allemagne*.

It seems to me there should be a prologue and three acts. We must raise the curtain on the burning of the town of Aquileia, with a chorus of townsfolk and of Huns. The people pray, the Huns threaten them etc. etc. Then Ildegonda appears, then Attila etc. and the prologue ends.

I should like to begin the first act in Rome, and, instead of having a scene of festivity, show an interior scene with Azzio meditating on the future etc. We could end the first act with Ildegonda giving Attila the poisoned goblet, which Attila thinks she does for love of him, but which she really does in order to avenge the deaths of her father and brothers etc.

It would be marvellous, in the third act, to have the whole of the scene with Leo on the Aventine, with the battle raging. But this may not be allowed,[1] so we must try to conceal the point as best we can. This is how the scene should go, however.

I don't like the finale of the fourth act, but I shall think about it and see if I can come up with something better. You think about it, as well as me.

The three main characters are wonderful: Attila, who must not be altered in any way; Ildegonda, a beautiful character who wants to avenge her parents, brothers and lover; Azzio is handsome, and I like his duet with Attila when they propose to divide up the world. We need to invent a fourth character, and I think this could be Gualtiero, who thinks Ildegonda is dead, who flees, and who can be used among the Huns or among the Romans. He can have one or two fine scenes with Ildegonda. He could perhaps be in the scene of the poisoning, but above all in the fourth act, when he learns that Ildegonda wants to kill

---

[1] The reference is to the political censorship.

Attila. I don't want Azzio to die first, as I need him in the fourth act with Ildegonda etc.

It seems to me that this could be a really fine work and, if you give it serious study, you will do a really beautiful libretto. But you must take care with it. I shall send you the original Werner play in a few days, and you must have it translated, for there are passages of tremendous power in it. In short, make use of everything you can, but do a good job. Above all, read De Staël's *De l'Allemagne*, which will throw great light on it for you. If you can find the original Werner play in Venice, that will save me some trouble. Let me know.

I advise you to study this subject thoroughly, and to keep everything well in mind: the period, the characters etc. etc. Then make your sketch, but in detail, scene by scene, with all the characters, so that all you have then to do is turn it into verse. That way you will encounter less difficulty. Read Werner, especially the choruses which are magnificent.

[7]

*To Francesco Maria Piave, Venice*                         *Milan, 22 May, 1844*

[This letter refers to *I due Foscari* which Verdi and Piave wrote for the Teatro Argentina, Rome, where it was given its première on 3 November, 1844. It was based on Lord Byron's play, *The Two Foscari*.

Giovanni Pacini (1796–1867) composed 73 operas, of which *Saffo* was the most successful. His *Lorenzino di Medici*, with libretto by Piave, was produced in Venice in 1845.]

I have already sent the outline to Rome, and hope they will approve of it. Nevertheless, you can stop work for the time being because I have plenty of other things to do. So think carefully, and try to continue as you have begun. So far everything is going beautifully, except for one small thing. I notice that, up to here, nothing has been said about the crime for which Foscari is sentenced. It seems to me that should be emphasized.

In the tenor's cavatina, there are two things which don't work well: the first is that, having finished his cavatina, Jacopo remains on the stage, and this always weakens the effect. Second, there is no contrasting idea to set against the adagio. So write a little bit of dialogue between the soldier and Jacopo, and then have an officer say 'Bring in the

prisoner'. Follow this with a cabaletta; but make it a strong one, for
we are writing for Rome. And then, as I say, the character of Foscari
must be made more energetic. The woman's cavatina is excellent. I
think that here you should insert a very short recitative, then a solo
passage for the Doge and a big duet. This duet, coming at the end,
should be quite short. Work yourself into a proper state of feeling and
write some beautiful verses. In the second act, write a romanza for
Jacopo, and don't forget the duet with Marina,[1] then the great trio,
followed by the chorus and finale. In the third act, do just as we agreed,
and try to make the gondolier's song blend with a chorus of citizens.
Could it not be arranged for this to happen towards evening, so that
we could have a sunset too, which would be beautiful?

By all means agree to write for Pacini, but try not to do *Lorenzino*,
because this we can do together some other time. But if you can't avoid
it, then do *Lorenzino*. Act in your own interests.

[8]

*To Salvatore Cammarano*                                    *23 May, 1844*

[Salvatore Cammarano (1801–1851), Neapolitan librettist, had already
achieved a certain fame for his work with Donizetti, Mercadante and
Pacini. He was to collaborate with Verdi on four operas.

*Alzira*, based on Voltaire's play, *Alzire*, was first performed at the Teatro
San Carlo, Naples, on 12 August, 1845, with Eugenia Tadolini (born 1809)
as Alzira. (See *Personalia*.)]

I have received the synopsis of *Alzira*, and I am completely satisfied
with it. I have read Voltaire's tragedy which, in the hands of a Cammarano, will make an excellent libretto. I am accused of liking a great
deal of noise and handling the singing badly. Pay no attention to this.
Just put passion into it, and you will see that I write reasonably well.
I am surprised that Tadolini is not singing. I ought to let you know that
in my contract article 3 reads as follows: 'The company to be engaged
for the opera to be written by Signor Verdi will be chosen by him from
those singers under contract to the management.' So, if Tadolini is
under contract, Tadolini will have to sing, for I shall certainly not
cede my rights for anything in the world.

---

[1] Thus the *Copialettere*. This is a misprint for Maria, the name of Jacopo's wife in
Byron's play. Eventually, in the libretto, her name was altered to Lucrezia.

I should like this to be kept secret for the moment, and I should also be grateful if you could elucidate this matter for me, and also let me know what kind of singer Bishop is.

To return to *Alzira*, may I ask you to send me some more verses quickly? There's no need for me to say keep it short, for you understand the theatre better than I do. We shall meet soon at Naples, meanwhile all my esteem.


[9]

*To the Noble Society of Milan*                          Milan, *10 July, 1844*

[The Society had invited Verdi to compose a Cantata for a soirée to be held in connection with a Scientific Conference in Milan. The text, entitled *Flavio Gioia*, was provided by the famous librettist, Felice Romani (1780–1865), on whose libretto *Il finto Stanislao* Verdi had already written the opera *Un giorno di regno*. *Flavio Gioia* was in three parts, the first of which contained no fewer than six pieces. Verdi, in fact, did not set any of this text.]

I have the honour to present to the Noble Society the first part of the Cantata, or to be more exact, the Drama, which Romani sent to me. In view of the plot, the shape and the length, this can be called a drama, as it is, in fact, written in verses like *La straniera* or *Il pirata*.

Due to the shortness of the time available, my present engagements and, above all, my health, which at the moment is not very good, I cannot take on a work of this size on my own. I would only be able to set one part of this Cantata to music. I would prefer to choose one of the last parts.

Very respectfully yours


[10]

*To Cavaliere Felice Romani*                          Milan, *10 July, 1844*

I have received the first part of the Cantata, or to be more exact, the drama, which is splendid as are all your works. Admiring as I do your pieces, indeed masterpieces, I have read and reread with close attention your new composition, which I find admirable in every way.

I do not know what kind of work the Noble Society asked you to compose for this cantata, but instead of a cantata for a special occasion as I expected, I find a drama which, in the short time available and, above all, because of my health (which at present is not very robust), it is impossible for me to work on. This morning I have written to the Noble Society, explaining that I could not set the whole Cantata to music on my own, and could only set one part of it. I thought, Signor Cavaliere, that I ought to let you know the position.

　　With feelings of the most profound esteem,

Your devoted servant

You cannot imagine, Cavaliere, how sorry I am to have to refuse this work, but I believe it is right to inform the Society in time, so that they can make other arrangements, instead of undertaking a work which I could never have completed in so short a time.

[11]

*To Giuseppina Appiani*　　　*Busseto, 28 August, 1844*

[*I due Foscari* had its first performance at the Teatro Argentina, Rome, on 3 November, 1844.]

Just a word or two to let you know that very soon I shall be in Milan. As soon as my health improves a little, I shall set out for the Lombardian capital. The air of my native district isn't doing me any good. What a deserted place this has become. It's hardly even on the map. What more can I say? Be patient for a while and believe that no one will stand in my way, and that I am not making myself anyone's slave.

　　Are all your sons working furiously? I am dissatisfied with myself because I am doing nothing, and there's still so much for me to do on *I due Foscari*! Poor me!

[12]

*To Salvatore Cammarano*　　　*Milan, 18 April, 1845*

[The opera referred to is *Alzira*.]

Dear Cammarano,

　　I have been in bed with a stomach ache for two days. I have been submitted to blood letting, God help me! I feel better, however, but at the moment I cannot work.

I have received the Finale, which is splendid. I await some pieces of clearing up (as you promised), and the synopsis, at least, of the last act.

It will be necessary to persuade the management to delay the performance of the opera for at least a month, because, when I am able to work again, I shall have to proceed gradually.

Believe me always your most affectionate friend

[13]

*To Vincenzo Flauto*                                      Milan, 14 May, 1845

[Verdi was not in good health while writing *Alzira*, and, when his usual nervous headaches, sore throats and stomach pains came on, he was obliged to ask the Naples management for a postponement of the première by two months. This was granted by Flauto, the impresario, only with the greatest reluctance. Not disposed to take Verdi's illnesses seriously, Flauto wrote telling him his health would be sure to improve in sunny Naples.]

I am terribly sorry to have to inform you that my illness is not as minor as you think it is, and the absinthe tincture will be of no use to me.

You say that the stimulating air of Vesuvius will improve my health, but I can assure you that what I need to get well again is calm and rest.

I am not able to leave immediately for Naples, as you invite me to, because, if I could, I would not have sent you the medical certificate. I inform you of this so that you can take whatever steps you think necessary during this period while I am trying to recover my health.

Yours very truly

[14]

*To Salvatore Cammarano*                                 Milan, 14 May, 1845

[See note to letter No. 13.]

Dearest Cammarano,

I have today received a rather curious letter from Sig. Flauto. Without replying to my question, which was supported by a medical certificate, about delaying the performance of the opera by a month, he invites me to go directly to Naples. Furthermore, this letter of his is written in a style which I do not like. I have answered him in the same manner, and have told him that, for the time being, I cannot go to Naples.

I wish this impresario would accept the situation in good part, and appreciate that I usually fulfil my obligations scrupulously, and that if it were not for a very bad stomach ache, which has prevented and which still prevents me from working, I would by now have had the good fortune to have finished my opera and be in Naples. If it were not for the pleasure of setting your libretto to music and writing for that theatre, I should have followed the advice of the doctor who advised me to rest all summer.

If you can contact the impresario and explain the matter, I should be very grateful, since, to put it briefly, I cannot come now, and the opera cannot be produced in June.

Forgive me for inconveniencing you. Reply quickly to your great friend and admirer


[15]

*To Salvatore Cammarano*                                    *Venice, 27 May, 1845*

[See also note to letter No. 8.]

I received your very kind letter somewhat late, as it was readdressed to me here from Milan. The lines for Alzira's cavatina are extraordinarily beautiful, especially in the recitative and first part. Please be so kind as to let me know more about the characters, and how many acts there will be. I'm sure there's no need for me to recommend brevity and a fine rôle for Coletti.

The management has written to say that until the end of July, they have no other leading lady except Bishop. If Tadolini is not singing, there's no point in talking about it, but if Tadolini is a member of the company, then I would choose her without a second thought. I shall be leaving shortly for Milan, so please address your next letter to me there.

PS. If you will forgive the observation: don't you think three cavatinas one after the other are too much? Forgive me for saying so.

(which would be a question of 40 or 50 thousand francs)? What fool would insist that she should come to Busseto instead and sing for free?

I repeat that my name should not have been used in their petition, particularly since it looks as though I am ambitious to have a theatre named after me, with a bust of myself in it. And I think almost everyone in Italy knows how I oppose that kind of publicity as much as possible.

Please dissuade them from sending the project for me to endorse as security for them, for I should reply that at present I feel obliged simply to put my name down for a donation of 20 or 30 thousand francs.


[19]


*To Andrea Maffei*                                                      *30 July, 1845*

[Andrea Maffei (1798–1885), husband of the Countess Clarina Maffei, was a poet of some elegance, and a respected translator from English and German. He was responsible for part of the *Macbeth* libretto, and also for the libretto of *I masnadieri*. The Maffeis separated in 1846, but Verdi remained on friendly terms with them both.

Verdi wrote this letter from Naples.]

I have finished the opera,[1] except for the orchestration, so it will be ready for performance towards August 9th. I am unable to give you an opinion about this opera of mine, because I have written it without any great care or much exertion, so if it fails I shan't mind very much. But don't worry, it won't be a fiasco. The singers enjoy singing it, so it must be quite tolerable, after all. I shall write to you immediately after the first performance. I shall be in Milan, about August 17th, but I shall say nothing here about my departure. The Neopolitans are strange: one part of them is rough, almost uncivilized, whom you almost have to beat to get them to respect you; the other part almost chokes you to death with its kindness. To tell the truth, I cannot complain, as the management here have been very good to me.

I wanted to introduce you to a certain Beneventano[2] who went to

---

[1] *Alzira*, which reached the stage not on 9th August but on the 12th (1845).

[2] Giuseppe Beneventano (1824–1880), baritone, is known to have sung the title rôle in *Nabucco* in its first New York performances in 1848, Giorgio Germont in *La traviata* when London first heard the opera in 1856, and Count Walter in *Luisa Miller* in its first London performances in 1858.

Milan to sing, but then I decided not to bother you with anything so irksome.

[20]

*To Jacopo Ferretti*                      *5 November, 1845*

[The poet Jacopo Ferretti (1784–1852) was the librettist of Rossini's *Cenerentola* and of four operas by Donizetti.]

I am very grateful for the news you have given me about that unfortunate *Alzira,* and even more for the suggestions you are kind enough to make. In Naples I too saw those weaknesses before the opera was produced, and you can't imagine how long I thought about them. But the flaw is too deeply rooted, and retouching would only make it worse. Then, how could I? I hoped that the Overture and the finale of the last act would to a great extent outweigh the defects of the rest of the opera, but I see that in Rome this was not so. So that's the way it was.

I have read your sonnet. Beautiful! I am really embarrassed by the kindnesses you show me, particularly as I can never display my gratitude as I should like to.

I am very much occupied with *Attila*! What a beautiful subject! The critics may say what they like, but I say 'What a beautiful musical libretto!'

[21]

*To Vincenzo Luccardi*                  *11 February, 1846*

[The sculptor, Vincenzo Luccardi, a life-long friend of Verdi, was a professor at St Luke's Academy in Rome. He died in 1878.]

I owe you a reply to your very welcome letter and I'm sending it very late, but perhaps you know that I have been ill since the 2nd of January, and have only been going out and beginning to write again in the last few days. I must ask a great favour of you. I know that in the Vatican, either among the tapestries or the Raphael frescos there must be a representation of the meeting of Attila and St Leo. I need to have a little sketch of Attila, so do one with a couple of strokes of your pen, and add a written note of the colours he is wearing. Above all I need to know his hair-style. If you do me this favour, I shall give you my holy blessing. No news here. *L'elisir*, the other evening, was greatly acclaimed as usual. I am tired of staying in Venice: this sullen, quiet melancholy has got to the stage where it puts me in an impossible mood. Farewell, dear scatterbrain. My greetings to all our friends.


[22]


*To Countess Maffei*                                        *18 March, 1846*


[The Countess Clarina Maffei (1814–1886) and her husband Andrea Maffei (see note to letter 19) were lifelong friends of Verdi. The Countess's salon in Milan exerted an influence on the musical and political life of that city for fifty years. Her father was a Count, and the title of Countess was extended by courtesy to his daughter.

This letter was written from Venice, the day following the première of *Attila*. Verdi had completed and rehearsed the opera in a state of ill-health: after a bout of rheumatism in December, he had succumbed to a severe form of gastric fever. He finished composing the opera in bed, in what, with a certain exaggeration, he referred to as 'an almost dying condition'.]

*Attila* had a fair enough success. The applause and the calls were too much for a poor sick man. Perhaps it was not completely understood, but it may be this evening. My friends would say that this is the best of my operas. The public questions that. I say it is not inferior to any of the others. Time will tell.

My health is improving day by day. Maffei, who is very well, will write to you tomorrow about the outcome of this evening's performance, and then we shall leave for Milan together as soon as possible.


[23]


*To Benjamin Lumley*                                    *Milan, 9 April, 1846*


[Benjamin Lumley (1811–1875) was an English operatic impresario who was in charge of Her Majesty's Theatre, London, in the 1840's and 50's. Lumley had asked Verdi to compose an opera for Her Majesty's Theatre, and the composer had considered writing *King Lear*, on the understanding that the great French-Irish bass, Luigi Lablache, would be available to sing the title-rôle. Verdi had intended travelling to London immediately after launching *Attila* in Venice. His health, however, continued to be poor, and his doctors forbade him to travel. He appears, temporarily, to have succumbed to that nervous exhaustion to which his temperament rendered him peculiarly vulnerable.]

Sig. Lumley,

I know that the news I am about to give you will not come as a surprise to you. Due to my illness while I was in Venice, I am unable to come to London, let alone write an opera. This very day Sig. Lucca[1] will send on to you the two medical certificates I gave him, which will authenticate the matter.

You cannot imagine how sorry I am to have to renounce the honour of composing for London. My health is improving very slowly, and I am unable to take up even the slightest amount of work. I have to rest and follow a very strict course of treatment, and later I shall have to go to Recoaro to take the waters there etc.

I hope that by inconveniencing you now, I shall by no means be ending our relationship, and I look forward to receiving a few lines from you.

Very truly yours

[24]

*To Benjamin Lumley*                    *Milan, 22 May, 1846*

[Lumley was not disposed to take Verdi's illness too seriously. On 14 April, he had replied to Verdi's letter of the 9th (No. 23), expressing sympathy, but continuing: 'I dare to hope that in a few days you will be back to normal and that, very soon, you will arrive here by short stages in the best of health—at the time of year when we enjoy our best weather, with a sky less blue than Italy's but also an air less exciting . . . I am sure that a change of scenery and a visit to London in such a beautiful and prosperous season (I've never known such a brilliant time in our theatre) will be better for you than all the remedies imaginable.'

---

[1] Verdi had agreed to write, for Lucca to publish, the opera which Lumley was to stage in London.

On 13 May, Lumley wrote again to Verdi, pointing out that he was awaiting a reply to his earlier letter, and attempting to entice the composer with the news that the previous evening he had presented *I Lombardi* with great success.]

Sig. Lumley,

I read with surprise that you were awaiting a letter from me, but I must confess openly that I had not thought of writing about a matter which I consider completely settled, as per my letter of April 9th to which I have received no reply. On the contrary, having handed over the medical certificates to Sig. Lucca, and received acknowledgment, I thought I had done everything necessary.

My natural curiosity to see a city as extraordinary as London, my self-respect and my own interests were sufficient motives for me to want to fulfil the contract made with Sig. Lucca. But my health has not allowed this, and I need complete rest.

I am glad to know that *I Lombardi* has been well received by the English, and I thank you sincerely for your flattering words. I hope for a continuation of your happy successes with operas in the future.

Yours respectfully

[25]

*To Emilia Morosini*                                    *Recoaro, 14 July, 1846*

[Emilia Morosini (1804–1875) was the wife of the nobleman Giovanni Battista Morosini. Their son Emilio died heroically at the siege of Rome in 1849. Carolina and Peppina were daughters of Emilia Morosini. Peppina is Giuseppina (1824–1909) who, in 1851, married Count Negroni-Prati.

For six months after the production of *Attila*, Verdi slowly fought his way back to health after a nervous collapse. He spent part of the summer of 1846, accompanied by his friend Maffei, taking the waters at Recoaro, a spa near the slopes of the Venetian alps, about thirty kilometres north-west of Vicenza.]

I was very pleased to receive your news, but at the same time mortified to find I had not written to you before. This was due partly to Venice, partly to Maffei whom I knew had written to you as soon as we arrived. Venice is delicious at present in the evenings, but not for too long. I am dying of boredom here. So many people about, that those who arrive now are being turned away from the hotels. But they all keep to themselves. There is no society in the evenings, so after supper one goes to bed. I find this valley very pretty, but what is it compared with Como, Varese and so on? We take long walks, using the map which Peppina gave me as a present. I do not understand what benefit I shall derive from the waters: I think they are like that malvino ointment which does no good and no harm. I find them very easy to take, and we must hope they will be of future benefit.

I was pleased to hear that Carolina is better, but sorry that Peppina is unwell. Why don't they come to Recoaro? Then we would all be happy, we could form our own little social group, and amuse ourselves in spite of Recoaro. What is good about this place is that no-one plays music or talks about it. It was a real inspiration not to bring a harpsi-chord here. I don't feel like myself any more: I cannot believe I am able to write music or compose good and bad pieces, and I don't know whether I shall ever be able to return to work. Perhaps one morning I shall awake a millionaire. What a lovely, full-sounding word. How empty by contrast are the words fame, glory, talent etc. I shall prob-ably leave Recoaro on Thursday.


[26]


*To Vincenzo Flauto*                              *Milan, 2 August, 1846*


[After *Alzira*'s première in Naples in 1845, Verdi had agreed to write another opera for Naples to be produced in June, 1847, and it is this to which he refers in the second paragraph of this letter. In fact, four operas were to intervene before *Luisa Miller* which was produced in Naples in December, 1849.

In the third paragraph, Verdi alludes to the Neapolitan coffee-house gossip which had irritated him at the time of *Alzira*'s production. His weak pun is on Verdi-verde (green).]


I am deeply affected by the affectionate care with which you ask for news of my health. I am perfectly well. I don't know how my enemies will feel about this information, but as far as my friends are concerned I shall take advantage of your kindness and ask you to inform them.

Regarding the change of date you would like to make for the opera I am to write for San Carlo, you know that I have obligations both before and after this one, and so at the moment I am not able to give you a positive answer. However there's plenty of time, and this is something we can talk about a few months from now.

I thank you for the friendship you show me. As for the good humour you wish me to display to the Neapolitans, I'm not certain what you mean, but I assure you I am in the most hilarious mood. Why should I feel bad-humoured towards the Neapolitans, or the Neapolitans to me. Do they lack colours in their prism that they have need of Verdi? As for me, I hope to find some scruffy little theatre for the time being. If nothing else offers, the Paris Grand Opéra will not disdain to open its portals to me, as I can show you in a letter from Pillet.[1] Meanwhile, let me have frequent news of you, tell me if I can be of service, and believe me, yours affectionately

[27]

*To Alessandro Lanari*                                    *Milan, 19 August, 1846*

[The impresario Lanari had his headquarters at the Teatro della Pergola in Florence, and also controlled theatres elsewhere in Italy.

Verdi would have liked to have had Mariani (see note to letter 116) conduct *Macbeth*. He was, in fact, still undecided whether to write *Macbeth* or *I masnadieri* for Lanari: this was to depend on which singers were available. For *Macbeth* Verdi wanted a baritone, for *I masnadieri* a strong tenor. Thus circumstances dictated the eventual choice of *Macbeth*. The singers at the première were Barbieri-Nini (Lady Macbeth) and Varesi (Macbeth).]

I am sorry and surprised that you did not reply to my letter complaining about Mariani's requests. But if you have not replied, it must mean you have good reasons not to do so, and that is an end of the matter.

Time is running out, and there is something we have to decide: there would appear to be just enough time to complete a work of this importance. Therefore, if you have settled the contract with Fraschini, nothing could be better, and I shall begin to compose one of the two subjects we have already discussed. In the event of your not having settled anything with Fraschini, I do not wish to take a chance on other tenors, and so I would wish to write a subject which did not require a tenor. In that case, I should definitely need these two artists: Loewe and Varesi.

Varesi is the only singer in Italy who can play the rôle I am thinking

---

[1] Leone Pillet, administrative director of the Paris Opéra was, the following year, to be succeeded by Duponchel and Roqueplan. He died in Venice in 1860.

of, not only because of his singing, but also by virtue of his temperament and his appearance. All the other singers, even those better than
he, would be less suitable. I do not wish to say anything against Ferri
who is better looking, has a more beautiful voice, and is perhaps a
better singer, but he would not play the rôle as well as Varesi. Try,
therefore, to engage Ferri elsewhere, then everything can be settled.
The subject is neither political nor religious: it is a fantasy. Decide,
therefore, either to engage Fraschini (and then I should want Barbieri),
or if you cannot engage Fraschini, try to obtain Varesi. If you wish, I
personally will deal with Varesi in order to facilitate matters. The
remainder of the company will have to be composed of good secondary
performers, but I need a good chorus. Anyway, we can talk about this
later on. Hurry, hurry, and reply by return so that all my efforts and
labours on this damned subject will not be in vain.

[28]

*To Benjamin Lumley*                    Milan, 11 November, 1846

If the Naples management allows me to postpone until the autumn the
opera I am supposed to write for the month of June next year, 1847,
then I am ready on my part to write for Her Majesty's Theatre, London,
an opera to be produced about the end of June, with the proviso that I
be allowed to choose the singers from your company, which must
include Lind and Fraschini. You realize, also, that the opera I shall write
will belong to the publisher Francesco Lucca with whom it will be
necessary for you to make all your arrangements.

With all esteem, your devoted

[29]

*To Francesco Lucca*                    Milan, 3 December, 1846

[Before deciding on *I masnadieri* for London, Verdi had at first intended that
the opera he was to write for Lucca to publish and Lumley to stage would be
based on Byron's poem, *The Corsair*. When he considered the subject in
close detail, however, he began to have doubts about its suitability for opera.
By this time, Lucca had warmed to the idea, and attempted to hold the composer to it.

When, after London and *I masnadieri*, Verdi found himself in Paris supervising the production of *Jérusalem* at the Opéra in November, 1847, he decided to stay on in Paris and write as quickly as possible the opera for which Lucca was by that time clamouring even more insistently than before. *Il corsaro* was staged in Trieste on 25 October, 1848, but Verdi did not attend the première. He remained in Paris, making the excuse that a bad cold prevented him from travelling.]

Take good care, when you write to Lumley, to remind him of the condition concerning the singers, which he promised me verbally and in secret, and to which I called his attention in my letter of November 11th. It is now necessary for Mr Lumley to write me a letter specifically assuring me I shall have those singers, and at the same time leaving me the right to choose from the company.

Regarding the subject, you know that I have changed my mind about *Il corsaro* and have had a new libretto written: *I masnadieri*, of which I have composed nearly a third of the music. You know this very well, and I am greatly astonished that you mention it again. Here are the conditions which have already been accepted: I am to write *I masnadieri*, and Lumley is obliged to give me from his company the two singers he has promised me.

With all esteem

[30]

*To Benjamin Lumley*                                      *Milan, 4 December, 1846*

The opera which I was supposed to write for Naples, for the spring of 1847, has been postponed to another season, and I should therefore be free to write for London in June, if nothing else of any importance arises to prevent it.

Last year I chose *Il corsaro* as a subject, but when it was put into Italian verse I found it cold and lacking in scenic effect. I changed my mind, therefore, and decided, even if it meant doubling my expense, to have another libretto made: Schiller's *I masnadieri*. As last year I had to cancel the contract due to my ill-health, I think I should now consider myself free to choose another subject, particularly as this is known to Sig. Lucca, who also knows I have already completed half of *I masnadieri*. This opera will be more effective, is better suited to your company, and, as I say, I have almost half finished it.

Let me repeat that I am not compelled to set any particular subject to music, and that if I have to write for London, I have just time to finish *I masnadieri*, but not to write *Il corsaro*.

If you agree to *I masnadieri* I shall consider myself from this moment under an obligation to write it for London, provided that you write to me agreeing to my choosing the cast from your company, which will include Lind and Fraschini, as previously agreed in Milan. Looking forward to receiving your prompt reply.

Yours very truly

[31]

*To Alessandro Lanari*                                              *22 December, 1846*

I am in good health except that, as I told you in my last letter, I am somewhat tired. Barbieri[1] must have a little patience: if she likes the opera, she'll do well out of it.

Farewell, farewell.

PS. Please note that the ghost of Banquo must come from under the earth, and must be performed by the same artist who plays Banquo in the first act. He should be covered in a very fine grey silk veil, with his hair ruffled and a few wounds visible on his neck. I found all this out from London where they have been performing this tragedy continually for more than 200 years.

[32]

*To Giovanni Ricordi*                                              *Milan, 29 December, 1846*

[The publishing house of Ricordi bought Verdi's first produced opera, *Oberto*, for publication, in 1839, and remained his principal publishers for the rest of his life. Giovanni Ricordi (1785–1853) was the founder of the firm. His son Tito Ricordi (1811–1888) was also at this time a member of the firm and eventually succeeded his father. Tito's son, Giulio Ricordi (1840–1912), was the last Ricordi to manage the business.

The most recent opera by Verdi to have had its première at La Scala was *Giovanna d'Arco* in 1845. So complete was the composer's dissatisfaction with

---

[1] Marianna Barbieri-Nini, Verdi's first Lady Macbeth.

the standards of production, management, orchestral playing and general discipline that he announced he would henceforth have nothing to do with La Scala. He was determined not to allow any more of his operas to be given their first performances there. A quarter of a century passed before he relaxed his attitude, and it was not until 1887 and *Otello* that La Scala was able to claim another Verdi world première.]

Dear Ricordi,

I approve the contract you have drawn up for my new opera *Macbeth* which is to be produced during next Lent in Florence, and I consent to your proceeding to use it, on the condition, however, that you do not permit this *Macbeth* to be performed at La Scala.

Far too many examples already have persuaded me that they either can't or won't produce operas decently, especially mine. I cannot forget the foul manner in which they produced *I Lombardi, Ernani, I due Foscari* etc. And I have another example before my eyes with *Attila*! Ask yourself if, despite a good company, this opera could possibly have been more badly staged.

I repeat, therefore, that I cannot, indeed I must not, allow a performance of this *Macbeth* at La Scala, at least until things have changed there for the better. I feel myself obliged to point out to you that this condition I have made concerning *Macbeth* will apply in future to all my operas. Farewell, yours affectionately

[33]

*To Tito Ricordi*                                                      *January, 1847*

[Perrone was the designer of the décor for *Macbeth*. In the Italian text in the *Copialettere*, Harold is described as 'Aroldo, detto Re di lepre' (Harold, known as King of the Hares); and a footnote comments: 'Non "Re di lepre", ma "piede di lepre" (Hare-foot) fu detto Aroldo.' But it is hardly likely that Verdi wrote 're di lepre'. It is, on the other hand, very likely that his spidery hand-writing was misunderstood when the letter was transcribed for publication, and that what Verdi wrote was, correctly, 'pie di lepre' (Hare-foot).]

Please let Perrone know that the era in which *Macbeth* takes place is much later than Ossian and the Roman Empire.

Macbeth assassinated Duncan in 1040, and he himself was killed in 1057.

In 1039, England was ruled by Harold, called Harefoot and of Danish extraction. He was succeeded in the same year by Hardicanute, half-brother of Edward the Confessor.

Don't forget to tell Perrone all of this, because I believe he is making a mistake about the period.


[34]

*To Alessandro Lanari*                          *Milan, 21 January, 1847*

I was not able to write to you earlier, as I have been excessively busy. Undoubtedly I shall write to Romani[1] very soon, and ask him to undertake the production. But, as I don't want to upset the librettist, I shall wait for a few more days before writing to him. I must also tell you that a few days ago I was talking to Sanquirico[2] about *Macbeth*. I explained to him how I wanted to stage the scene of the apparitions, and he mentioned various ways to me of which I am sure the finest is the phantasmagoria.[3] He assured me that a very beautiful and appropriate effect can be achieved by this means, and he himself has agreed to talk to the optic specialist Duroni, and arrange for the machinery to be used.

You know what a phantasmagoria is, so I don't need to describe it to you. By God, if the effect is as successful as Sanquirico's description of it, many people will come to the theatre simply to see it. As for the cost, I am assured that it will be only a little more expensive than the ordinary machinery. What do you think?

Within a week, you will receive the whole of the third act, the beginning of the fourth, the complete libretto and also, I hope, the costume designs. I want the costumes to be very well made, and to ensure that they are authentic I have sent to London, and I have consulted the foremost authorities on the period and the costumes, which can be designed by Hayez[4] and other members of the Committee.

When you receive the music, you will see that there are two choruses of the greatest importance: don't try to economise on the size of the chorus and you won't regret it. Note that the witches must always be divided into three groups, the best numbers being 6, 6 and 6, 18 in all

[1] Musical Director of the Teatro della Pergola (see *Personalia*).
[2] La Scala's stage designer.
[3] A species of magic lantern.
[4] Francesco Hayez (1791–1882), portrait painter, was responsible for the *Macbeth* costume designs.

etc. . . . Choose carefully the tenor who is to sing Macduff, and be sure too that the secondary singers are good, because the ensembles call for good voices. And I am greatly concerned about these ensembles.

I can't tell you precisely when I shall be in Florence, because I want first to finish the opera here in peace. I assure you I shall be there in good time. Hand out the solo and the chorus parts so that, when I arrive, we can work with the orchestra after the first two or three rehearsals, because I shall need many orchestra and stage rehearsals.

I am annoyed that the singer who is to play Banquo does not want to appear as his ghost! Why is this? The singers must be engaged to sing and act: what's more, it's high time we stopped being so easy-going about this kind of thing. It would be monstrous to have someone else play the ghost, for Banquo must continue to look like the same person when he appears as a ghost.

Farewell, farewell, write to me at once. I repeat that I hope soon to send you some more music. Meanwhile, my greetings to Romani to whom I shall write soon.


[35]

*To Antonio Barezzi*                                              *25 March, 1847*

For a long time now I have intended to dedicate an opera to you who have been father, benefactor and friend to me. It was a duty I ought to have carried out earlier, and I would have done so had I not been prevented by certain imperious circumstances. Now here is this *Macbeth* which I love much more than my other operas and which I therefore consider more worthy to be presented to you. It is offered from the heart: may it be accepted by the heart and be a testimony for all time to the gratitude and love borne to you by your most affectionate


[36]

*To Francesco Lucca*                                     *Milan, 10 April, 1847*

I am glad that Lind is going to London, though it seems to me she is going very late, and I don't want the season to be too far advanced before my opera is produced.

Take careful note that I will not tolerate this, nor am I disposed to tolerate the slightest default. I have not been very well treated in this business, so if the opera is not put on at the proper time and in a decent manner, I tell you frankly I shall not allow it to proceed. With all esteem

## [37]

*To Giovanni Ricordi*                    *Milan, 20 May, 1847*

[The opera referred to is *La battaglia di Legnano* which was produced at the Teatro Argentina, Rome, on 27 January, 1849.]

In reply to yours of April 26 last.

As I am no longer bound by contract to write an opera for the Naples management, I am willing to write it instead for you, to be performed by a first-rate company in one of the leading Italian theatres, with the exception of La Scala. So that you will not have to suffer the entire loss if the outcome is not a happy one, I wish to share the expenses.

Here are my conditions for the contract:

1. The opera shall be given in one of the leading Italian theatres (except La Scala) with a first-rate company, during 1848. I shall be responsible for the libretto.
2. You shall pay me, for all the material, 12,000 francs in 600 gold Napoleons, upon delivery of the score, that is on the day of the dress rehearsal of the opera.
3. During the first season in which the opera is presented under my direction, you will pay me 4,000 francs in 200 gold Napoleons.
4. Whenever the opera is presented in countries where literary and musical works are protected by copyright, you will pay me 300 francs per theatrical season continuously for ten years. After the first ten years, complete ownership of the score will pass to you.
5. For all other countries not covered by the copyright convention, you will pay me a part of the 300 francs you will receive in rental fees.
6. If you sell the rights to the score of the aforementioned opera in France, you will pay me 3,000 francs in gold Napoleons. If you sell it in England, another 3,000 francs. In all other countries, it cannot be sold without my approval, as I shall wish to have a share in the sale.

7. This opera may not be produced at La Scala without my permission.

8. In order to prevent the alterations which theatres make in musical works, it will be forbidden to insert anything into the aforementioned score, to make any cuts, to transpose into different keys, higher or lower, or to make any kind of alteration which would affect the instrumentation. I shall impose a fine of 1,000 francs, which I shall expect you to extract from any theatre which makes any such alteration to the score.

If these conditions are acceptable to you, I shall consider myself bound to them until Saturday 22nd inst.

[38]

*To Countess Maffei*                                    *postmark 9 June, 1847*

[Verdi travelled to London to stage and conduct the first performances of *I masnadieri* at Her Majesty's Theatre. His travelling companion was Emanuele Muzio, his young pupil and amanuensis (see *Personalia*).]

I have been in London scarcely two days. I had a ghastly trip, but it amused me. When I arrived in Strasbourg the coach had already left, so rather than wait twenty-four hours I took the journey along the Rhine and thus did not get tired. I saw the delightful scenery, stopping in Mainz, Cologne, Brussels, two days in Paris, and at last here I am in London. In Paris I went to the Opéra. I have never heard more awful singers or a more mediocre chorus. The orchestra itself, if our lions will permit me to say so, was little better than mediocre. What I saw of Paris I quite liked, and above all I like the free life one can live in that country. I can say nothing about London because yesterday was Sunday and I haven't seen a soul. This smoke, however, and the smell of coal upset me. I feel as though I were on a steam-boat all the time. In a few moments I'm going to the theatre to find out how my affairs are going. Emanuele (Muzio) whom I sent ahead of me has found me such a homoeopathically minute suite of rooms that I can't move about in them. Nevertheless, it's quite clean, like all the houses in London.

I can't tell you how fanatical they are about Lind. They are already selling boxes and seats for tomorrow evening. I can't wait to hear her. My health is excellent. The journey didn't affect me very much because I took my time over it. It's true that I arrived late, so the impresario could complain, but if he says a single word to me that I don't care for, he'll get ten in reply and I shall leave immediately for Paris, regardless of the consequences.

[39]

*To Giuseppina Appiani*                                  *London, 27 June, 1847*

[On the same day, Verdi wrote an almost identical letter to Clarina Maffei. It is published in Alessandro Luzio's *Studi e bozzetti di Storia letteraria e politica* (Milan, 1910, p. 408).]

Long live our sun, which I have always loved greatly, but which I now adore, since I've been suffering this fog and smoke which suffocates me and depresses me as well. Apart from that, what a magnificent city! There are things here at which you can only stare as though turned to stone—but this climate paralyses such beauty. Oh, if only the Naples sky were here, you wouldn't need to ask for Paradise. I haven't yet begun the rehearsals for my new opera because I haven't had time to do anything. And I really mean *to do anything*. That tells you all. However, Lind has not cancelled out other impressions; I am still loyalty personified. Don't laugh, by God, or I shall fly into a rage.

The theatres are packed out, and the English enjoy performances which—and they pay so much!! Oh, if I could stay here a couple of years, I'd like to carry away a bagful of these *most holy* pounds. But there is no use my thinking about such lovely things, for I couldn't stand the climate. I can't wait to go to Paris, which has no particular allurement for me, but which I shall enjoy very much because there I can live as I like. It's a great pleasure to be able to do whatever you want!! When I think that I shall be several weeks in Paris without getting mixed up in musical business, without hearing anyone talk of music (because I shall throw all publishers and impresarios out of the door), I almost swoon at such consolation.

In London, my health is really not bad, but I am always afraid that misfortune will overtake me. I stay in the house a great deal to write (or at least with the intention of writing), go very little into society, and very seldom to the theatre to save myself as much trouble as possible. Oh, if I had the time, I should like to write about so much to you. But now I can only press your hand earnestly, and tell you I'm your friend for life.

[40]

*To Countess Maffei*                              *London, 17 July, 1847*

You will be surprised to hear that I am still in London, and that the opera has not yet been staged. But the smoke and the fog are to blame, as well as this diabolical climate which robs me of all desire to work. But now, at last, everything is finished, or almost finished, and on Thursday 22nd, the opera will definitely be staged. I have had two orchestral rehearsals, and if I were in Italy I would know by now whether the work was good or not, but here I understand nothing. Blame the climate . . . . . blame the climate! As you can imagine, I want to leave London as soon as possible and stay in Paris for a month. So you can address your letters to me in Paris, poste restante. For the rest, I'm quite pleased at the state of my health, although if I survive London this time, I'm not likely to come back again. Still, it's a city that in some extraordinary way I like.

It's true that they have offered me 40,000 francs for another opera, but I have not accepted. Don't be surprised however, because that's not really an exorbitant sum, and if I have to come back here I shall ask for much more.

[41]

*To Giovanni Mario*                               *London, 24 July, 1847*

[Member of an old and noble family, Mario, Conte di Candia (1810–1883), achieved fame as a tenor, using the stage name of Giovanni Mario.[1] After witnessing his London début in Donizetti's *Lucrezia Borgia* in 1839, Chorley wrote: '. . . . physical beauty and geniality, such as have been bestowed on few, a certain artistic taste, a certain distinction—not exclusively belonging to gentle birth, but sometimes associated with it—made it clear, from Signor Mario's first hour of stage-life, that a course of no common order of fascination was begun.'

Verdi had made certain alterations to the part of Jacopo to suit Mario when he sang it in Paris in 1846. Mario sang the rôle again in London at Covent Garden in June, 1847.]

----

[1] The Italian editors of the *Copialettere* give his stage name incorrectly as Giuseppe Mario.

Sir,

I was very surprised and sorry to read that you think I have complained about your behaviour to me, for if you knew me better you would be reassured that what I think is completely different. To relieve my conscience, I shall relate to you the circumstances which may have given rise to the gossip of which you complain in your letter. As someone noticed that I was not in touch with you, who are such an important figure in the artistic world, I found it necessary, in order to be rid of the query, and not to be charged with haughtiness, to reveal what had happened between us.

Last carnival season, you asked me, through Prince Poniatowski, if I would write that well-known cabaletta for you to sing in *I due Foscari* in Paris, for which I did not charge you. In fact I thought you had forgotten to acknowledge it, as it was two months later that you wrote to me, asking what you should do with that piece. I was very sorry, however, to find that you used it again in London, even though you knew I had not given you any rights in this music. This was what I complained of in conversation, and the frankness of my character does not permit me to conceal any part of it.

You should therefore not blame me in this matter, and I should be upset if you were to think my conversation was guided by financial interest. I should prefer both my work and all gossip about it to be forgotten, and I trust that, like myself, you will not mention this in future.

[42]

*To Emilia Morosini*                                        *Paris, 30 July, 1847*

[The day before this letter was written, Verdi had written one of similar content to the Countess Maffei. See Luzio, *op. cit.*, p. 409.]

No doubt you will be angry with me, and who knows with what ill-humour you will receive this letter from me. This time you are right, and I cannot use as excuses either my work or the London climate or my ill-health or bad moods etc. I am wrong, I am wrong, and if you will extend your hand to me in forgiveness I shall be happy.

Although I found the London climate horrifying, nevertheless I was extremely delighted with the city. No, it's not a city, it's a world. There's nowhere else to compare with it for size, richness, the beauty

of the streets, the well-kept houses. You are struck dumb with astonish-
ment and made to feel very humble when, in the midst of all these
magnificent sights, you survey the Bank and the Docks. Who could
resist such a nation? The surroundings and the country around London
are terrific. I'm not so keen on a number of the English customs: or,
to be more exact, they don't suit us Italians. How ridiculous it is in
Italy when some people imitate the English!

Without having caused a furore, *I masnadieri* was well received, and
I should have returned to London next year to write another opera if
the publisher Lucca had been willing to accept ten thousand francs to
release me from my contract with him. As matters stand, I can't go
back for two years. I'm sorry about it, but I can't break my contract
with Lucca.

I've been here for two days, and, if I continue to be as bored as this,
I shall be back in Milan immediately. The July festivities seem to me a
most unfortunate affair.

If you are going to favour me with a letter, send it to Paris, poste
restante.


[43]

*To Benjamin Lumley*                          *Paris, 2 August, 1847*

[Lumley had asked Verdi to return to London as musical director of Her
Majesty's Theatre, at a very large salary, and to compose for that theatre one
opera per year for ten years. Insufficiently enthusiastic, Verdi proposed
exorbitant terms, and nothing came of the offer.]

I have delayed answering the proposal you made to me before my
departure from London because, in the case of so lengthy and important
a contract, I wanted to think carefully about it before coming to a
decision.

I am not very keen on undertaking the musical direction for the
entire season, because this would allow me to write only one opera
a year, which could be damaging to me. Nevertheless, I would be
willing to accept your proposal, to agree to write one opera a year for
the three consecutive years 1849, 50 and 51, and at the same time
conduct all the operas in the season which runs from mid-February to
mid-August. I would require for all this, the sum of ninety thousand
francs for each season, that is 60,000 for the new opera, and 30,000 for

conducting all the operas performed during the season, plus a house in the country and a carriage.

The librettos would have to be written by a really fine poet at your expense, as agreed orally. If you are agreeable to the above, we can then arrange how the payments should be made, how you want the orchestra to be handled and the performances staged.

I take this opportunity to let you know how grateful I am for your kindness during my stay in London. Whether or not we satisfactorily conclude this present business, I trust it will not affect our friendship which I beg you to put to the test in any circumstance where I can be of service to you.

Very respectfully yours

[44]

*To Giuseppina Appiani*                    *Paris, 22 August, 1847*

I owe you a number of letters, but you are sure to excuse me when I tell you all that I have had to do here. It's different from the Opera in London. Just think: you find yourself all day between two poets, two managers, two music publishers[1] (they always go in twos here) trying to contract a prima donna, devise an idea for the libretto etc., and I tell you it's enough to drive you out of your senses. However, I don't wish to be driven out of my senses, and I face up to the whole of the theatrical world, all the Parisians, all the newspapers—those for me and those against me—and the comic pieces in *Charivari* and *Entre-Acte*. Apropros *Entre-Acte*, they published a quite funny article about me. I think Emanuele [Muzio] has taken it to Milan, so ask him for it.

I shall be here until about the 20th November, but by the end of the month I shall be admiring the cupola of the Duomo.

Though my health is better here than in London, I don't like Paris as much as London, and I have an extreme antipathy to the boulevards (quiet, don't let anyone overhear such blasphemy).

You ask me about Donizetti,[2] and I shall tell you frankly, although

[1] The two poets are Alphonse Royer and Gustav Vaez, librettists of *Jérusalem*. The two impresarios of the Paris Opéra are Charles Duponchel and Nestor Roqueplan, and the two music publishers are Léon and Marie Escudier, Verdi's French publishers.

[2] Donizetti was at this time living in a sanatorium at Ivry, suffering from general paralysis of the insane. In 1847 he was taken back to his home town of Bergamo to die.

it is not a pleasant story. I have not seen him yet, as it was thought ill-advised, but I assure you I very much want to, and if the opportunity presents itself for me to see him without anyone knowing of it, I certainly shall. His physical appearance is good, except that his head is constantly bowed over his chest and his eyes kept shut. He eats and sleeps well, but says hardly a word, and when he does it's very indistinct. If someone goes up to him, he opens his eyes for a moment. If they say, 'Give me your hand', he extends it, and so on. Apparently this is a sign that his mind has not completely gone, although a dear friend of mine who is a doctor tells me that he does these things simply out of habit, and that it would be more encouraging if he were animated or even violently mad. There may perhaps be hope, but in his present condition it would take a miracle to improve him. Still, he is no worse now than he was six months ago, or a year ago. No better, either. So that's the truth about Donizetti's condition. It's distressing, simply too distressing. If his condition improves, I shall let you know immediately.


[45]


*To Giovanni Ricordi*                                             *Paris, 15 October, 1847*


[*Jérusalem,* a revised version of *I Lombardi* with a new French libretto, and some new music, was first performed at the Opéra on 26 November, 1847. An Italian translation, *Gerusalemme* had its première at La Scala, Milan, in 1850.]


Dear Ricordi,

I shall indulge in neither preamble nor excuses for not having written earlier, for I have not much time, but I shall come directly to the question of this opera *Jérusalem* which I was asked to write, and which will be produced here at the Académie Royale, probably before November 15.

I shall then make over to you the above-mentioned score for the entire musical world except England and France. For this material, you will pay me 8,000 francs in 400 gold Napoleons either in Paris or Milan, whichever I indicate, in the following manner; 100 gold Napoleons on 1 December 1847; 100 on January 1st; 100 on February 1st; and the final 100 on March 1st, 1848.

For hiring fees, you will pay me for the first ten years as follows: for the first five years, you will give me 500 francs per hire, and for the other five years, 200 francs per hire.

If I can find an Italian poet here, I shall have the Italian translation done myself. If not, I shall send you the French score on condition, however, that you engage Emanuele Muzio to fit Italian words to the music.

It is forbidden to add to the score, or to make any cuts, with the exception of the ballet music which can be omitted, under penalty of a fine of 1,000 francs which I shall extract from you every time the penalty is incurred by a theatre of the first rank. In second-rank theatres, the clause still exists and you will be obliged to discover a method of extracting the fine when necessary. But, if you fail to collect it, you won't be obliged to pay me.

Farewell, farewell!


[46]

*To Giuseppina Appiani*                    *Paris, 9 March, 1848*

[1848 was the year of spontaneous political uprisings throughout Europe. Verdi witnessed the unrest in Paris which resulted in Louis Philippe retiring to England, and the beginning of the Second Republic. Adolphe Thiers was the leader of the new government.]

I gather from the few lines you have written me that you did not receive my last letter. This is now the third or fourth letter that has been lost. I simply can't understand why. I realize that we are in the middle of a revolution, but what has that to do with letters? In my last letter I asked on Custine's account why you had not replied to three letters of his, whose dates he had given me. If you now write to Custine, make some reference to it. It is more than a month since I saw him, but I believe he is perfectly well.

You know all about what's going on in Paris: since February 24th, nothing has happened. The procession that accompanied the funeral of those killed to the memorial column of the Bastille was imposing, indeed magnificent, and although there were neither troops nor police guards to maintain order, the whole thing passed without the slightest trouble. The big National Assembly to choose the government will meet on April 20th. I still can't understand why it was not called earlier: I am too hard-headed or perhaps too malicious. One hears no talk at all about Thiers, but, who knows, perhaps his snout will suddenly pop up!!

I can't conceal that I am enjoying myself very much and that so far nothing has disturbed my dreams. I do nothing, go for walks, listen to meaningless gossip, buy nearly twenty newspapers a day (though, of course, I don't read them) to avoid being persecuted by the paper sellers, because when they see me coming with a bundle of newspapers in my hand, they don't offer me any. And I laugh, and laugh, and laugh. If nothing important calls me to Italy, I shall stay here for the whole of April to see the National Assembly. I have seen everything that has happened so far, both serious and comical (please believe that by 'seen' I mean with my own eyes), and so I want to see April 20th.

[47]

*To Countess Maffei*                                    *Paris, 24 August, 1848*

[Lombardy had revolted against its Austrian overlords, but the Austrian army, under Radetzky, had defeated the Piedmont and Lombard forces. Verdi, still in Paris where he was living with Giuseppina Strepponi whom he was much later to marry, was one of several Italians in France who signed a petition to General Cavaignac to intervene with military aid for Italy. But the French government was reluctant to move.

Verdi and his music were to become closely identified with the *Risorgimento*, the political movement towards a free and united Italy. His only direct musical contributions to the cause were a patriotic song, 'Suona la tromba', and the opera *La battaglia di Legnano*; but audiences read topical references into many an aria or chorus in his other works, and Verdi was quite happy that they should do so.]

Your letter pleased me enormously, because I did not know what was happening to you. Now that I know you are safe and in good health, I am relieved.

You want to know French public opinion about the events in Italy? Good Lord, what can I say to that? Those who are not against us are indifferent: I must say further that the idea of a United Italy frightens these little nobodies who are in power. It is certain that France will not intervene with arms unless some unforseen event occurs to force it in that direction. Anglo-French diplomatic intervention can be nothing but unfair, shameful for France and ruinous for us. Indeed, such intervention would tend to make Austria abandon Lombardy and content itself with Venetia. If Austria could be persuaded to give up Lombardy (at present this seems possible, though perhaps she would sack and burn everything before leaving), that would be a further dishonour for us, the devastation of Lombardy, and one more prince in Italy. No, no, no: I have hopes neither of France nor of England. If I have hopes of anything, it is, can you imagine?, of Austria: of confusion within Austria. Something serious must be emerging there, and if we know how to seize the moment and wage the war that should be waged, the war of insurrection, Italy could be free again. But God save us from having to rely on our kings or on foreign nations.

Italian diplomats are arriving here from all over the place: Tommaseo yesterday, Picciotti today. They will achieve nothing; it seems impossible that they should still hope for anything from France. To put it briefly, France does not want to see a united Italy.

So there's my opinion, but please don't attach any importance to it, for, as you know, I don't understand politics. For the rest, even France is in the abyss, and I don't know how she will get out of it. The inquisition which followed the events of May and June is the most wretched and disgusting thing that exists. What a miserable, puny age, even in its crimes! I believe that another revolution is imminent: you can sense the odour of it everywhere. And another revolution will completely finish off this poor republic. Let us hope it will not happen, though there are good reasons for fearing that it will.

Carcano is already in Switzerland, and perhaps you have seen him. Emanuele[1] writes to me that he can no longer stay in Milan, and perhaps he will be here tomorrow or the day after.


[48]

*To Salvatore Cammarano*                    *Paris, 18 September, 1848*

[The opera on which Verdi and Cammarano were working was *La battaglia di Legnano*, first performed at the Teatro Argentina, Rome, on 27 January, 1849.]

I cannot persuade myself that your letter of the 9th was written seriously. What? *I am always obliged to write and deliver the music four*

---

[1] Muzio.

*months after receiving the libretto*? So if the Naples management frivol-
ously decides to postpone production of my opera for a year, two, three
or ten, I shall have to continue to be the most humble servant, at the
disposition of the management? I should have to abandon all other
projects until the management deigns to send me the libretto? Oh,
admit it: you were not being serious! Do you know what the first
clause in my contract says? 'The work will be performed in October
1848, and Signor Verdi is to send the complete score by the end of
August, having received the complete libretto four months before this.'
Then they talk to me of litigation . . . . . the process of the law! So be it.
I am not frightened by these threats.

Because of my friendly feelings for you, I am sincerely sorry that
you have to suffer, and I assure you that insofar as it depends on me I
shall do everything possible to deliver you from this mess. On the
other hand, I myself am in a worse mess than you. You know that I
have placed this opera elsewhere in the event of its not being produced
in Naples at the time agreed. I have taken on other engagements here at
the Opéra which it is impossible to defer even for an hour. If you had
not imposed two months indolence upon me without sending me one
word of text, I should by now have finished this opera. Having found
now that it is almost impossible to fulfil this engagement, I find greater
difficulty in accepting the project you propose to me. Nevertheless, I
shall do all I can to adjust matters amicably, but what is necessary now
is that you lose not one more instant in sending me the rest of the
libretto.

With all esteem, Yours


[49]

*To Salvatore Cammarano*                    *Paris, 24 September, 1848*

[On the same day, Verdi wrote two letters to Cammarano.]

Dear Cammarano,

The Naples management, by means no more legitimate than they
are humane, wishes to obtain complete fulfilment of the conditions of
the contract.

You, an honest man, father of a family and a distinguished artist,
would be the victim of all these ignoble intrigues.

I, protected by my contract, am able to be scornful of the management's threats, and to forget the whole business, but for your sake, *purely for your sake*, I shall write the opera for Naples next year, even if I have to steal two hours every day from my rest, and so from my health!

I cannot at the moment say exactly when I shall give the opera to Naples (this will depend on the manner in which I can either postpone or get rid of other engagements), but you may assure the management of the date next year that they themselves have requested of me, on condition that you are not made to suffer anything by it, since it is for you alone that I am making this sacrifice. Otherwise, I shall not consider this letter binding.

Let me end my letter by saying to you that, from his acute intelligence, his business knowledge and, for that matter, the manner in which he has bungled these negotiations, I should have expected Signor Flauto to proceed differently.

Farewell, my dear Cammarano, and send me some more text as soon as possible. Ever yours

[50]

*To Salvatore Cammarano* [*24 September, 1848*]

[*La battaglia di Legnano*, ostensibly about the defeat of Barbarossa and his German army by the Italian cities of the Lombard League in 1176, was rightly to be understood by its first Italian audiences to refer to the situation in 1848, in which Italy was fighting a war of resistance against Austria. After its first performances, the opera did in fact succumb to the Austrian censorship. When it surfaced again, it was as *L'assedio di Haarlem*, in which Barbarossa had become the Duke of Alba, and Italy was transformed into sixteenth-century Flanders.]

If by any chance you have in the meantime come to an agreement with the management, I implore you in the name of friendship not to make use of my letter, as it is only with the greatest possible difficulty that I could find time to write this opera.

But if you cannot dispense with it and I am obliged to write it, do at least remember that I shall need a short text, full of interest, movement and, in particular, passion, which will make it easier for me to set it to music. I rely on you; meanwhile continue to send me the drama you have begun to write and tell me this: if the Censor should not pass it, do you think that, with the title and locale etc. changed, all or most of the text could be retained? For the time being, let's proceed and work on it as it is.

Allow me to beg a favour of you concerning the last act: at the beginning outside the Church of St. Ambrose, I would like to combine two or three different tunes. I would like, for example, the priests inside and the people outside to have a part in one metre, and Lida to have a tune in a different metre. Leave it to me to put them together. Perhaps you could also, if you agree, have some little verses in Latin for the priests. Do as you think best, but remember that this scene must make an effect.

[51]

*To Giuseppe Mazzini*                                    *Paris, 18 October, 1848*

[Giuseppe Mazzini (1805–1872), Italian revolutionary leader, had lived in exile in London for ten years before returning to Italy in 1848 to fight for a united Italian Republic. After the armistice, Mazzini fled to Switzerland. Verdi, who had met Mazzini in London in 1847, composed a patriotic song of battle on a poem, 'Suona la tromba', by the young romantic poet of the *Risorgimento*, Goffredo Mameli, who was to die in the fighting in Rome in 1849 at the age of twenty-two. Verdi's battle hymn arrived after the fighting was over, and, although Mazzini had it published, it was certainly not 'sung on the plains of Lombardy, amid the music of the cannon'.]

I am sending you the hymn, and, although it is a little late, I hope it arrives in time for the purpose. I have attempted to make it as popular and easy as possible. Make whatever use of it you wish to, but burn it if you don't think it worthwhile. If, however, you publish it, see that the poet changes a few words at the beginning of the second and third stanzas. 'Noi lo giuriamo . . . . Suona la tromba' etc., etc., then, if you think it a good idea, finish the verse with a word whose accent falls on the third last syllable. In the fourth verse of the second stanza, he will need to remove the interrogative and ensure that the sense of it ends with the verse. I could have set it to music as it stands, but then the music would have been difficult, and therefore less popular, and we would not have achieved our object.

May this hymn soon be sung on the plains of Lombardy, amid the music of the cannon.

Please accept the sincere greeting of one who holds you in complete veneration.

PS. If you decide to print it, you can apply to Carlo Pozzi in Mendrisio. He is Ricordi's agent.

[52]

*To Vincenzo Flauto*                                        *Paris, 23 November, 1848*

[Verdi refers in this letter to his experiences in Naples in the summer of 1845, when he was there for the production of *Alzira*. He did not, in fact, produce another work for the Paris Opéra until *Les Vêpres siciliennes* in 1855.]

I am sorry to seem to you to be difficult or precious. I am extremely frank, decided, sometimes irascible, even savage if you like, but never difficult or precious, and if I appear to be so it is not my fault but that of the circumstances. You paint a flattering picture of the manner in which I would now be received in Naples; but, pardon me, might it not be that, suffering as you do with nerves, you are liable to have visions and to work yourself into a state in which you are capable of seeing pink where there is only black? I would certainly be lying if I were to tell you I was satisfied with Naples last time: but, believe me, what disgusted me was not the outcome, but the endless petty wrangling that had nothing to do with any opera. Why attack me because I went to a popular café, or was seen on a balcony with Tadolini, or wore light-coloured shoes instead of black, or a thousand other trifling matters which were certainly not worthy of a serious public or a big city? Do you imagine that my presence can influence the result? Don't you believe it! I repeat what I said to you at the beginning, that I am somewhat savage, and that if Naples remarked on so many defects the first time, they will do so again a second time. It is true that I have been in Paris for eighteen months, in this city where one is said to acquire some civilized manners, but let me admit I am even more of a bear than I was. For six years I have been composing continually, wandering from country to country, and I have never said a word to a journalist or approached a friend or paid court to rich people in order to achieve success. Never, never! I have always despised means such as these. I write my operas as well as I can, and let things go their way without ever trying to influence public opinion in the slightest.

But let us leave this exordium which has nothing to do with our affairs. I want now to convince you that, if I do not come to Naples, this is not of my volition. I would sincerely like to be able to prove to the Neapolitans that I can achieve something not unworthy of their theatre. But listen, and then tell me yourself whether I can take on new obligations. You know that at the end of last year I signed a contract here to write a grand opera for the Opéra. I myself sent off to Guasco in St Petersburg a contract for a three year engagement at 80,000 francs a year, which was accepted. Guasco should have been here at the end of October, but various circumstances which it would be pointless to mention have prevented him from arriving. Because of this, there have been delays, and alterations to my contract. Therefore I am unable to be definite about my being here at a certain time, so I cannot give you a definite no, or make any promise to you until this is over.

This is the true situation, but don't make it known except to those you think it necessary to speak to about it. For the rest, make your own arrangements freely, because this correspondence cannot be legally binding on either you or me. If the future changes, then I too shall change. I am writing to Cammarano about various points concerning *Macbeth*. You too should attend the rehearsals, and don't object to an additional one: this is an opera a little more difficult than my others, and the manner in which it is produced is important. I confess to you that I have a preference for this opera over my others, and I should be sorry to see it go down the drain. Tell them it belongs to a genre which usually either goes wonderfully well or perilously. That is why the greatest care is necessary in performing it.

Farewell, farewell, yours affectionately

[53]

*To Salvatore Cammarano*                            *Paris, 23 November, 1848*

[The opera Verdi and Cammarano were working on was *La battaglia di Legnano*. Cammarano was at this time producing Verdi's *Macbeth* in Naples. Despite the composer's advice, Tadolini sang the rôle of Lady Macbeth in these Naples performances.]

I am still waiting for a reply to my letter which I sent after receiving the third act, as indeed I asked you in that letter to add a scene for the leading lady. I am still hoping that your friendship will lead you to do me this favour. In case you did not receive my letter, I will repeat my suggestions here. Since the woman's rôle seems to me to be less important than the other two, I should like you to add after the death chorus a big agitated recitative in which she expresses her love, her desperation at knowing Arrigo is to die, her fear of being discovered etc. etc. After a beautiful recitative, have the husband arrive for a moving little duet, make the father bless his son or something of the kind, etc. etc.

One final, tiny favour I ask of you. At the end of the second act, I should like four verses for Arrigo and Rolando (together) before

> Infamati e maledetti      (Dishonoured and accursed
> voi sarete in ogni età      You shall be forever.)

I should like to give some significance to this passage before the finale, so I don't want at this point to repeat words. I require these verses to be strong and full of energy. The idea I want them to express is this: 'A time will come when your descendants will shrink in horror from bearing your name' etc. etc. . . . then 'Dishonoured and accursed' etc.

If you can write these verses and send them to me immediately, you will be pleasing me greatly for I have no time to lose.

And tell me (don't be frightened to!): in the ensemble of the introduction I need to have another voice, a tenor. Could one include, for example, one of Arrigo's retinue? The same voice could also, perhaps, be used in the last finale. He could help Arrigo when he is wounded. Let me know about this.

I understand you are rehearsing *Macbeth*, and, as this opera interests me more than my others, please allow me to say a few words about it. Tadolini, I believe, is to sing Lady Macbeth, and I am astonished that she should have undertaken the part. You know how highly I regard Tadolini, and she herself knows it, but for the sake of us all I feel I must say this to you: Tadolini's qualities are far too fine for this rôle. This may seem to you absurd, but Tadolini has a beautiful and attractive figure, and I want Lady Macbeth to be ugly and evil. Tadolini sings to perfection, and I don't want Lady Macbeth to sing at all. Tadolini has a wonderful voice, clear, flexible, strong, while Lady Macbeth's voice should be hard, stifled and dark. Tadolini's voice is angelic; I want Lady Macbeth's to be diabolic. Please bring these comments to the notice of the management, of Maestro Mercadante who will understand my ideas better than anyone, and of Tadolini herself, then do in your wisdom what you think best.

Tell them that the two most important numbers in the opera are the duet between Lady Macbeth and her husband, and the Sleepwalking

Scene. If these two numbers fail, then the entire opera fails. And these numbers must definitely not be sung:

> they must be acted and declaimed
> in a voice hollow and veiled:
> otherwise the effect will be
> lost. The orchestra muted.

The stage extremely dark. In the third act, the apparition of the kings (I have seen this in London) must take place behind a special opening at the back, with a thin, ash-coloured veil in front of it. The kings must not be puppets but eight men of flesh and blood. The spot they pass over must be a kind of mound, and you should be able to see them ascend and descend. The stage must be completely dark, especially when the cauldron disappears, with light only where the kings are moving. The music from underneath the stage will have to be reinforced for the large San Carlo Theatre, but take care that there are neither trumpets nor trombones. The sound must seem far away and muffled, so it must be composed of bass clarinets, bassoons, contrabassoons and nothing else. Farewell, farewell. Always yours affectionately

[54]

*To Filippo Colini*                                           *Paris, November, 1848*

[The Roman baritone Filippo Colini, who had sung frequently at the Teatro Argentina in Rome, was to create the leading baritone rôle of Rolando in *La battaglia di Legnano* at its première there. He had been the first Giacomo in *Giovanna d'Arco* in 1845, and in 1850 was to sing Stankar in the first performances of *Stiffelio*.]

I don't know how the arrangements about the opera were made, but I do know that I have received various letters which I have found extremely mortifying. It seems that they have been put to great bother, it seems that this management has done me a great favour in accepting my score. Dear Colini, you know that I have never put myself under an obligation to anyone, I have never asked managements to accept my scores, nor have I ever received favours or charity from anyone, not even six years ago when I had need, indeed great need of them. You can therefore imagine that I am not going to put up now with even the slightest humiliation. As you know, I am under contract to write an opera for Ricordi. I have no other obligation. So, if I have intervened in this matter, it has been to help to get things settled, and if I have agreed to come to Rome it is not out of self-interest, but quite the reverse: I am making a sacrifice, for, as you know, a thousand francs is certainly not enough to defray the expenses of the journey from Paris to Rome and from Rome to Paris. I say all this to you, who are only my deputy in this matter, so that, if I have to come to Rome, you will know what the situation is.

[55]

*To Giovanni Ricordi*                                    *Paris, 19 April, 1849*

[This letter typifies Verdi's business correspondence with the firm of Ricordi.]

I can hardly express my surprise on receiving your statement. Why exchange francs into Milanese lire? To facilitate payment I would have accepted, for each golden napoleon of twenty francs, four silver napoleons plus half a franc, as you yourself did in the statement of December 14, in respect of *Gerusalemme*; but I cannot accept silver napoleons exchanged with Milanese lire at 7.4. I could give you plenty of reasons, but there is no point in talking to you, a businessman. You know what is right, and it is unjust that I should have to lose money on the exchange, in view of the fact that I also had to wait for payment. Will you please be so kind as to pay me the rest of the sum you owe in golden napoleons worth 20 francs each, as previously agreed. Permit me in turn to set out for you how matters stand.

You owe me:

1. The balance in respect of *Gerusalemme*, as stated by you etc.

2. The loss on the exchange of 150 golden napoleons which were paid in silver on behalf of Signora Strepponi. The difference in money has to be the same amount as the difference in value of the golden napoleons on January 26th, the day when payment should have been made.

3. The balance of payment in respect of the opera, *La battaglia di Legnano*: 650 golden napoleons worth 20 francs each.

4. The Florence contract: 400 gold francs (that is, 20 golden napoleons of 20 francs) as agreed in my letter of June 24, 1847, from London.

5. Rome contract: paragraph 4 of my letter of May 20th 1847 from Milan refers to this, and you agreed in your letter of December 29th 1848, in which you authorized me to ask the management in Rome on your behalf for the amount of 3,000 francs, and you wrote: 'therefore deducting from this amount (the above 3,000 francs) the 400 francs due to you on the contracts of the first two years, I have paid you 2,600 francs in respect of this opera.'

You are too reasonable not to agree with me about this. What I find embarrassing is your proposal to pay me in June only 300 golden napoleons. If I did not need this money, I would give you easy terms and I would only require one or two thousand francs a month till the entire amount had been paid. Unfortunately, however, I owe a large sum of money, and I must insist that you pay me the whole amount due to me.

In proof of what I am saying, let me tell you that I am in debt to a certain Jewish gentleman named Levi in Soragna. The debt is approximately 600 golden napoleons, and is due for payment in mid-June. If you would like to deal with this debt, I should be very glad, as I prefer to have no further contact with this Levi who is very rich and who may well agree to let you have this amount of money, provided that you pay his interest etc. etc. In this case, Emanuele could be very useful and could perhaps manage this affair. Write soon to let me know what you think about this.

I am surprised that Emanuele has not received your letters. Perhaps you didn't stamp them? Please note that for Parma and for San Donnino, letters require stamps. I myself have posted the letter for London with the two signatures etc. etc.

In Havana there are various theatres,[1] and therefore it is difficult to know whether the opera will be performed in one or more of them. Anyway, you know that during certain months in the year, the company moves from one country to another, so I think it would be more convenient to fix a price for the whole of Havana. Therefore, you will pay me 2,000 francs in 100 golden napoleons. In the event of the opera being performed in New York, you will pay me the sum of 300 francs in 150 golden napoleons. In that case, the contract would be for the whole of America.

Concerning the money you will be sending to my father at the beginning of May, please make sure it is in golden napoleons. Towards

[1] The leading Italian opera house in Havana was the Gran Teatro Taccon, under the management of Dr Francesco Marty y Torrens.

the end of this month I will let you know how much to send, in addition to the amount of 300 or 400 francs.

Farewell, farewell.


[56]

*To Carlo Verdi*                                   Paris, *19 April, 1849*

[Verdi's father, Carlo Verdi (1785–1867), was the village inn-keeper at Le Roncole. He married Luigia Uttini (1787–1851). Two children were born of the marriage: Giuseppe in 1813, and a girl, Giuseppa Francesca, in 1816. As the result of meningitis in childhood, Giuseppa became mentally deficient, and died in 1833 at the age of seventeen.

Verdi had purchased the Villa Sant'Agata, and his parents were acting as caretakers. He planned that his parents should live in a small farmhouse on the property.]

Dearest Father,

As I wrote to you in my letter of the 11th., Ricordi will send you the money you need to make the payments, and you will receive either 271 silver napoleons or 60 gold napoleons.

Ricordi will write to tell you when you must be in Piacenza, and you should pay Signor Bonini at the same time.

Give this letter to Emanuele, and he will tell you what it means. Try to adjust the accounts properly with Merli, and send me, after May 11th, a note of all the expenses incurred.

Farewell, farewell! A kiss to mama.


[57]

*To Salvatore Cammarano*                          Paris, *17 May, 1849*

[The opera referred to is *Luisa Miller*.]

I have just received your scenario, and I confess to you I would have preferred two prima donnas, and I should also have preferred more emphasis on the prince's mistress, exactly as in Schiller. There would have been a contrast between her and Eloisa, and Rodolfo's love for Eloisa would have been more beautiful. I do realise, however, that I cannot always have what I want, and I am very pleased with it as it is. It seems to me, however, that all that devilish intrigue between Walter and Wurm, which dominates the whole of the play, doesn't here have the same colour and force that it has in Schiller. Perhaps in verse it will be different, but in any case let me know yourself whether you think I am right or not. Finally, it seems to me that when Eloisa is compelled by Wurm to write the letter instead of saying she was Wurm's mistress it would have been more meaningful, also more natural and credible, if she had said she was in love with someone else—anyone except Wurm.

Deal with these remarks of mine in any way you wish, but let me say that in the first act finale, I am against having a stretta or cabaletta. The situation doesn't require one, and a stretta would probably lose all its effect in this position. The beginning of the piece and the ensembles you can deal with as you wish, but at the end you should stick as closely as possible to Schiller.

Rodolfo: Through death! Go back, I entreat you, I implore you etc.
Walter: Wretched fellows? Do you hesitate?
Rod: Father, if he goes to prison, your son goes with him.
Walter: Do it!
Rod: I shall draw my sword on you——
Walt: Do it.
Rod: Ah, my father, I would pierce you through the heart rather than——
Walt: Do it.
Rod: God is my witness etc. etc. . . . . . how you became Lord Walter (*He rushes out desperately*)
Walt: Let that woman go, and follow me. Rodolfo! Rodolfo! (*He goes*)

Here a general exclamation from everyone, and the curtain falls.

You can make this finale as long as you like; since I don't have to repeat the piece (or rather cannot), the length does not matter.

In the second act, take great care with the duet between Wurm and Eloisa. Make a strong contrast between Eloisa's terror and desperation and Wurm's diabolic frigidity. It seems to me that if you can give to the character of Wurm a slightly comic touch, the situation will become even more terrifying. After the other duet between Walter and Wurm, are you having a quartet? I think you need one here for unaccompanied voices.

I think you should do an aria for Rodolfo's scene. The first part of the piece is all right, but I have the impression that the end will be cold.

Antonio Barezzi

Giovanni Ricordi, from
a drawing by Bignoli

Countess Clarina Maffei

Antonio Ghislanzoni

To lower the curtain on two people alone, after having had a grand finale in the first act! Think of this. I believe we'll have to find something here.

The third act is superb. Try to develop further the duet between father and daughter: make it a duet to bring tears to the eyes. The duet which follows is superb and tremendous, and I think it will be necessary to end with a trio with the father.

When Walter enters, he should have as few lines as possible. If, in order to develop these two pieces, you find it necessary to make them a little longer, do so. In the piece for the three basses, I think the principal part should be that of Eloisa's father, so make it a good part. Then Walter, and finally Wurm. Don't forget, in the part of this last character, to keep a certain comical something which will serve to give greater emphasis both to his manners and his villainy.

All I have to say to you now, in a loud voice, is to send me your verses as soon as possible. Farewell, farewell.

## [58]

*To Vincenzo Luccardi*                    *Paris, 14 July, 1849*

[Verdi, living in Paris with Giuseppina Strepponi, was at work on *Luisa Miller*. Things went badly for the liberal cause in Italy in 1849: a recurrence of the fighting in the north led to the abdication of the King of Sardinia and Piedmont, and the victory of Austria. In July, Rome fell, and Verdi wrote to his friend Luccardi, the sculptor, in Rome.]

Dear Luccardi,

For three days I have been waiting impatiently for your letters. You can well imagine how the catastrophe in Rome has weighed heavily in my thoughts, and it was wrong of you not to write to me immediately. Let's not speak of Rome! . . . . . . what good would it do? Force still rules the world! Justice? . . . . what can it do against bayonets!! We can only weep at our disgrace, and curse those responsible for so much disaster.

Talk to me then about yourself; tell me of your vicissitudes. What are you doing now? In short, tell me everything that our new masters will allow you to tell. Tell me, too, about my friends.

Write this very moment, don't lose a minute, for I have an inferno within me.

c

[59]

*To Vincenzo Flauto*                              *Busseto, 7 September, 1849*

[*Eloisa* is *Luisa Miller*. Although, in this letter to the Naples impresario, Verdi agrees to write another opera for Naples, and the first mention of Hugo's *Le Roi s'amuse*, the source of *Rigoletto*, occurs, Verdi in fact never wrote another opera for Naples after *Luisa Miller*. *Rigoletto* was first performed in Venice, and it was Piave, not Cammarano, who was to write the libretto.]

Dear Flauto,

I have little time to write at length, and will only say that I shall do as you require, and shall write, after this *Eloisa*, another opera to be produced the day after Easter, 1850. Send me, therefore, the contract, as required by my last letter (26 July). All that remains to be fixed is the rate of payment for your rights in the score for the Kingdom of Naples, and this should be divided into three equal instalments: the first to be paid on the day of my arrival on the scene (which should be about a month before the date of production), the second on the day of the first orchestral rehearsal, and the third on the day after the dress rehearsal. Take care that the paragraph regarding your rights for the Kingdom of Naples and my rights for the rest of the musical world is quite clearly worded.

As for the opera I'm writing now, I shall be in Naples about the 8th or the 10th October in order to stage it by the end of the same month. Arrange matters so that I can begin rehearsals the day after I arrive, as I shall be bringing with me the score which is finished except for the instrumentation. In the matter of the payment for this opera, you should refer to the very first contract of all.

Now we must think seriously about the libretto for the opera to be produced the day after Easter, because, in order to do things properly, Cammarano will have to have completed a rough sketch and sent the first part to me by the end of October, when this *Eloisa* will be staged, and when I shall be leaving Naples for a time, and would like to take the poetry with me to set to music. As for the subject, suggest Victor Hugo's *Le Roi s'amuse* to Cammarano. It's a fine play with stupendous situations, and with two magnificent rôles for Frezzolini and De Bassini.[1] Farewell, farewell

[1] The two magnificent rôles were, of course, Gilda and Rigoletto, but they were not to be created by Frezzolini (see *Personalia*) and De Bassini. The baritone Achille de Bassini (1819–1881) had created the rôle of the Doge in *I due Foscari* in 1844, and

PS. It's understood that, for the opera to be written after Easter, I shall have the right to choose the singers from among the company. Don't forget to put this clause in the contract.

[60]

*To Vincenzo Flauto*                    *Naples, 1 November, 1849*

[Cammarano had warned Verdi of the management's financial difficulties. Flauto responded to this letter by threatening to invoke a curious law which forbade any artist to leave Naples unless authorized to do so. Verdi predictably refused to be intimidated, and announced his intention of taking himself and his opera on board one of the French warships in the bay, and demanding protection against the Kingdom of the Two Sicilies. Flauto capitulated.]

Dear Flauto,

It has come to my knowledge that the affairs of the management are not improving, and so I have resolved to come to a decision; though not without informing, through you, the management with whom I have a contract. The sacrifices I have made, and the damages I have suffered, are known to you. You also know my obligations. You know that I came to Naples in answer to your requests, and to render a small service to Cammarano. You know that I could have profited from the offers you have made me thousands of times, and that I have not done so. Finally, you know that I no longer write operas for 3,000 ducats, and that I could have refused to write this one. Nevertheless, I submitted voluntarily to the sacrifices; I should like now, however, to be sure that I shall not have to suffer from it in the future. I know the critical circumstances of the management, and, if they are finding it difficult to pay me the first instalment, it will be even more difficult for them to make the other two payments, particularly if their hopes of having a great success with my new opera are not realized. Great successes are difficult to come by in Naples, and above all for me. Now, in order to settle things with the fewest possible ill-effects, it seems to me there are only these two ways: either for you to deposit the three thousand ducats owing to me with some person I can trust, or to dissolve my contract.

---

Seid in *Il corsaro* (1848), and was to sing Luisa's father in *Luisa Miller*, at the première on 8 December, 1849. In 1862, he was to be the Melitone of the St Petersburg première of *La forza del destino*.

You will see that I couldn't be more reasonable. Discuss it with the management and the Superintendent so that they can all, each on his own part, come to a decision. Today, I shall go again to the rehearsal, but I don't know if I shall go tomorrow. If you think that the contents of this letter should be kept secret between you, me, the management and the Superintendent, I give you my word that on my part they will be. Farewell, farewell.

[61]

*To Giovanni Ricordi*                          *Busseto, 31 January, 1850*

[The opera referred to in the final paragraph is *Stiffelio*, which was to be produced at the Teatro Grande, Trieste, on 16 November, 1850. The libretto, however, was not by Cammarano but by Piave. With Cammarano, Verdi began discussions about the possibility of composing an opera on Shakespeare's *King Lear*.]

Dear Ricordi,

I have no doubt at all that what you tell me in your letter of the 26th is true. I know very well that these are critical times, that you have to carry enormous expenses, and that you are employing solicitors everywhere (though not only on my account); but you also know that I have ten years ahead of me, and during that time the situation of our theatres may improve, as I have reason to believe from various letters I've received. Besides, without reserving these rights for myself, at one time I might have made other conditions for *Gerusalemme* and *La battaglia di Legnano*. But I don't wish to bore you with the thousands upon thousands of reasons which I could produce to my advantage, and I am only surprised that, after Emanuele had written to me that you had agreed on 50%, you now reduce me to 30. This is too much! Nevertheless, I don't wish to be obstinate, and I accept your proposals to pay me for ten years 30% of all hire fees you receive, and 40% of sales in all countries, so long as you intend to include *Luisa Miller* in this ten-year arrangement, and handle it in the same way as *Gerusalemme* and *La battaglia di Legnano* or *Assedio d'Arlem*. In this manner, it seems to me the burden can be shared. You must realize how fair I am being, and just how much faith I have in the reasons you offer. If this suits you, we shall have to adjust our accounts up to the present, then you can compile a list of all the hire agreements and sales you make, which I or someone delegated by me will examine twice yearly: at the end of June and December, you will remit any sums due to me. This agreement shall begin to operate today, and my rights will subsist for ten years commencing on the dates on which the above three operas had their first performances.

As for the other opera I was to have written for Naples, I got out of it in disgust at the unworthy method of procedure of the management and the direction. Nevertheless, the subject having already been agreed with Cammarano, I shall write it in any case, and I hope to have it finished in four or five months. I shall hand it over to you willingly, and leave you with the task of having it produced sometime in November of the present year, 1850, in any one of the leading Italian theatres (with the exception of La Scala, Milan) by a first-rate company, and with my promise to attend rehearsals in person. In recompense, you will pay me 16,000 francs (sixteen thousand) in 800 gold napoleons of twenty francs each, either on the day the opera is produced or in monthly instalments to be agreed between us, as soon as you have accepted the principal conditions. Furthermore, you will pay me 30% of all hire fees you obtain, and 40% of all sales in every country, for ten consecutive years beginning on the day of the first performance of this opera, which will be, I repeat, during November, 1850. These conditions regarding the hire fees of the opera to be written shall go into effect as soon as you have accepted those concerning the other three operas, and so all four will be bound together by the same agreement.

[62]

*To Salvatore Cammarano*                    *Busseto, 28 February, 1850*

[Verdi had first thought of composing an opera on *King Lear* in 1843, when the Teatro La Fenice had asked him for a new work. As he wanted to write the rôle of Lear for a baritone, and there was no really first-rate baritone among the Venice company, he shelved the project. It came up again in 1846, when Verdi was corresponding with Benjamin Lumley about the opera he was to compose for London. He agreed to write *Lear* for Luigi Lablache to sing in London, but the venture was postponed because of Verdi's ill-health, and the opera which finally got written for London was *I masnadieri*. For a discussion of Verdi's life-long interest in *King Lear*, which he never composed, the reader is referred to the present editor's *The Complete Operas of Verdi* (London 1969; New York 1970.)]

Dear Cammarano,

*King Lear* at first sight is so vast and intricate that it seems impossible one could make an opera out of it. However, on examining it closely, it seems to me that the difficulties, though no doubt immense, are not insuperable. You realize that there is no need to make *King Lear* into the usual kind of drama we have had up until now: rather, we must treat it in a completely new manner, on a large scale, and without regard for mere convenience. I believe the rôles could be reduced to five principal ones: Lear, Cordelia, the Fool, Edmund, Edgar. Two secondary female roles: Regan and Goneril (though perhaps the latter would have to be made a second leading lady). Two secondary bass rôles (as in *Luisa*): Kent and Gloucester, the rest minor rôles.

Would you agree that the reason for disinheriting Cordelia is rather infantile for the present day? Certain scenes would definitely have to be cut, for instance the one in which Gloucester is blinded, the one in which the two sisters are carried onto the stage etc. etc., and many others which you know better than I do. The number of scenes can be reduced to 8 or 9: let me draw your attention to the fact that in *I Lombardi* there are 11, which has never been any bar to performance.

### Act I, Scene i

Great Stateroom in Lear's palace. Lear on his throne. Division of the Kingdom. Demonstration by the Earl of Kent. Rage of the King who banishes the Earl. Cordelia's farewell.

### Scene ii

Edmund's soliloquy. Gloucester enters (without seeing Edmund) and deplores the banishment of Kent. Edmund, encountering Gloucester, tries to hide a letter. Gloucester forces him to reveal it. He believes that Edgar is plotting. Edgar enters; and his father, blind with fury, draws a sword against him. Edgar flees, after trying to assuage his father's anger with soothing words.

### Scene iii

Hall (or vicinity) of Goneril's castle. Kent is seen dressed as a beggar. Lear arrives and takes him into his service. Meanwhile, the Fool with his bizarre songs mocks Lear for having trusted his daughters. Goneril enters, complaining of the insolence of her father's knights, whom she refuses to allow to stay in the castle. The king erupts with anger when he realizes his daughter's ingratitude. He fears he will go mad . . . . . but remembering Regan, he calms himself and hopes to be treated better by her. The arrival is announced of Regan, who has been invited by her sister. Lear approaches her and tells how Goneril has wronged him. Regan cannot believe this and says he must have offended her. The sisters unite to persuade Lear to disperse his followers. Then Lear, realizing his daughters' heartlessness, cries: 'You think I'll weep; no, I'll not weep.' He swears vengeance, exclaiming that he will do terrible things, 'what they are yet,' he knows not, 'but they shall be the terrors of the earth.' (The noise of a tempest begins to be heard.) The curtain falls.

## Act II, Scene i

Country. The tempest continues. Edgar, a fugitive, banished and accused of an attempt on his father's life, laments the injustice of his fate. Hearing a noise he takes refuge in a hut.—Lear, Fool and Kent.— 'Blow, winds, and crack your cheeks . . . . Rumble thy bellyful! Spit, fire! Spout, rain! Nor rain, wind, thunder, fire are my daughters. I tax you not, you elements, with unkindness; I never gave you kingdom, call'd you children!' The Fool (still joking): 'O, nuncle, court holy-water in a dry house is better than this rain-water out o' door.' He enters the hut and is frightened when he sees Edgar, who feigns madness and utters cries of woe. Lear exclaims: 'What, have his daughters brought him to this pass? Couldst thou save nothing? Didst thou give them all?' (magnificent quartet.) Someone bearing a torch approaches. It is Gloucester who, in defiance of the decree of the daughters, has come in search of the King.

## Scene ii

Hall in Goneril's castle. Huge chorus (in various verse metres): 'Do you not know? Gloucester transgressed the command! . . . . . Well then? A terrible punishment awaits him!! What? . . . . to have his eyes put out!! Horror, horror!! Wretched age, in which such crimes are committed.' The events relating to Lear, Cordelia, Kent, Gloucester etc. are recounted, and finally all fear a horrifying war which France will wage against England to avenge Lear.

## Scene iii

Edmund: 'To both these sisters have I sworn my love; each jealous of the other, as the stung are of the adder. Which of them shall I take? Both? one? or neither?' etc. etc. Goneril enters and, after brief dialogue, offers him command of the army, and gives him a token of her love.

## Scene iv

A poor room in a cottage.

Lear, Kent, Edgar, the Fool, and peasants. The Fool asks Lear, 'Whether a madman be a gentleman or a yeoman.' Lear replies: 'A King, a King!!'—Song—Lear, in a state of delirium, continually obsessed with the idea of the ingratitude of his daughters, wishes to set up a court of justice. He calls Edgar 'most learned justicer', the Fool 'sapient sir' etc. etc. Extremely bizarre and moving scene. Finally, Lear tires and gradually falls asleep. All weep for the unhappy King. End of second act.

## Act III, Scene i

The French camp near Dover.

Cordelia' has heard from Kent of her father's misfortune. Great sorrow on Cordelia's part. She sends messenger after messenger to see if he has been found. She is ready to give all her possessions to whoever can restore his reason; she invokes the pity of nature etc. etc. The doctor announces that the King has been found and that he hopes to cure him of his madness. Cordelia, intoxicated with joy, thanks heaven and longs for the moment of vengeance.

## Scene ii

Tent in the French camp.

Lear asleep on a bed. The doctor and Cordelia enter very quietly. '[He] sleeps still . . .' After a brief dialogue very sweet sounds of music are heard behind the scenes, Lear awakes. Magnificent duet, as in the Shakespeare scene. The curtain falls.

## Act IV, Scene i

Open country near Dover. The sound of a trumpet from afar.

Edgar appears, leading Gloucester: moving little duet in which Gloucester recognizes that he has been unjust to his son. Finally, Edgar says: 'Here, father, take the shadow of this tree for your good host; pray that the right may thrive.' (Exit) Sound of trumpet nearer, noises, alarm; finally the signal to assemble is given. Edgar returns: 'Away, old man; give me thy hand; away! King Lear hath lost, he and his daughter ta'en.' (March) Edmund, Albany, Regan, Goneril, officers, soldiers etc. enter in triumph. Edmund gives an officer a letter: 'If thou dost as this instructs thee, thou dost make thy way to noble fortunes.' An armed warrior with lowered vizor (Edgar) enters unexpectedly and accuses Edmund of high treason: in proof, he offers a letter to Albany. A duel takes place. Edmund is mortally wounded:

before he dies he confesses all his crimes, and tells them to hurry to save Lear and Cordelia . . . . . 'For my writ is on the life of Lear and on Cordelia—nay, send in time.'

### Final scene
### Prison

Moving scene between Lear and Cordelia, Cordelia begins to feel the effects of the poison: her agony and death. Albany, Kent and Edgar rush in to save her, but too late. Lear, unconscious of their arrival, takes Cordelia's corpse in his arms, and exclaims: 'She's dead as earth. Howl! Howl!' etc. Ensemble in which Lear must have the leading part. End.

[63]

*To Guglielmo Brenna*                    *Busseto, 18 April, 1850*

[Guglielmo Brenna was the Secretary of the Fenice Theatre. C. D. Marzari was President, or chief administrator, of the Fenice Theatre.]

Dear Brenna,

You will see from the letter to Sig. Marzari that everything has now been arranged. I seek only a few days' postponement of the performance because I cannot begin rehearsals before February 1st. For the rest, if the singers are good and willing, do not doubt that everything will go quickly. I shall certainly cause no delay.

Take good care in engaging the company; I say this as much in my own interests as in those of the theatre itself. See that it goes well. For the women, if neither Frezzolini nor Barbieri is free at that time why not try to get De Giuli?[1]

In *Luisa Miller* there is a rôle for a contralto, but it is very small. I cannot make promises, but I have no objection to writing for a contralto. It will depend on the circumstances and on the subject that we have to choose.[2]

[1] The soprano Teresa de Giuli-Borsi (1820–1877) had sung Lida in the first performances of *La battaglia di Legnano* in 1849. None of the three sopranos mentioned in this letter sang Gilda in the *Rigoletto* première. The Gilda was to be Teresa Brambilla.

[2] The President of the Fenice had requested that there be a contralto rôle in the opera for a singer named Annetta Casaloni, who was in the company, and who was also to sing the small rôle of Federica in *Luisa Miller* in the same season.

If you are drawing up the contract, make it brief and very clear. Do not include clauses on the dress rehearsal, costumes and lighting etc.

If the management is sending me the contract, in order to save time tell Piave that, if he has not found the Spanish drama[1] I mentioned, I suggest *Kean*,[2] one of the finest plays of Dumas. It would be possible to do many good things with this play without losing time. I could start work a month from now.

Farewell. Believe me always yours affectionately

[64]

*To Giulio Carcano*                                        *Busseto, 17 June, 1850*

[Giulio Carcano (1812–1884), poet and translator of Shakespeare, was an old friend of Verdi. In 1855 he wrote the libretto for Muzio's opera, *Claudia*.]

My dearest Carcano,

How many sad and tender memories are contained in the few lines which you sent to me! My Carcano! It is impossible to forget the past, and the future, I don't know what it will bring.

I would dearly like to associate my name with yours, and I know that if you are proposing I should compose *Hamlet*, the adaptation will be worthy of you. Unfortunately, these huge subjects demand too much time, and I have had, for the time being, to give up *King Lear* as well, leaving the commission with Cammarano to adapt the drama at some other more propitious moment. Now, if *King Lear* is difficult, *Hamlet* is even more so. And, pushed as I am by two commissions, I have had to choose easier and shorter subjects to be able to fulfil my obligations. I do not give up all hope, however, that one day I can get together with you and work on this masterpiece of the English theatre. I should be proud to clothe your verses in my music and thus present the operatic theatre with a beautiful work of poetry.

---

[1] *El Trovador* by Antonio Garcia Gutiérrez.

[2] Dumas's play is about the English actor Edmund Kean. Although Verdi was intrigued by the play, he never used it as the subject of an opera.

[65]

To C. D. Marzari, Venice                    Busseto, 5 December, 1850

[*La maledizione* was eventually to be called *Rigoletto*.

Many of the early performances of *Stiffelio* had to be given without the final act, which was considered blasphemous. The first scene in the act has Lina addressing her clergyman husband as 'ministro' and confessing to him as a priest. The final scene is set in a church, and the clergyman preaches from the pulpit a sermon in which he quotes from the New Testament.]

The letter which arrived with the decree completely banning *La Maledizione* was so unexpected that I almost went out of my mind. In this matter, Piave was at fault: completely at fault! He assured me in several letters, written as long ago as May, that approval had been obtained for it. This being so, I set to music a large part of the play, working with the greatest zeal in order to finish at the time agreed. The decree forbidding it drives me to desperation, because now it is too late to choose another libretto. It would be impossible, absolutely impossible, for me to set another subject to music this winter. This was the third time I was granted the honour of writing for Venice, and the management knows with what punctuality I have always carried out my duties. It knows that when I was almost dying I gave my word I would finish *Attila*, and I did so. Now I repeat on my oath that it is impossible for me to set a new libretto, even if I were to slave away to the point of endangering my health. Nevertheless, to demonstrate my good will, I offer the only thing that I can do. *Stiffelio* is an opera new to Venice. I suggest presenting it, and I would myself come to produce it at whatever time the management thinks opportune, during the carnival season of 1850–51. There is in this opera one very great difficulty (also due to the censor), and that is the final scene. It cannot be staged as it is; but if it is not possible to obtain permission from Vienna to do it as I intended, I would be willing to change the ending which would thus be completely new for Venice. I request the management to accept this proof of my good will, and to believe that the damage and the displeasure I am caused by this prohibition are greater than I have words to describe.

[66]

*To C. D. Marzari, Venice*                    *Busseto, 14 December, 1850*

[The character Triboletto was finally to be called Rigoletto. The opera, after a compromise had been reached in which the situations in Hugo's play were left intact, though the names of characters and the locale were changed, was produced at the Fenice on 11 March, 1851.]

In order to reply immediately to yours of the 11th, let me say I have had very little time to examine the new libretto. I have seen enough, however, to know that in its present form it lacks character, significance, and, in short, the dramatic moments leave one completely cold. If it was necessary to change the characters' names, then the locality should have been changed as well. You could have a Duke or Prince of some other place, for example a Pier Luigi Farnese, or put the action back to a time before Louis XI when France was not a united kingdom, and have a Duke of Burgundy or Normandy etc. etc., but in any case an absolute ruler. In the fifth scene of Act I, all that anger of the courtiers against Triboletto doesn't make sense. The old man's curse, so terrifying and sublime in the original, here becomes ridiculous because his motive for uttering the curse doesn't have the same significance, and because it is no longer a subject who speaks in so forthright a manner to his King. Without this curse, what scope or significance does the drama have? The Duke has no character. The Duke must definitely be a libertine: without this there is no justification for Triboletto's fear that his daughter might leave her hiding-place, and the drama is made impossible. What would the Duke be doing in the last act, alone in a remote inn, without an invitation, without a rendezvous? I don't understand why the sack has gone. Why should a sack matter to the police? Are they worried about the effect? But let me say this: why do they think they know better than I do about this? Who is playing the Maestro? Who can say this will make an effect and that won't? We had this kind of difficulty with the horn in *Ernani*. Well, did anyone laugh at the sound of that horn? With that sack removed, it is improbable that Triboletto would talk for half an hour to a corpse, before a flash of lightning reveals it to be his daughter. Finally, I see that they have avoided making Triboletto an ugly hunchback!! A hunchback who sings? Why not? . . . Will it be effective? I don't know. But, I repeat, if I don't know then they who propose this change don't know either. I thought it would be beautiful to portray this extremely deformed and ridiculous character who is inwardly passionate and full of love. I chose the subject precisely because of these qualities and these original traits, and if they are cut I shall no longer be able to set it to music. If anyone says to me I can leave my notes as they are for this new plot, I reply that I don't understand this kind of thinking, and I say frankly that my music, whether beautiful or ugly, is never written in a vacuum, and that I always try to give it character.

To sum up, an original, powerful drama has been turned into something ordinary and cold. I am extremely sorry that the Management did not reply to my last letter. I can only repeat and beg them to do what I asked then, because my artist's conscience will not allow me to set this libretto to music.

I have the honour to sign myself, your devoted servant

[67]

*To Giovanni Ricordi*                      *Busseto, 5 January, 1851*

[*Stiffelio* was not performed at La Scala during this season.]

Dear Ricordi,

The news I hear that they want to stage *Stiffelio* at La Scala displeases me because, ordinarily, operas which are not written expressly for that theatre are too badly treated there: *Gerusalemme* is a recent example of this. Why do they omit the little duet at the beginning? Why do they omit the *Ave Maria*? (to say nothing of the washed out performances of chorus and orchestra). If a score doesn't please them, better not to perform it at all. To return to *Stiffelio*, if it really must be performed there, the Censors will first have to persuade themselves that the libretto contains nothing harmful to politics or religion; and they must leave the original libretto as it is, with all its words and stage directions intact. There should be neither alteration nor expurgation, and everyone must really put his best effort into it. It must particularly be noted that, in the final scene, the effect depends on the manner in which the chorus is distributed about the stage, so they must have not just one stage rehearsal as usual, but ten or twenty if necessary.

Unless these conditions are agreed to, I cannot permit *Stiffelio* to be performed at La Scala, and you should also note that, if it should make no effect through defects in performance, I shall hold you, Sig.

Giovanni Ricordi, responsible for any damage that may be caused by it. Farewell, farewell.

PS. It's impossible for me to come to Milan to stage *Stiffelio*.


[68]

*To Doctor Ercolano Balestra*                    Busseto, *21 January, 1851*

[Dr Balestra was a notary in Busseto.]

From a reliable source, I have learned that my father goes around saying that things have been arranged between you in one of the two following ways: namely, that I have assigned to him the administration of my property, or that I am going to lease it to him. I do not believe that, between you and me, Doctor, there can be any misunderstanding over this, nor do I believe that you have proposed any of these things: nevertheless, I should like to repeat, mainly to reassure myself, that I do not agree to either of these suggestions. I intend to be quite separate from my father both in domestic and in business affairs. Finally, I can only repeat what I said to you yesterday in person: to the outside world, Carlo Verdi must be one thing and Giuseppe Verdi another. I have the honour to sign myself, with all esteem, devotedly yours


[69]

*To Salvatore Cammarano*                         Busseto, *9 April, 1851*

[This letter is about *Il trovatore*, based on the play *El Trovador* by Gutiérrez. The other subject, which Verdi mentions in his penultimate paragraph, is *La Dame aux camélias* by Dumas *fils*.]

Dear Cammarano,

I have read your synopsis, and, as a man of talent and very superior character, you will not be offended if I, in my most niggardly fashion, take the liberty of saying to you that, if we cannot retain for this subject all the novelty and bizarre quality of the Spanish drama, it would be better to abandon it.

It seems to me that, unless I am mistaken, several of the situations lack their former force and originality, and, above all, that Azucena no longer has her strange and novel character. It seems to me that this woman's two great passions, filial love and maternal love, are no longer present in all their power. For example, I would not like to have the troubadour wounded in the duel. This poor troubador has so little individuality that, if we take away his valour, what remains to him? How could he interest Leonora, a well-bred lady? I wouldn't like Azucena to address her narrative to the gypsies, nor, in the third act ensemble, to say 'Tuo figlio fu arso vivo etc. etc. .... ma io non v'era' etc. etc. (Your son was burned alive ... but I was not there), and finally I don't want her to be mad at the end. I should like you to leave the big aria in!! Eleonora has no part in the Miserere and the troubador's song, and this seems to me one of the best places for an aria. If you are afraid of giving Eleonora too big a rôle, leave out the cavatina. To express my thoughts better, let me expand into more detail about how I feel this subject should be treated.

### Part I—Prologue

1. Opening number.—The chorus and introductory narrative are fine. Suppress Leonora's cavatina, and write an imposing

2. Trio, beginning with De Luna's recitative, then the troubadour's song, Leonora's scene and challenge, etc. etc.

### Part 2

Gypsies, Azucena and the troubadour who has been wounded in battle.

3. Gypsies sing a strange, fantastic chorus. While they are carousing, Azucena intones a lugubrious song. The gypsies interrupt because it is too sorrowful. 'Funesta come la storia che ne fu l'argomento! Voi non la conoscete ... (Sarai vendicata!)' (Just as sad as the story that inspired it ... You don't know her .... You shall be avenged.) These words agitate the troubadour who, until this moment, has been standing lost in thought. Day dawns and the gypsies disperse over the mountainside, repeating a part of their chorus etc. The troubadour, left alone with his mother, begs her to tell him the story which so horrified him. Narrative etc. Duet with Alfonso which must keep to free and new forms.

4. Duet with Alfonso.—It seems to me inappropriate for Azucena to recount her narrative in the presence of the gypsies and let slip the few words about her having abducted De Luna's son and having sworn to avenge her mother.

5. Scene of Leonora's taking the veil etc. etc., and finale.

## Part 3

6. Chorus and De Luna's *romanza*

7. Ensemble. The dialogue, or interrogation in the Spanish play, reveals the character of the gypsy very clearly. On the other hand, if Azucena reveals who and what she is, she immediately puts herself into the hands of her enemy, and loses her chance of vengeance. It's good to have Fernando arouse the Count's suspicions, and to have the Count, when he refers to himself as De Luna, startle Azucena. In this manner, she is recognized by Fernando and does not betray herself, except with the phrase which escapes her: 'Taci, che se lo sa m'uccide!' (Quiet, if he knows that he will kill me.) Very simple and beautiful are Azucena's words when asked: 'Dove vai?' (Where are you going?) Nol so: vissi sulle montagne: avea un figlio: m'abbandonò: vado a cercarlo . . .' (I don't know. I lived in the mountains, had a son, he left me, and I am going to look for him.)

8. Leonora's recitative. Recitative and narrative of Manrique's dream, followed by

9. Duet between him and Leonora. He reveals to his bride-to-be that he is the son of a gypsy. Ruiz announces that his mother is in prison. He rushes off to save her etc. etc.

## Part 4

10. Leonora's big aria, interwoven with the chant for those about to die and the troubadour's song.

11. Duet for Leonora and De Luna

12. Don't make Azucena mad. Exhausted with fatigue, with sorrow, terror and lack of sleep, she is unable to speak rationally. Her senses are overwrought, but she is not mad. You must keep in sight right to the end this woman's two big passions: her love for Manrique and her wild desire to avenge her mother. When Manrique is dead, her feeling of revenge becomes gigantic, and she cries in exaltation: 'Si . . . egli era tuo fratello . . . Stolto! . . . Si vendicata, o madre!' (Yes, he was your brother. Fool! Mother, you are avenged.)

I beg you to forgive my rash words. I am no doubt wrong, but I could not refrain from at least telling you how I feel about it. Besides, my first suspicion that you didn't like this play is probably true. If this is so, we still have time to change our minds rather than work on something you don't like. I already have another subject, simple but affecting, which can be said to be almost finished. If you like, I'll send it to you, and we'll think no more of *Trovatore*.

Let me have a word from you about this. And if you have a subject, tell me of it. Farewell, farewell, my dear Cammarano. Write to me immediately, and believe me yours affectionately for life.

[70]

*To Salvatore Cammarano*                    *Busseto, 9 September, 1851*

[The 'serious misfortunes' included the death of Verdi's mother on 30 June, 1851.]

An accumulation of serious misfortunes has prevented me from thinking seriously about *Il trovatore*. But now that things are beginning to right themselves again, I must give some thought to music and business. Both Rome and Venice have asked me for operas. Rome offers me the singers De Giuli, Fraschini and Colini; Venice, Frezzolini and Coletti. The Rome company is more suitable for *Il trovatore*, except that they lack an actress for Azucena, and you know how demanding I am about Azucena! Gabussi[1] would be fine in the rôle, but I don't know whether she is free, or engaged by Naples or somewhere else. If she were free, perhaps I could engage her for Rome. If she were engaged by the San Carlo Theatre with other first-rate artists, I could re-open the negotiations with them that I broke off last winter, when I was irritated by the patronizing tone they adopted in writing to offer me the contract. But this would be a delicate matter, which is why I turn to you, dear friend, who are so tactful, and ask you to deal with this, so that my dignity as man and artist need not suffer for it.

[71]

*To Vincenzo Luccardi*                    *Busseto, 1 December, 1851*

[In the autumn of 1851, *Rigoletto* had been performed in Rome in a version mutilated by censorship requirements, much to Verdi's indignation. Angiolini was conductor of the orchestra at the Teatro Apollo, Rome.]

---

[1] Rita Gabussi (b. 1812) was the wife of the baritone De Bassini. When *Il trovatore* finally reached the stage in Rome on 19 January, 1853, none of the singers mentioned in this letter was in the cast.

Dear madman,

I shall not come to Rome this year, as you and I had hoped I could. An accumulation of adverse circumstances prevents me from having the pleasure of greeting you, and my other friends, and seeing the eternal city. I hope that another time things will work out better, but I don't wish to accuse anyone, the fault is all mine! Understand? I know that not only was *Stiffelio* ruined in Rome, but also *Rigoletto*. These impresarios just aren't intelligent enough to understand that, if operas cannot be performed exactly as their composers intended, then it's better not to perform them. They don't realize that the transposition of a scene, or even of one number, almost always leads to a non-success. Imagine what happens when they change the plot!! It's surprising that I haven't yet made a public declaration to the effect that, as given in Rome, *Stiffelio* and *Rigoletto* are simply not my music. It's as though someone had placed a black band across the nose of one of your beautiful statues.

Greetings to all my friends, especially Angiolini.

[72]

*To Antonio Barezzi*                                        *Paris, 21 January, 1852*

[Verdi's old benefactor and ex-father-in-law, Antonio Barezzi, had taken the composer to task for not legalizing his union with Giuseppina Strepponi, the singer with whom he had been living for some years, and who was now installed in his villa at Sant'Agata. (They eventually married, in 1859.)]

Dearest Father-in-law,

After waiting such a long time, I hardly thought I would receive from you a letter so cold, and containing, if I am not mistaken, so many wounding phrases. If this letter had not been signed Antonio Barezzi, whom I wish to think of as my benefactor, I should have replied most strongly or not have replied at all. But since it is signed by that name which I shall always consider it my duty to respect, I shall do everything possible to persuade you that I do not merit such a reproof. In order to do this, it is necessary for me to refer to things in the past, to speak of other people, of our native district, and so my letter will be somewhat prolix and boring, though I shall try to be as brief as possible.

I do not believe that, of your own accord, you would have written a letter which you knew could only cause me displeasure. But you live in a district that has the bad habit of continually interfering in other people's affairs, and disapproving of everything which does not conform to its own ideas. It has never been my habit to interfere in other people's business unless asked to, precisely because I require that no one should interfere in mine. This is why there has been gossip, whispering and disapproval. This liberty of action, which is respected even in less civilized communities, I claim as a right in my own vicinity. You be the judge, and be a judge severe, yet calm and dispassionate: what harm is done if I live in isolation, if I prefer not to make visits to titled people, if I don't take part in festivities, in the pleasures of others, if I manage my own property because it pleases and entertains me? I repeat, what harm is done? In no instance has anyone else suffered any damage.

That said, I come now to a sentence in your letter: 'I understand very well that I am not a man for commissions, because my time is already past, but for little things can I not still be useful?' If by that you mean to say that I used to give you important commissions, while now you serve me only in small things, alluding to the letter enclosed in yours, I can find no excuse for this, and though I should do the same for you in similar cases, I can only say I have learnt my lesson for the future. If your sentence is meant as a reproof because I have not entrusted you with my affairs during my absence, permit me to ask you: how could I ever be so importunate as to place heavy burdens upon you, who never even set foot in your own farmyards because your business affairs are so pressing? Should I have commissioned Giovanino?[1] But is it not true that last year, while I was in Venice, I gave him full power of attorney in writing, and that he never once set foot inside Sant'Agata? Not that I am complaining of him, he was perfectly right. He had his own affairs which were sufficiently important, and so he could not take care of mine.

This has revealed to you my opinions, my actions, my wishes, my so-to-speak public life, and since we are making these revelations, I find no difficulty in raising the curtain which veils the mysteries hidden within my four walls, and speaking to you about my domestic life. I have nothing to hide. In my house there lives a lady, free and independent, who, like myself, prefers a solitary life, and who has a fortune capable of satisfying all her needs. Neither I nor she is obliged to account to anyone for our actions. But who knows what our relations are? What affairs? What ties? What rights I have over her or she over

[1] Giovanni Barezzi, one of Antonio's two sons.

me? Who knows whether she is my wife or not? And if she is, who knows what the reasons may be for not publicly announcing the fact? Who knows whether that is a good or a bad thing? Might it not be a good thing? And even if it is a bad thing, who has the right to ostracize us? I will say this to you, however: in my house she is entitled to as much respect as myself, more even. And no one is allowed to forget that, for any reason. And finally she has every right, both because of her conduct and her character, to that consideraton she habitually shows to others.

With this long chatter, all I have meant to say is that I claim my freedom of action, because all men have a right to it, and because my nature rebels against mere conformity. And to say, too, that you, who are fundamentally so good, so just and so kind-hearted, must not let yourself be influenced, must not absorb the ideas of a community which—it really needs to be said—at one time did not even consider me worthy to be its organist, and is now complaining and gossiping about me and about my business. This cannot continue. But if it should, I am a man who can look after himself. The world is big enough, and the loss of 20- or 30,000 francs would never prevent me from finding somewhere else to live. There can be nothing offensive to you in this letter, but if anything in it displeases you, then consider it not written, because I swear to you on my honour that I have no wish to displease you in any way. I have always considered you my benefactor, and still do, I consider this an honour and I boast of it.—Farewell, farewell, in our customary friendship

[73]

*To Giovanni Ricordi*                                    *Busseto, 23 March, 1852*

Dear Ricordi,

You have written me a long letter to explain things that I already know very well. I know very well that you own the libretto of *Miller*, and the music, and that you can have a translation made and sell it to Sig. Alaffre[1] or whomever you wish, and have the opera produced wherever you please. I repeat, I know all this, but that is not the point.

---

[1] Benjamin Alaffre, a professor at the Lycée in Toulouse, translated the libretto of *Luisa Miller* for its French production.

I told you, and I tell you again, that if I had realised those two documents (and note well the second of these documents) gave you control of a French translation, I would not have signed them. Whether or not I am able to do a French translation is not for you to say. What I am saying is that the words of your letter—'I wish, therefore, to delay the aforesaid performance in an Italian theatre, which we can settle when you are convinced. For this reason, I enclose two papers, which, if you accept, you should sign for the Escudiers etc.'—no, by God, these words do not mean that you can sell a French translation. You speak to me of semi-colons, full stops, and so on, but this is cavilling of a kind which I think should not exist between you and me. I do not know whether we shall work together again, but, if we do, I warn you frankly that, in order to avoid semi-colons, full stops and all that misery, I shall not in future sign any more papers of that kind. I will conclude by saying that you were not being honest with me when you made me sign those papers in the belief that they were merely obstructing an Italian performance, whereas they referred also to the sale of a French translation. You believed you had made a good bargain, but you have forgotten that you called yourself my friend, and that I trusted your word. You now propose a settlement, but I do not want to make concessions. I have signed something I did not wish to sign, and it is your duty to return it to me.

I hope to see you here in my humble home. I should consider myself fortunate and, above all, honoured if you were to come with your Signora Marietta:[1] be assured we shall not discuss business. I owe Signora Marietta a thousand apologies, as I have forgotten to buy the scarf she asked me for. It's completely my fault. I was so worried about the above-mentioned affair with Alaffre and a hundred other things, that it was not until my last days in Paris that I asked Peppina[2] to buy that scarf, but it was too late for her to make the purchase. The fault is certainly mine, and it is a grievous one, but on the first possible occasion I shall set matters right.

With the usual compliments, farewell, farewell.

[1] Giovanni Ricordi's wife.    [2] Giuseppina Strepponi.

[74]

*To Cesare de Sanctis*                              *Busseto, 3 May, 1852*

[Cesare de Sanctis, one of Verdi's Neapolitan friends, was born in Rome but lived most of his life in Naples.

Cammarano, whose illness is referred to in the last paragraph, was not completely recovered. He died in July, and, in another letter to De Sanctis, Verdi wrote: 'I was thunderstruck by the sad news of Cammarano. I can't describe the depth of my sorrow. I read of his death not in a letter from a friend but in a stupid theatrical journal. You loved him as much as I did, and will understand the feelings I cannot find words for. Poor Cammarano. What a loss' (in Alessandro Luzio: *Carteggi Verdiani* I p. 9). Verdi paid Cammarano's widow six hundred ducats instead of the agreed five hundred, and, through De Sanctis, engaged a young Neapolitan poet, Leone Emanuele Bardare, to complete the libretto.]

Dear De Sanctis,

I'm afraid that this time, too, we shall not manage to conclude anything for Naples. Things have gone on for too long, I cannot wait any longer, and I shall tell you why. About ten days ago, Ricordi came here, entrusted by the management of La Scala to commission me to write an opera for Milan. Two days later, the Secretary of the Fenice arrived here to ask me to write for Venice. A few days later, Lanari was here asking for an opera for Bologna in the autumn. I haven't signed any contracts yet, but it wasn't possible for me not to say something, and to commit myself to a certain extent. Now, if I am to write for Naples, I must have a contract from the management by the 25th or 26th of the current month. You know that the post takes nine or ten days to arrive here. My conditions would be as follows:

Subject: *Il trovatore*. The company would have to include De Giuli, Mirate, Ferri and another prima donna, someone like Gabussi, to play the rôle of Azucena.[1] First performance between 20th and 30th November, 1852. I would come to Naples in October. The management would own the rights to the entire score and libretto for the whole of the Kingdom of the Two Sicilies. For other countries, both music and libretto will remain entirely mine. Cammarano will be paid for the libretto, half by the management and half by me. For the performance rights in the Kingdom of Naples, the management will pay

---

[1] *Il trovatore* did not have its first performance in Naples, but in Rome. Verdi was to write no more operas for Naples.

for my travelling expenses, work on the production etc., three thousand ducats in three equal instalments: the first when I arrive on the scene, the second on the day of the first orchestral rehearsal, and the third on the day of the dress rehearsal. Please reply immediately.

I haven't had any more news of Cammarano, so I think he must be completely recovered. Ask him to send me the remainder of the libretto as soon as possible, and tell him that, when this is finished, if he would like to do another one for me, I should be delighted. Please reply to all these points, and see that your answer reaches me by the 25th or 26th of this month. Farewell, farewell.

[75]

*To Carlo Antonio Borsi*                          *Busseto, 8 September, 1852*

[Carlo Antonio Borsi, husband of the soprano Teresa de Giuli-Borsi, had written to Verdi requesting that he compose an aria for De Giuli-Borsi to introduce into *Rigoletto*.]

My dear Borsi,

If you could be persuaded that my talent was so limited I did not know how to do better than I have done in *Rigoletto*, you would not have requested of me an aria for this opera. Miserable talent, you may say ... and I agree; but there it is. Then, if this *Rigoletto* can stand as it is, a new aria would be superfluous. And where would one put it? Verses and notes can be provided, but unless they are at the right time and in the right place, they will never make any effect. We may know of a place, but God forbid! We should be flayed alive. Is there any need to show Gilda with the Duke in his bedroom? Do you understand me? Whatever one did, it would have to be a duet. A magnificent duet!! But the priests, the monks and the hypocrites would all cry scandal. Oh, how happy were the times when Diogenes could say in the public square to those who asked him what he was doing: 'Hominem quaero!!' etc. etc.

As for the cavatina in the first act, I do not understand where you find any agility in it. Perhaps you have not understood the tempo, which should be an *allegretto molto lento*. At a moderate tempo, and sung quietly throughout, it should not be difficult. But to return to your first proposition, let me add that I conceived *Rigoletto* without arias, without finales, as a long string of duets, because this was how I wanted it. If anyone adds: 'But one could do this here, and that there' etc. etc., I reply: 'That would be fine, but I did not know how to do any better'.

Please pass on to De Giuli my respectful greetings, and believe me always yours affectionately

[76]

*To Nestor Roqueplan*                                     *Busseto, 10 November, 1852*

[Roqueplan, a director of the Paris Opéra, had revived *Jérusalem* in September 1852, reduced to three acts. *France Musicale* wrote that it was impossible to pass over in silence the inexplicable mutilations to which the opera had been subjected. The performance was said to be 'distressingly weak'.

*Luisa Miller* was, in fact, performed at the Opéra on 2 February, 1853, with a cast consisting of Bosio, Masson; Gueymard, Morelli, Merly and Depassio.]

My dear Roqueplan,
    Do you think that my silence indicates a tacit consent to let you perform *Miller*? You are mistaken. I took you at your word: you promised me often, and quite clearly, that you would never produce *Miller* without my consent, so I didn't worry. Notwithstanding this, you are now going to perform *Miller* at the Opéra. I am writing to you not to complain, but to tell you that this is against my wishes.
    Do you wish to popularize my name in France? You will certainly not do so with this translation, which I do not know, but of which I have grave doubts when I remember how you handled *Jérusalem* the second time. What is certain is that, in the whole of my already lengthy career, I have never had so much trouble with other theatres as with the Opéra. If I could put an end to this, I should be very glad. It is in your hands, so if you wish to, I am perfectly prepared.
    Yours truly

[77]

*To Cesare de Sanctis*                                       *Busseto, 1 January, 1853*

[The libretto referred to is that of *Il trovatore*, completed, after the death of Cammarano, by Leone Emanuele Bardare, who had been recommended to Verdi by De Sanctis.]

We are agreed, then, on the finale of the second act, which I shall have printed as I have transcribed it to you. I should like nothing better than to find a good libretto as well as a good poet (we have such need of one!); but I will not conceal from you that I read without pleasure the libretti that are sent to me. It is impossible, or almost impossible, for anyone else to know what it is I want. I want subjects that are new, great, beautiful, varied, strong. . . . and really strong, with new forms etc. etc. and at the same time suitable for music. If someone says 'I have done it like this, because that's how Romani, Cammarano etc. did it', then we no longer understand each other. It is precisely because those great men did it that way that I want it done differently. For Venice I have written *La Dame aux camélias* which will probably be called *La traviata*. It's a contemporary subject. Another composer would perhaps not have done it because of the costumes, the period or a thousand other foolish scruples, but I did it with great pleasure. Everyone complained when I proposed putting a hunchback on the stage. Well, I wrote *Rigoletto* with great pleasure. The same with *Macbeth* etc.


[78]

*To Countess Maffei*                        [*Sant'Agata, 29 January, 1853*]

[Verdi was at work on *La traviata*. *Il trovatore* had had its première in Rome on 19 January.]

Dear Clarina,

Here I am again in my desert, awkwardly for a few days only. I'm tired enough from the journey yet I have to start work again.

You have heard about *Il trovatore*: it would have been better if the full company had been available. They say this opera is too sad, and that there are too many deaths in it. But after all, everything in life is death! What else is there? . . .

I have seen the little Marchioness Patrizi who is an angel of beauty and virtue, as she was when she was a girl, although her physiognomy is completely changed. I have also seen Count Somaglia[1] a few times: he was in good humour, and friendlier to me than perhaps he has ever been.

[1] The Count and Countess Somaglia were friends of the Maffeis. Their daughter Nena ('the little Marchioness') married the Marquess Patrizi of Rome, but died a year later.

If you have occasion to see the Countess, commend me to her memory and her friendship.

My dear Clarina, I have to leave you now. I must return to my notes which are a real torment to me.

[79]

*To Emanuele Muzio*                                    *Venice, 7 March, 1853*

[*La traviata* had its first performance at the Teatro La Fenice, Venice, on 6 March, 1853. The first-night audience had laughed at the thought of the prima donna Fanny Salvini-Donatelli, an extremely stout woman, dying of consumption. The tenor, Lodovico Graziani, was not in good voice, and the baritone, Felice Varesi, who had been Verdi's first Macbeth and Rigoletto, felt unhappy with his rôle of Germont père, and apparently merely 'walked through' it.

Verdi's letters to his friends, reporting a 'fiasco', were written the next morning before any newspaper reviews had appeared. The reviews, though mixed, were by no means entirely unfavourable.]

Dear Emanuele,

*La Traviata* last night—fiasco. Was the fault mine or that of the singers? Time will be the judge.

[80]

*To Tito Ricordi*                                  [*Venice, 7 March, 1853*]

Dear Ricordi,

I am sorry to have to give you sad news, but I cannot conceal the truth. *La traviata* was a fiasco. Let's not enquire into the reasons. That's what happened. Farewell, farewell.

I am leaving the day after tomorrow, so write to Busseto.

[81]

*To Vincenzo Luccardi*                             *Venice, 9 March, 1853*

[Vincenzo Jacovacci was impresario of the Teatro Apollo in Rome.]

Dear Luccardi,

I did not write to you after the first performance of *La traviata*. I am writing to you after the second. The outcome is a fiasco! A definite fiasco! I do not know whose fault it is, it's better not to speak of it. I will say nothing to you about the music, and allow me to say nothing about the performers also. Give this news to Jacovacci, and that will serve as a reply to his last letter in which he asked me something about these singers.

Farewell, my dear lunatic. Wish me well always. I leave tomorrow for Busseto.

[82]

*To Giuseppina Appiani*                    *Paris, 25 February, 1854*

I have read *Graziella*: it's a short play in one act. In my opinion, it has little interest and no dramatic movement. I read *Les Confidences* four or five years ago, and I seem to recall that I derived great pleasure from it. The style and the language are everything in it, but in a play style and language are worth nothing without action. The moment of greatest interest is in the final scene, but it is too heroic and tragic and clashes terribly with the preceding scenes. In short, I don't like it, but Eugenia[1] must not pay any attention to my opinion.

To give advice is usually a mistake, because just as people's mouths, noses and faces differ from one another, so do their hearts differ, and so no two people see and feel in the same way. The artist must give himself completely to his own inspiration, and if the artist has real talent, he will feel and know better than anyone else what he needs. I should set to music with perfect confidence any subject that moved me, even if it had been condemned by every other artist as unsuitable for music. This is why, I repeat, Eugenia should pay no attention to my advice, and if this subject pleases her let her proceed without hesitation. If she wishes, I shall send it to her.

I am extremely sorry to have to tell you that I shall not write for La Scala!

If I find a subject I like, I certainly intend to send it, with whatever

---

[1] Eugenia was one of Giuseppina Appiani's four daughters. Apparently she composed, and was interested in a play by Lamartine called *Graziella* on which her mother had asked Verdi's opinion. *Les Confidences* is *Les Fausses confidences* by Marivaux.

observations occur to me, but let me advise you never to pay too much attention to them.

I write very slowly, in fact it may be that I shall not write. I don't know why, but I know that the libretto is there, still there in the same place.


[83]

*To Countess Maffei*                                                      *Paris, 2 March, 1854*

I cannot tell you what pleasure it gives me to think of you, although this pleasure must be tempered with remorse for not having written to you for so long a time. I have been so remiss to you that I shall need all your kindness and all your generosity to forgive me. Not long ago, I heard from Giulini[1] of Count Somaglia's illness, and you can imagine with what sorrow. Oh, I can clearly picture the solicitude, the kindness, the resignation of the Countess in bearing it all, and alleviating his pain. Poor Countess, so kind and generous and so warm-hearted. When you see her, do pay my respects to her.

I have never seen Lugo, so I don't know where he is. Enrico ran into him in the street at the beginning of the year: since then I've not seen him.

Shall I write for La Scala? No. If I were asked my reason, I would find it embarrassing to reply. I could say I have little desire to write, or better still that I loathe signing contracts. But it is not, as people have said, because I have obligations here until after '56; I have no other commission after I finish the opera I am writing. Nor is it the desire (as people have also said) to *put down roots* here!! *Put down roots*? That's impossible! . . . . . . And, in any case, what would be the point of it? What purpose would it serve? Fame? I don't believe in it. Money? I make as much, and perhaps more, in Italy. And even if I wanted to, I repeat, it's impossible. I'm too much in love with my desert and my own sky. I don't raise my hat to counts or marquesses, or to anyone. Finally, I haven't got millions, and the few thousand francs I have earned through my own labours I shall never spend on publicity, on claques and such filth. And they seem to be necessary for success! A few days ago, even Dumas wrote in his newspaper about Meyerbeer's new opera: 'What a pity that Rossini did not give us his masterpieces in 1854! It is also true to say that Rossini never had that German

[1] Count Cesare Giulini (1815–1862) was a member of the provisional Government of Lombardy in 1848. Cavour thought very highly of him.

vivacity which knows how to bring a success to the boil six months before the event in the cauldrons of the newspapers, and thus time the explosion of interest precisely for the first night.' That is very true. I was at the first performance of this *Etoile du Nord*, and I understood little or nothing, while the good public here understood everything, and found it all beautiful, sublime, divine! . . . . And this same public, after 25 or 30 years, has not yet understood *Guillaume Tell*, and so it is performed in a bungled fashion, mutilated, with three acts instead of five and in a production unworthy of it! And this is the world's leading opera house. . . . But, without realizing it, I am talking to you of things which cannot interest you. So I shall finish by telling you I have a fierce desire to return home. I say this to you, secretly, because I am sure you will believe me. Others will believe it an affectation on my part. But I have no interest in saying what I do not feel. Our Milanese *lions* however, have such an exaggerated idea of what goes on in Paris! Well, so much the better. Good luck to them! The season was beautiful during the three days· of carnival, and after that crowds on the boulevards.

[84]

*To Dr Ercolano Balestra, Busseto*                    *Paris, 8 April, 1854*

I need your help, and hope I am not being too forward in asking for it.

I believe that from the sale of my wheat and wine you should have a tidy little sum, and since I have no need of money at the moment, I should like you, on my behalf, to acquire the land belonging to Signora Sivelli, on the south side of my estate. This land, as you will see, is fairly poor and infertile. It produces good grapes but only in small quantities. (Giovanino Menta can tell you all about this.) All that matters to me are the fields adjoining Brunelli's property. I have dealt in other small matters with Signora Sivelli, and I have found her rather difficult. I want to pay a fair price, but no more. As long as Signora Sivelli asks a price, not based on her own affection for the land, but on its value—for, as I say, it's neither beautiful nor fertile—then you can conclude an agreement on my behalf for what seems to you to be right. As for the completion date, fix one that you think most convenient. The same applies to the payment. Whether I pay now or at St Martin's Summer, whether I take possession now, next summer or last, doesn't matter to me. I should like, however, to settle the deal as soon as possible, simply because I detest things that drag on for a long time, and because, as soon as I get the land, and in any case before May 11th, I shall want to dismiss the peasant who is currently working the Sivelli land. For your information, Giovanazzo has spoken to me and indeed speaks for me in this business, so if you need any further details, please ask him. As I have said, I wish to pay for this land with the money you have obtained from the sale of the wine, but, should you be short of money, I shall be receiving some more at the end of this month, and a further amount in June. This is for your guidance. It is understood that you, Doctor, will draw up the contract and sign it in my name.

[85]

*To Giuseppina Appiani*                                    *Paris, 21 October, 1854*

[This letter marks the sad ending of Verdi's friendship with Giuseppina Appiani. She had evidently offended him by addressing a letter to 'Giuseppina Strepponi' care of him, instead of to 'Madame Verdi', presumably, though Strepponi was not then entitled to that name.]

It was by chance, by pure chance that your letter reached Peppina. As the address you chose to put on it is unknown at the door of this house, your gracious letter was in danger of being lost if, I repeat, I had not by chance run into the postman, who, seeing a name ending in 'i', asked me about it. I retrieved it, and carried it to its destination. Peppina said to me that, having renounced letters and the arts, and keeping up a correspondence only with her family and a few very intimate friends, she would be grateful if I would make her apologies and reply to so *spirituelle* a letter. And here am I, who cannot write like you or like Peppina, in the greatest embarrassment at having to reply to a letter so well-written, so fine, and, I repeat, so *spirituelle*. My rough style does not allow me to make a show of wit or of spirit, so I shall tell you briefly that we are in a great hurry to pack our bags, that Cruvelli's[1] flight from the Opéra has obliged me to ask to be released

[1] Sophie Cruvelli (1826–1907) was to create the rôle of Helène in *Les Vêpres siciliennes* at the Paris Opéra on 13 June, 1855. The opera was already in rehearsal, but Cruvelli suddenly disappeared from rehearsals without explanation. Verdi asked to be released from his contract, but, before he could leave Paris, Cruvelli as suddenly reappeared. She had, it appears, merely gone off for a few days in the country with Baron Vigier, whom she later married.

from the contract, which I hope will happen, that I shall go straight to Busseto but stay there for only a few days. Then where shall I go? I can't say. Now that my bag of news is empty, I press your hands.

[86]

*To Nestor Roqueplan*                                    *Paris, 28 October 1854*

[Mlle Cruvelli's disappearance from the rehearsals of *Les Vêpres siciliennes* (see note to letter 85) was the cause of the situation discussed in this letter. The original is in French.]

Time, which passes and pushes on, does not allow me to hesitate any longer, and obliges me to come to a decision regarding my dealings with the Opéra.

The two propositions which His Excellency the Minister of State has been good enough to put to me, i.e.; to translate one of my Italian scores, or to write a new one in three acts are (I regret so say) unacceptable to me. Circumstances have rendered my position in France excessively difficult. It would be much better for me to be *unknown* rather than *badly-known*! Now there is only one course open to me: to bring off a great *coup*—a decisive one, and to present myself on your stage with a Grand Opera: it will mean success or it will finish me forever!

It will be very difficult to replace Mlle Cruvelli, at least for the moment—so I must use my time sensibly and leave for Italy. I have spent two years in France during which time I could have written two Italian operas. Now that we too have artistic copyright, with Italian theatres all over the world as well as publishers of our operas, the material interests accruing from them are much more considerable. One of our Italian operas today brings five or six times as much as it would have ten years ago. I tell you this to make you understand that I have withstood a loss much greater than you could imagine: and I am sure that the Directors of the Opéra would not wish, would not in fact allow, me to undergo further sacrifices! This is why I ask for the formal cancellation of my contract. I also ask that every copy of my score be returned to me and that all the parts extracted from it be destroyed.

If, at a later date, it suits both of us to present this opera, I could ask for nothing better. That is in my interests too; for I tell you frankly that an opera in five acts, five acts so as to accord with the traditions of your theatre, would not go down well anywhere else! It is, however, impossible for me to fix a date, which might prevent me from concluding some other important business. So I must be at complete liberty in this matter.

I know that the Opéra would wish to resolve these differences in the most amiable way: as for myself, I have never, in the twelve years of my career, had lawsuits with either Directors or publishers in my native land and I should be most upset to be involved in them for the first time in France.

I could have explained myself better in my own language, but your intelligence will help you to understand what I have not been able to express well in French.

Please be kind enough to make my views known to whomever needs to know them, and let me have your answer as soon as possible.


[87]


*To Louis Crosnier*                                      *Paris, 3 January, 1855*


[In November, 1854, Roqueplan was dismissed from his post at the Opéra, and Louis Crosnier, who had directed the Opéra Comique from 1834 to 1845, became Director of the Opéra.

The famous librettist and playwright, Eugène Scribe (1791–1861), who during his lifetime wrote nearly four hundred plays, had agreed to provide a libretto for *Les Vêpres siciliennes*. The Opéra refused to release Verdi, and Scribe made none of the required changes. Rehearsals dragged on for another five months, and the opera was finally produced on 13 June to enormous initial success.]


Monsieur Crosnier,

I feel it my duty to let no more time pass without making a few observations concerning *Les Vêpres siciliennes*.

It is both upsetting and mortifying for me that M. Scribe will not take the trouble to improve the fifth Act, which everyone agrees is uninteresting. I fully realise that M. Scribe has a thousand other things to concern him which are perhaps more important to him than my opera! But if I had been able to foresee his complete indifference I should have stayed in my own country where, really, I was not doing so badly.

Giuseppina Strepponi

anuele Muzio, from an oil
nting by Giovanni Boldini

Domenico Morelli

Angelo Mariani

I had hoped that M. Scribe would find it possible to end the drama with one of those moving scenes which bring tears to the eyes, and whose effect is almost certain, since in my opinion the situation lends itself to that. Please note that this would have improved the entire work, which has nothing at all touching in it except the romanza in the fourth Act.

I had hoped that M. Scribe would have been kind enough to appear at rehearsals from time to time, to be on the look out for any unfortunate lines which are hard to sing, to see whether anything needed touching up in the numbers or the Acts and so on. For example, the second, third and fourth Acts all have the same form: aria, duet, finale.

Finally, I expected M. Scribe, as he promised me at the beginning, to change everything that attacks the honour of the Italians.

The more I consider this, the more I am persuaded it is dangerous. M. Scribe offends the French because Frenchmen are massacred; he offends the Italians by altering the historic character of Procida into the conventional conspirator beloved by the Scribe system, and thrusts the inevitable dagger into his hand. Good Lord, there are virtues and vices in the history of every race, and we are no worse than the rest. In any case, I am first of all an Italian, and whatever happens I will not become an accomplice in offending my country.

It remains for me to say a word about the rehearsals in the foyer. Here and there I hear words and remarks which, if not actually wounding, are at least inappropriate. I am not used to this, and I shall not tolerate it. It is possible there are people who do not think my music worthy of the Opéra. It is possible there are others who think their rôles unworthy of their talents. It is possible that I, for my part, find the performance and style of singing other than I would have wished! In short it seems to me, unless I am strangely mistaken, that we are not at one in our way of feeling and interpreting the music, and without perfect accord there can be no possible success.

You see that everything I have just said is serious enough for us to stop and consider how to avoid the catastrophe which menaces us. For my part, I see but one means and I do not hesitate to propose it: the dissolution of the contract. I quite realize you will answer that the Opéra has already lost some time and money, but that is little in comparison with the year I have lost here, during which I could have earned a hundred thousand francs in Italy. You will go on to say it is all very well to annul a contract when there is a deficit, to which I reply that I should by now have paid it if my losses and expenses here were not already too great.

D

I know you are too just and reasonable not to choose the lesser of two evils. Trust my musical experience: under the conditions in which we are working, a success is really improbable. A half-success profits no-one. Let each of us try to make up for lost time, try to arrange everything calmly, and we may both gain by it.

Accept, sir, the assurance of my great esteem.

PS. Excuse my bad French. The important thing is that you understand.

[88]

*To Countess Maffei*                                    *Paris, 28 June, 1855*

*Les Vêpres siciliennes* seems to me to be going not too badly. You agree with me about the good and the bad (if any aspect of opera can be good or bad), I am aware of that, for I know you too well and so I am grateful, and send you the affection I shall always feel for you.

Criticism here has been either moderate or favourable, except from three Italians: Fiorentini, Montazio and Scudo.[1] My friends say 'What injustice!' But no, the world is too stupid to be infamous.

Ristori is causing a furore, and I am very pleased. She has annihilated Rachel, and in fact she is truly superior to Rachel, and the French themselves agree about this—an unheard of thing. The difference is that Ristori has a heart, while Rachel in the same place has a piece of cork or marble.

I haven't seen the Exposition properly. I have glanced at the rooms containing Italian things, and I must say, reluctantly, that I could have hoped for something better. Nevertheless, there is one object which is beautiful and sublime, the *Spartacus* of Vela.[2] All glory to him!

Farewell, my dear Clarina. I hope to be in Italy in a fortnight.

[89]

*To G. B. Benelli*                              *Enghien, 11 September, 1855*

[G. B. Benelli, theatrical agent, had his office in Paris. See also note to letter 91.]

---

[1] The first of these three Italian journalists was a Neapolitan, the second from Tuscany, the third from Venice.

[2] This *Spartacus* is by the Ticinese sculptor, Vincenzo Vela.

Dearest Benelli,

I have much respect for your very great experience, but until now I have not given you the right to suggest whom I should take counsel with, and whom I should confide in. For many years now, I have been used to managing my own affairs, and if you had known me better you could have saved yourself this trouble.

If by 'those who love arguments' you mean Messrs Escudier, let me tell you that a business man like yourself should have understood that the Escudiers, publishers of my operas, have an interest in getting these works performed. If the operas are performed, even in a mediocre fashion, there are prospects of more business. If they are not performed, everything is lost.

What are you trying to say to me about conducting? A few days ago, you talked about conducting for a fee of 24 thousand francs etc. etc. My dear Benelli, you should first of all know that 24 thousand francs is not sufficient for me, and that in any case I am not a director of orchestras, of singers or of productions. If a proposition has been made to me by the Théâtre Italien, it was concerning something quite different, and you have no right to question me or talk to me about it.

As for Sig. Salvi,[1] I know nothing about him, and I have nothing to do with him. I know only, from reading the *Revue Franco-Italienne*, that he doesn't want to give my operas. If that is so, we are in perfect agreement.

You say that the management of the Théâtre Italien will explain why they do not perform my operas. If this is a threat, do whatever you wish.

Amen, then, and let us speak no more on this subject.

No one could wish you more success and good health than I do.

[90]

*To Dr Ercolano Balestra*                              *Paris, 21 October, 1855*

[The 'well-known English affair' was the long-drawn-out legal action over an unauthorized performance of Bellini's *La sonnambula* in London, which reached its conclusion after twelve years when, on 1 August, 1855, the House of Lords decreed that there could be no copyright protection for an opera written by a foreigner, unless the composer himself supervised the first

---

[1] Matteo Salvi, composer and conductor, worked for a number of years in Vienna.

production in England. English impresarios had anticipated this ruling, and Ricordi had had occasion, in March, 1854, to protest against the threat of an unauthorized production of *Il trovatore* in London.]

Dear Dr Balestra,

I have not answered your very kind letter, because I expected to be home before today, but as I now have to produce *Il trovatore* at the Théâtre Italien, I shall have to stay here for another fortnight. Meanwhile, allow me to speak to you again about the well-known English affair. At one time, there existed in that country a copyright for the works of composers, artists, authors etc. That is to say, if I, for example, wrote an opera, no one in England could publish or produce it without my permission. So, naturally, I was able to sell my opera to a publisher. Now, a recent law of the House of Lords forbids this copyright to any foreigner whose country does not have an international agreement with England. Thus these publishers find it more convenient to appropriate our operas without consulting the composer, which is understandable. During my two visits to London, it was suggested that I should apply for citizenship of either England or France, or even Piedmont (because France and Piedmont have international agreements with England), but I prefer to remain what I am, that is to say a peasant from Roncole, and I prefer to ask my Government to make an agreement with England. The Government of Parma has nothing to lose in an agreement of this kind, which is purely artistic and literary: it would only have to go to the bother of requesting it through its representative in England who is, I believe, either the Austrian or the Spanish Ambassador. That would be all. When you go to Parma, will you kindly arrange matters so that, when I return, I can know whether or not this is feasible? May we meet again soon, and believe me with esteem and friendship, affectionately yours


[91]


*To Tito Ricordi*                                        *Paris, 24 October, 1855*


[Letters 89, 90 and 91 all relate to the copyright problem. The details are too many and complex to be gone into in this context, but briefly the facts relating to the opening paragraph of letter 91 are these: Calzado, the Spanish director of the Théâtre Italien in Paris, had asked permission to perform Verdi's operas without paying the usual rate. To prevent *Il trovatore* being given,

Verdi engaged a legal attorney. The impresario Benelli (letter 89), acting in collusion with Calzado, threatened Verdi that he would publicly declare the composer's motive was spite that Salvi, and not he, had been asked to conduct the opera at the Théâtre Italien. Blanchet was Ricordi's representative in Paris.

The lacunae in paragraphs three and four are due to the copy in the original notebook being rendered illegible by fading.]


Dear Ricordi,

I did not deliver the power of attorney to Blanchet or to anybody else, because Calzado promised not to allow my operas to be performed without my consent. If I were not here, I am sure that *Il trovatore* would have been performed, and slaughtered at the Théâtre Italien! And this is certainly because your representative is not doing his job. So I have to prolong my sojourn in Paris and spend more money! As usual, the expense and the bother are mine, the profits are for others.

I found your proposal for Bordeaux very odd! When you wanted to have *La traviata* performed in Vienna, because you thought it would be useful for the future of that opera in Germany, you did not consult me, and you showed no concern over my reputation. But now, before performing *Il trovatore* in Bordeaux, where interest in it is slight or non-existent, you are worried about my reputation!! Regarding *Il trovatore* Escudier insists on having it translated into French, and he tells me that you will let me have a third of the composer's royalties.

'Let me have' is hardly the right phrase, as I do not think you have any rights in respect of the translation. But even pretending for the moment that you have, your offer is hardly generous. I shall explain: if the translation of *Il trovatore* is so successful that it is also performed in the provinces, in a twenty-year period it will produce a profit of 25 to 30 thousand francs (I may have over-estimated this amount). In compensation for all my labour, loss of time and the expenses I have to incur here, I shall earn in twenty years from eight to ten thousand francs. And you earn the same amount while you are strolling around Lake Como. If the translation is a failure, everything is lost. Why should I bear all the inconvenience but merely share in the profits? This is not right. If, instead of being a composer, I were a publisher ———— also for nothing. But when I think that, for *Il trovatore* ———————— a thousand francs and you four or five times more, I cannot help but reflect on it, and shall become more demanding in future, if I find that offers are not reasonable enough.

And, while I'm busy complaining, I may as well pour it all out. It will be for the last time. Why, since I have rights in the sale of my score to foreign countries, do you no longer sell the score, but a copy? In this way you deprive me of all benefit. You may answer that the foreign publishers only want the copy, but they used to buy the entire score of my first operas, and the last could have been handled the same way if you had wanted it. Another thing (though I am not sure if it is true): I am told that when you sign contracts you often add an amount for printing charges or something. For instance, last carnival season, in the contract for *Il trovatore* at La Scala, there was a sum of ———, and then you added another small sum in order to recompense yourself for printing costs. If that is true, permit me to say that it is behaviour unworthy of a great business man. The same thing happened another time with *Luisa Miller*. This is nothing better than evasive quibbling. I know that you can say 'I have the right to do this. The law allows it.' I know, I know. But I hoped that you would not behave like this to me. Many and many a time I have done things for you that I was not obliged to. I, after all, am the main source of your colossal fortune. Don't deny it. Examine your books, and observe the profits you have gained from my operas.

I wish to lodge a bitter complaint about the editions of my latest operas which have been produced in a slovenly manner, and with countless misprints. Above all, I must protest that you have not yet withdrawn the first edition of *La traviata*. This is an unpardonable negligence. If I had not by chance visited Escudier on business, this edition would be circulating in France. Who knows whether or not it is circulating in Germany, Spain, and other countries? You know this edition should have been withdrawn two years ago!! It was on condition that this was done (a condition in the contract—I asked no money for it), that I made an agreement with Coletti.[1] But who cares about the reputation of a composer? I can't help reflecting and feeling heartily discouraged. Throughout my long career I have always found impresarios and publishers hard, inflexible, always inexorable, and ready to invoke the law on their side when necessary. Always fine words and very bad deeds. I have never been treated as anything but an object, a tool to be used as long as it brings profits. This is sad but true.

Let us turn to *Il trovatore*. I don't believe that anyone can translate it at the moment, since I'm opposed to it, and I am not prepared to do it

---

[1] Filippo Coletti (1811–1894) was the baritone in the revival of *La traviata* at the Teatro San Benedetto in Venice, on 6 May, 1854. The soprano was Maria Spezia, and the tenor was Landi.

myself. As I am the composer, I wish to retain the copyright, and it seems to me that you should be content to receive the profit from further editions etc. You could yourself purchase the score for France.

If we should come to an agreement to do this translation, I make the following conditions:

1. You renounce your claim, just or unjust, on the copyright.

2. If you wish to receive one third of the copyright, you will pay me for four thousand francs towards my labours and expenses here.

3. You sell to me ownership of the score for France, Belgium and Holland, for a sum to be agreed, which I shall ask to be sent immediately.

Accept or refuse these conditions, but reply quickly because there isn't a moment to lose.

Farewell, farewell

[92]

*To Tito Ricordi, Milan*                    *Paris, 11 November, 1855*

To all my accusations (as it pleases you to call them) you reply with a very nice letter, but you do not justify yourself. My accusations remain unanswered. It seems that you think it a valid reason to say that I gave my consent to Merelli. But when? How? Merelli spoke to me on the stage of the Opéra about doing *La traviata* in Vienna, and I replied that, if we reached an agreement, I would need Boccabadati, Piccolomini or Spezia. Was this an agreement? Anyway, did I not write a thousand times to you that Bendazzi[1] would never make a good Traviata? As far as the contract with Boracchi is concerned, allow me to say that I do not agree. A loss on the editions?

Because of the carelessness of your solicitors, if I hadn't intervened *Trovatore* would have been given with Mongini, and you can imagine what the result would have been.[2] It is also true that the edition of *La traviata* would have been published already if I had not intervened. You say it is not your fault but that of your representatives. That may be so, in which case you ought to take more care in choosing them in future, and then place your complete trust in them.

[1] See *Personalia* for notes on these singers.

[2] Pietro Mongini, tenor (1830–1874), may not have been very highly thought of by Verdi in 1855, but in 1871 he was the Radames in the première of *Aida* in Cairo.

Now we come to something important. I have never talked with you, at the Hotel Violet or anywhere else, about allowing a translation of *Il trovatore* in return for one third of the royalties. Léon Escudier mentioned this to me only after your departure. I made absolutely no reply to this proposition because I found it repugnant. You believed all the newspaper gossip about *Il trovatore* being given at the Opéra. If that had been true, I would have said so. I would do a translation for the provincial towns if I thought they could perform it. On principle, the Opéra does not allow translations unless absolutely necessary, so there is no need of one there. With the new ballet they are about to produce, that theatre will not need attractions for at least a year. It would be wasteful, therefore, to spend 180 or 200 thousand francs on *Il trovatore*. Nor would it be advantageous for me, as I should have to set *Les Vêpres* aside. Besides, *Il trovatore* would be almost impossible at the Opéra, as I will only give my consent to the performance when two prima donnas of the very highest standard have been engaged. Furthermore, the most certain proof that *Il trovatore* will not be given there is that in a few days it will be performed at the Théâtre Italien.

I repeat then, despite the assertion in your letter that this is going too far, that the publishers would have bought the score if you had insisted. But if, for an opera which has cost you 20,000 francs for all countries, you ask 12 or even 10,000 francs for France alone, it is obvious that you do not wish them to buy the score. On your calculations, an opera would be worth 100,000 francs!

In conclusion then, after having read the seven or eight pages of your letter, I have not found any categorical reply to the proposals made in my last letter. So I shall have to stay another ten or twelve days in Paris to await a fresh reply from you. Finally, if it is possible, I should like to purchase the French, Belgian and Dutch rights for *Il trovatore*. I shall pay you the ten thousand francs you were going to charge Escudier. It is understood that you will give me what profits you have received or expect to receive in France from this score. On the day I acquire the rights, you will order M. Blanchet to hand over to me the score and the parts which are now at the Théâtre Italien. At your convenience you will let me have a contract in writing. Reply immediately. Farewell.

PS. It is understood that I acknowledge the sale of the copies to Escudier by means of a reimbursement to me of the sum agreed in the contract with Escudier.

[93]

To Tito Ricordi                                    *Paris, 25 November, 1855*

Dear Tito,

I shall pass over in silence the many things mentioned in your letter. I shall say nothing about the jeers and witty remarks you aim at me, but I cannot ignore your sentence that talks of 'the sinsister influence of two-faced and four-faced Januses'. I cannot permit you to judge me a weak man, a good-for-nothing, an imbecile easily influenced. I want you to know, Mr Tito Ricordi, that I am accustomed, for good or bad, to come to my own decisions, and to do things as I wish and as I please.

You say that you paid 20,000 francs for the right to publish. Why then are you the owner of the score if you have paid only for the publication right? Why are you retaining the greater part of the hiring fees? By what right? By what merit? In heaven's name, have I any obligations to the firm of Ricordi? But if I've donated the ownership to you, you now have the nerve and the generosity to make me pay 10,000 francs for France etc??!! For France, where you have already made a profit of more than 12 thousand francs? Fortunately you recognize that the success of *Il trovatore* owes something to my assistance! Many thanks. I'll put it differently: without me *Il trovatore* would have had the same result as *Miller*. You are wrong if you expect that I will go to the same trouble with *La traviata* and *Rigoletto*. To disperse energy and money uselessly on behalf of someone else has no attractions for me. I know that you are counting on my self respect and on my reputation which would be compromised if these operas went badly. It is true that I am very proud of my reputation in France, but you must know that not only are the doors of the Opéra open to me but also the Opéra Comique and the Théâtre Italien, and that everything depends on my accepting the generous offers the three Directors make me to write operas for their theatres. You see, therefore, that my reputation does not depend on *Rigoletto* and *La traviata* which I can leave to look after themselves for better or worse, while I get on with writing new works.

Now let's conclude, if possible. Since I have already wasted so much time and money, and have begun the *Trovatore* translation, I can only agree to the barbed terms of your contract. You are very slow to settle accounts due to other people, but very quick at drawing up your own! You say that *Il trovatore* will fetch four or five thousand francs during the current season at the Théâtre Italien. If that is so, if it fetches five

thousand, I shall pay you the 10,000 francs you ask for the ownership.
If the profit is only four thousand francs, I shall pay you nine thousand.
If it brings in less than four thousand, I shall pay you eight thousand.
Whatever happens, not less than eight thousand. Please think about it
and let me have your answer by return, but remember I am staying here
only to conclude this business. Every day that passes is precious time to
me, and money wasted. The ownership should be for France, Belgium
and Holland. Ask Blanchet to give me the score and parts that are at
the Théâtre Italien, and send me this year's royalties etc. etc. Farewell.

[94]

*To Francesco Piave*                                    *Paris, 25 November, 1855*

[Verdi had by this time realized that *Stiffelio*, first performed in Trieste in
1850, was being hampered by its libretto. In 1854, he had written to De
Sanctis: 'Among my operas which are not in circulation, there are some I
must forget about, because their subjects were at fault. But there are two I
should not like to be forgotten: they are *Stiffelio* and *La battaglia di Legnano*'
(Luzio: op. cit., Vol. I, p. 25). But it was not until 1857 that the revised
*Stiffelio*, now called *Aroldo*, was staged, and then not in Venice but in Rimini.]

Dear Piave,
    I have received your letters. I anticipated that you might not be able
to come and see me, but I may be able to come to Venice. Your
proposal that I come to produce *I Vespri* could suit me, so long as it
doesn't prevent me from revising *Stiffelio*. Why not perform both of
them in Venice? I believe that might amuse the management. I would
come to Venice soon, first mount *I Vespri*, and then the revised *Stiffelio*.
    Discuss this with the management, and if they like it, the deal is on.
Send me a couple of lines of contract. The fee I would charge is 20,000
Austrian lire.

[95]

*To Sig. Calzado, Paris*                                  *Paris, 12 December, 1855*

[Calzado was the impresario of the Théâtre Italien in Paris.
    Verdi wrote this letter in French.]

I received your letter yesterday, and I thank you for it. I completely approve of the decision not to present *Rigoletto* or *Traviata* this year. I desire nothing better than to lend you (as you put it) my co-operation or concurrence, providing my own interests allow it, and providing *above all* that you are capable of selecting the appropriate artists for the performances: for a capable Director should be able either to choose the operas suitable for the artists he has engaged, or to choose the artists for the operas he is presenting. This is something much more difficult than may be imagined. Believe me from my long experience.

I cannot prevent *Ernani* being presented. If I could, I tell you frankly I should prevent it. Those who tell you that the performances will be good and thorough, deceive you, and deceive themselves. They do not know what they are talking about when it comes to music. I believe that the overall performances of *Ernani* will be bad. Understand me well—*overall*! For the rest, the takings will prove me right or wrong; and in this regard I wish nothing better than to be wrong. My pride as composer and your impresario's moneybags both stand to gain. I advise you again, I even beg you, to renounce the undertaking! . . . . .

[96]

*To Tito Ricordi*                           *Busseto, 17 February, 1856*

Dear Tito,

Piave will come to Busseto for the express purpose of revising *Stiffelio*, for which I intend to find a completely new subject which the censorship will pass. We shall therefore have to alter some of the music, write a few new pieces, make some cuts here and there, what-ever the new subject renders necessary. Before I set to work on this, however, taking up time, and throwing money away on a new libretto, I should like to know whether you agree to the following terms:

1. No further printing or hiring of *Stiffelio* to be allowed, as this is going to become, at any rate very largely, a new opera.

2. You will pay me for the new pieces I compose at the rate agreed for the last two operas I wrote for Italy.

3. You will let me have the rental fees from the theatre in which it is first performed. I shall stage the work.

4. Finally, I ask for a share of the profits resulting from hiring and sales, as was done with *Il trovatore* and *La traviata*, for the usual ten years, beginning on the date of the first performance.

Please let me know immediately if you agree to the above. I, on the other hand, cannot commit myself to anything until I have found a subject that satisfies me. Farewell, farewell.


[97]

*To Francesco Piave*                              Busseto, *10 March, 1856*

[Despite Verdi's injunction to Piave to think of 'something newer and more interesting', Stiffelio became the crusader Aroldo.]

Dear Piave,

I hope you are free at the moment, and can come to Busseto immediately. Before setting out, please obtain all the material necessary for rearranging *Stiffelio*. You know there are not many books here, nor is there any big library nearby. So arm yourself. I have already mentioned to you that I would not like to make Stiffelio a crusader. Something newer and more interesting. Think about it.

Come quickly then, and, if you can, bring a lion[1] with you, which you know will delight Peppina.


[98]

*To Vincenzo Torelli*                             Busseto, *22 April, 1856*

[Vincenzo Torelli wrote on music in his own Neapolitan newspaper, *L'Omnibus*. His review of *Alzira* in 1854 had been the least favourable, and he had been accused of partisanship. By 1856, he had become a strong supporter of Verdi.

Giuseppina Strepponi, writing to Torelli on Verdi's behalf in 1858, charmingly calls him 'a bitter-sweet sauce', and continues: 'Unfortunate is he who bumps into you and sets in motion the bitter substances; fortunate, however, is he that happens on the sweet ones' (Frank Walker: *The Man Verdi*, p. 229). Torelli was associated with the management of the Teatro San Carlo.]

Dear Sig. Torelli,

I thought that Galeotti did not receive any commission from the

_____
[1] *'Leone'*, slang for 'poodle'.

Naples management, but I wanted to be sure so that I would be aware of the circumstances for future negotiations.

I cannot help being flattered by all the kind things you say about me in your letter, and I should have been delighted, had my engagements permitted it, to come and spend a winter in your delightful Naples, even if I were not writing anything. But, alas, it is not possible. Next carnival season, I was to have written an opera for Italy, in fact for Naples; but the management, as well as having now engaged another composer, is under an obligation to offer all rights in operas written for the San Carlo Theatre or anywhere in the Kingdom of the Two Sicilies, to the publisher Cottreau. This has made it almost impossible to work out a form of contract. It is by no means certain that I shall be writing a work for Italy in 1857-58, so this time I am afraid I must give up all hope of returning to Naples. All I can say at the moment is that, if I find I can write a work for Naples in the following season, my terms would be:

1. A company of singers I was satisfied with.

2. Six thousand ducats to stage the opera. The management would own the score only in the Kingdom of the Two Sicilies. As for the method of payment, and all secondary details, these could be agreed at the time of the drawing up and signing of the contract, which would be the beginning of 1857.

I should like to compose *King Lear* if I can have the following artists:

A really fine baritone for the rôle of King Lear.

A leading soprano, not a dramatic soprano, but a singer of expressive quality for Cordelia.

Two good secondary performers.

A very good contralto.

A dramatic tenor with a good voice, for a less important rôle.

Regarding the soprano and the contralto, I hear Piccolomini and Giuseppina Brambilla well spoken of. Both are singers of feeling, and are young.

I should be very grateful if these preliminary negotiations could be kept a close secret, in order to minimize the difficulties.

Please pay my respects go Sig. Monaco,[1] and accept my protestations of friendship and esteem.

---

[1] President and Censor of the Neapolitan royal theatres.

[99]

*To Vincenzo Torelli*                                    *Busseto, 16 May, 1856*

I need not say how sorry I am not to be able to sign this contract right now, and to have to repeat what I said in my last letter: 'If I find I can write a work for Naples in the following season, my terms would be . . . .' etc. etc.

I note that you find my conditions no obstacle to our coming to an agreement, but I shall not be free to sign a contract before the beginning of 1857. If I find I can do so before then, I shall, and for that reason I shall not return the contract to you now. I do realize, however, that this uncertainty may be an embarrassment to the management of the San Carlo Theatre, so I wish you to feel free to enter into any other contract you may wish to, provided that you advise me at the time. On the supposition that the management is kind enough to wait until I am free to sign a contract, I can tell you positively the opera will be *King Lear*. For the title rôle we shall need a baritone who is an artist in every sense of the word: an artist such as Giorgio Ronconi was, for instance. If I had to choose between Coletti and Colini, I should prefer the former. The tenor would not have a large rôle, so Fraschini would be wasted in it. Lotti is excellent in strong, dramatic roles, but she would not do for Cordelia. I should very much like a contralto, and I repeat that Giuseppina Brambilla might be of interest to you. In addition to the new opera, she could also perform some of the important rôles in the old repertory, in *Il giuramento*, *Il trovatore* etc., and in many other operas as a leading lady. It's very important to keep all this secret. If it's a question of Piccolomini, I myself will approach her. Whether or not we proceed with this project, I shall always be very grateful for the kind and friendly manner in which you have carried on negotiations.

[100]

*To Sig. Monti*                                         *Busseto, 2 June, 1856*

[Monti was the Ricordi agent in Bologna.]

Dear Monti,
    Ricordi has in fact written to me about this, and I am very sorry that I cannot at the moment give you a clear answer. We may be able to go

ahead, as long as the management of the Teatro Comunale is not in too great a hurry.

For some time I have had another commission to stage one of my operas in Bologna in the autumn. What's more, I have to go away on important private business. All of this prevents me from giving you, as I said earlier, a firm answer. You may, however, inform the management that they can expect my answer in a couple of months.

If I can do it, the opera will be *Stiffelio*, with a different title, a new libretto, and a new fourth act. The company you propose is fine. Let me know what the male chorus is like, and how many there are of them.

Send me your answer, and believe me yours truly

[101]

*To Dr Ercolano Balestra (?)*                                    *Paris, August, 1856*

[The editors of the *Copialettere* consider that the recipient of this letter was probably Dr Balestra.

On 3 August, Verdi had left Italy for Paris, where Calzado, the director of the Théâtre Italien, was threatening an action.]

I have been in Paris for three or four days, and as usual I need your help. In the first place, I want to know if the Government of Parma has at last asked for that agreement on copyright. Second, I want to entrust you with a commission for Piccolomini.

You know that for a long time it has been in my mind to set *King Lear* as an opera. Great difficulties have presented themselves in the search for an appropriate cast, but the Naples management has offered me what I need. As you can well imagine, I've kept my eye on Piccolomini[1] for the rôle of Cordelia. I wrote to her about this, and she has replied with such kindness, such selflessness, that even a man less scrupulous than I would have been heavily embarrassed. I am, and shall remain, eternally grateful for such confidence, but my sense of delicacy will not allow me to accept such responsibility. I know her interests and I can predict her future, and not for all the money in the world would I have her suffer for this, and say to herself 'The sacrifice I made

---

[1] Maria Piccolomini (see *Personalia*) was much admired in *La traviata*.

was too great'. . . . . You know that my vision is so acute that sometimes I can read the hearts of others.

Ask her then to let me know her conditions in advance (so that they may be transmitted to Naples) freely and openly, as if I had nothing to do with this business. Tell her that I shall arrange for her to make her début in *La traviata* but that she will have to play the rôle for the first time at the San Carlo. She will only be committed from 15 October, 1857 to 15 March, 1858, which will make it necessary for them to have another prima donna under contract. She can say how many times a week she will perform, and what monthly fee she requires.

The rôle I intend her to play, as I've already said, is Cordelia in *King Lear* which she may know, or can get to know in Shakespeare. But if in any of this business, she believes there is the slightest disadvantage to her, she is not to worry, for I shall not be offended if she refuses.

[102]

*To Vincenzo Torelli*                                      *Paris, 11 November, 1856*

Dear Torelli,

You know that Medori[1] was to have sung at the Opéra in the French translation of *Il trovatore*, but she broke her contract. The Minister sent a deputation to Milan to hear Spezia and engage her, but her voice was thought not large enough for the Opéra, and I thought I was going to be free to return to the country, when suddenly they have proposed a prima donna who sang two years ago at the Théâtre Lyrique, and who I myself had once recommended to the Opéra.[2] So how could I leave? The prima donna was signed up, *ipso facto*, and consequently I am imprisoned here for about another two months, alternating between boredom, business at the Théâtre Italien, and the rehearsals of *Il trovatore*. What is satisfactory in all this is that, once *Il trovatore* is out of the way, I can write for the Opéra whenever I want to, and I can be free to come to Naples next year.

I could have signed and enclosed the contract, but there are a few items which need explanation. I don't really understand part of paragraph 5. What is the purpose of 'Compensation to composers for

[1] Giuseppina Medori (1828–1906)
[2] The prima donna was Deligne-Lauters. She sang in the French translation of *Il trovatore* at the Opéra on 12 January, 1857, when her husband, Louis Gueymard was the Manrico.

renunciation of benefit'. Would you explain that to me, and also explain what 'money outside of banks' means (forgive my ignorance)?

The company selected is still not adequate to perform *King Lear*. Penco, although she is an excellent artist, could not play Cordelia the way I see her. I know only three singers who could do it: Piccolomini, Spezia and Virginia Boccabadati. All three have weak voices but great talent, spirit and feeling for the stage. They would all be excellent in *La traviata,* and if the management thought of engaging one of them, she could play simply the two roles in *La traviata* and *King Lear*, for half the season from the beginning of January. I shall speak to Piccolomini here, and let you know the outcome. A contralto is also needed for the Fool, and it can only be Brambilla.

These difficulties have to be overcome, and you have until I have written the opera for Venice, that is to say, the whole of next March, and then (not in January, as the contract states) I shall send you the libretto for the approval of the censors. So find a soprano for Cordelia and a contralto for the Fool, and, pending signature of the contract, I shall consider this letter binding until the end of March.

A thousand greetings to Sig. Monaco, and believe me yours sincerely


[103]

*To Vincenzo Torelli*                              *Friday, 7 December, 1856*

[Rosina Penco had been engaged some months previously by Flauto, with the proviso that she would sing in Verdi's new opera. Meanwhile, Flauto had died.]

Sig. Torelli,

Just a few lines to reply to yours of 27th November, and to say that I cannot agree to the understanding you have come to with Penco. It is not my custom to allow artists to be foisted on me, not even if Malibran were to come back into this world. Not all the money on earth would make me relinquish this principle. I have the greatest esteem for Penco's talent, but I don't want her to be able to say to me 'Oh maestro, give me that rôle in your opera, I want it and I have a right to it'.

Yours truly

[104]

*To Tito Ricordi*                                          *11 April, 1857*

Ten years ago, I decided to compose *Macbeth*. I wrote the synopsis myself, and what's more I wrote out the entire libretto in prose, with its distribution into acts, scenes, vocal numbers etc. Then I gave it to Piave to turn into verse. As I was not entirely happy with his versification, I asked Maffei, with Piave's permission, to rewrite some verses and re-cast the witches' chorus in the third act, and the sleep-walking scene. Well now, would you believe it? Although the libretto did not carry the name of the poet, it was believed to be by Piave, and that chorus and the sleep-walking scene were the most abused and ridiculed of all. Perhaps both pieces could have been better done, but as they exist they are still verses by Maffei, and the chorus especially has a great deal of character. So there: so much for public opinion!

[105]

*To Cesare Vigna*                              *Busseto, 11 April, 1857*

[Verdi had dedicated *La traviata* to his friend the Venetian alienist, Dr Cesare Vigna (1819–1892). On 12 March, 1857, *Simon Boccanegra* had had its première in Venice.]

My dear Vigna,

   I, too, will be sincere with you (as I always am with you and with everyone), and tell you that I have not written to you before now, because from morning till evening I am always in the fields, in the woods, with the farm-workers and the animals . . . . . the nicer ones, however, are the four-legged ones. Coming back to the house tired, I can never find the time or the energy to take up my pen. That's the truth, and it's a serious fault, but you, out of friendship, will forgive me.

   Have the Venetians now calmed down? Who would ever have thought that this poor *Boccanegra*, whether a good or a bad opera, could stir up such a devil of a row?

   But I remain calm, and not offended by my enemies whether Jews or Christians of past, present or future, and, like you, I find the world fair enough.

What a great man is Signor Bartolo! And we, my dear Vigna, I at first and you a little later, shall become two little Bartolos.

The rumour that the libretto was written by me was really the end!!! A libretto that bears Piave's name is judged in advance as the worst possible poetry, but, frankly, I know I would be content if I could write verses as good as:

> Vieni a mirar la cerula
> . . . . . . . . . . . . . . . . . . .
> Delle faci festanti al barlume

and several others, with many such lines scattered here and there. I confess that, in my ignorance, I could not do so well.

But let's forget the Venetians and *Boccanegra* for the moment: a little later, towards the middle of May, I myself am going to Reggio to stage it: the business was settled yesterday here at Sant'Agata with Marzi[1] and Piave.

[106]

*To Vincenzo Torelli*           *Busseto, 9 September, 1857*

[Verdi did not proceed with this particular Spanish play, which was *El Tesorero del Rey Don Pedro* by Gutiérrez. Nor did he set Victor Hugo's play, *Ruy Blas*, though he was to consider it again in 1861.]

I am working day and night on the subject of the new opera. I have chosen a Spanish play and have already translated it. Now I am abbreviating it for the music, and then I shall have it put into verse. I should have liked to do *Ruy Blas*, but you are right, it would not have done to write a brilliant rôle for Coletti; on the other hand he could not have sung the title rôle.

[107]

*To Vincenzo Torelli*           *Busseto, 19 September, 1857*

I am in despair! In these last months I have read through so many plays (some of them very beautiful), but not one of them is right for my

---

[1] The Marzi brothers were impresarios of La Scala.

purpose. I settled on a very fine and interesting play, *The Treasurer of King Don Pedro*, which I immediately had translated, but when I made a scenario to reduce it to operatic proportions, I found various difficulties, and gave it up. Now I am working on a French play, *Gustav III of Sweden*, a libretto by Scribe which was done at the Opéra over twenty years ago.[1] It's grandiose and huge, and really beautiful, but it's in many ways conventional, like all of Scribe's works for music, which I've never liked but which I now find insufferable. I repeat, I'm in a state of despair, because it's too late now to find another subject, and in any case I don't know where to find one. I'm not inspired by any that I've read. I suggest, therefore, a way of settling the matter in the best interests of the theatre and my own reputation. Let us give up the idea of my writing a totally new opera this year, and substitute *La battaglia di Legnano*, rearranged with a new libretto, with new pieces added where necessary, as I did with *Aroldo*. If we did this, I could come and produce *Boccanegra*, then, if you like, *Aroldo* as well, and finally *La battaglia*. Thus, instead of one, you would have three operas which I would conduct; and, unless my *amour propre* is deceiving me, one or the other of them would be a success. Let me add that all three operas are perfectly suitable for your company.

If you accept this combination, I shall also, if you wish, agree to write *King Lear* for next year, provided you have the right singers, which you know is imperative. So as not to lose time, and to finish off everything at once, I propose now the following terms. For *King Lear* the contract can remain as it is, except for the changing of the dates. For *Boccanegra*, *Aroldo* and *Battaglia*, which belong to Ricordi, it will be necessary for me to contact him and obtain his agreement. I imagine he will give it, in which case you will have to deal only with me. You will have the performance rights of *Aroldo* and *Boccanegra* for the autumn and carnival season, 1857–58. You could have the rights, for the Kingdom of Naples, of the new version of *Battaglia*. My fee for the rights to *Boccanegra*, and for my staging it, would be 1,500 ducats. Similarly for *Aroldo*. 3,000 ducats for *La battaglia*. Think about this, and then say yes, because I think this is in your interests. I shall lose somewhat, by not having parts to sell to publishers, but that doesn't matter. But if you don't like this proposal, I shall have to write *Gustav*, which I'm luke-warm about.

[1] Scribe's libretto had been written for Auber's opera, *Gustave III, ou Le bal masqué*, which was produced at the Paris Opéra in 1833.

[108]

*To Vincenzo Torelli*                              *Busseto, 14 October, 1857*

[The libretto of *Un ballo in maschera* underwent countless vicissitudes because of the Neapolitan censorship. Eventually, Verdi offered the opera instead to Rome, where, after more changes by the Papal censors, it was produced in 1859. By this time, it had become an opera about fictitious characters, set in North America.]

I have sent your letter on to the poet,[1] and I don't believe it will be difficult to change the locale and the names. But, as the poet is hard at work at the moment, it is better to let him finish the libretto, and then we can think about the changes.

A pity! To have to give up the pomp of Gustav III's court! And it will be very difficult to find another duke as good as Gustav. Poor poets and poor composers!

[109]

*To Vincenzo Torelli*                           *Naples, 10 February, 1858*

First of all, tell me how you are. Second, tell me something about the libretto, if you know anything. This business has already been too long-drawn-out, and it's beginning to take on the air of a joke, not to mention a taunt.[2] Wouldn't it be better and more convenient to arrive at some kind of solution?

[110]

*To Vincenzo Jacovacci*                            *Naples, 19 April, 1858*

[The Roman impresario, Jacovacci, had been secretly negotiating with Verdi for *Un ballo in maschera*, knowing of the censorship difficulties the opera was experiencing in Naples. The approval of the Roman censor was,

---

[1] The librettist, Antonio Somma.
[2] With 'joke' and 'taunt', Verdi plays on the similarity of 'scherzo' to 'scherno'.

however, not easily obtained. Despite the despairing tone of this letter, the opera was finally staged in Rome on 17 February, 1859.]

Dear Jacovacci,

I do not have, nor have I ever had, anything to do with the newspapers, and if you knew me better you would have spared me that long exordium in your last letter but one.

In Rome, they will allow *Gustavo III* on the stage, but to set the same subject to music is not allowed!!! That is very strange! I respect the wishes of my masters, and I have nothing to say. But, if I didn't want to stage the opera in Naples because the libretto was altered, I cannot give it in Rome, since they also want to change it there.

Everything is settled here, and the dispute is over! I shall leave Naples by ship on Wednesday: I shall be in Civitavecchia on Thursday morning. Send to me there, to await me at the post office, the libretto of *Gustavo III* which is in your possession, and let's speak no more of this business, which has come to nothing and can be considered cancelled under clause 6 of our contract.

Believe me yours affectionately


[111]

*To Tito Ricordi*                                                          *4 February, 1859*

[*Simon Boccanegra* had been revived at La Scala on 24 January, 1859, with a mediocre cast.]


The fiasco of *Boccanegra* in Milan had to happen, and it did happen. A *Boccanegra* without Boccanegra!! Cut a man's head off, and then recognize him if you can. You are surprised at the public's lack of decorum? I'm not surprised at all. They are always happy if they can contrive to create a scandal! When I was twenty-five, I still had illusions, and I believed in their courtesy; a year later my eyes were opened, and I saw whom I had to deal with. People make me laugh when they say, as though reproaching me, that I owe much to this or that audience! It's true: at La Scala, once, they applauded *Nabucco* and *I Lombardi;* but, whether because of the music, the singers, orchestra, chorus or production, the entire performances were such that they were not unworthy of applause. Not much more than a year earlier, however, this same audience ill-treated the opera of a poor, sick young man, miserable at the time, with his heart broken by a terrible misfortune.[1] They all knew that, but it did not make them behave courteously. Since that time, I've not seen *Un giorno di regno*, and I've no doubt it's an awful opera, but heaven knows how many others no better were tolerated and even applauded. Oh, if only the public at that time had, not necessarily applauded, but at least suffered my opera in silence, I shouldn't have been able to find words enough to thank them! If they now look graciously upon those operas of mine that have toured the world, then the score is settled. I don't condemn them: let them be severe. I accept their hisses on condition that I don't have to beg for their applause. We poor gypsies, charlatans, or whatever you want to call us, are forced to sell our labours, our thoughts, and our dreams, for gold. For three lire, the public buys the right to hiss or to applaud. Our fate is one of resignation, and that's all! But, whatever my friends or enemies say, *Boccanegra* is in no way inferior to many other operas of mine which were more fortunate: perhaps this one needed both more care in performance and an audience which really wanted to listen to it. What a sad thing the theatre is!! But, contrary to my usual custom, I've inadvertently gone on chattering uselessly to you. Nevertheless, I'll send it to you, rather than rewrite the letter.

[112]

*To Vincenzo Jacovacci*                                    *Busseto, 5 June, 1859*

Dear Jacovacci,

You were wrong to defend *Un ballo in maschera* against the attacks of the newspapers. You should have done as I always do: not read them, or let them chatter away as they wish. Apart from that, the question is this: is the opera good or bad? If it is bad, and the journalists spoke unfavourably of it, they were right. If it is good, and they have not thought so because of their own petty feelings, or other people's, or for whatever reason, one should let them talk, and not worry about it. But you must admit that if anyone or anything needed defending during the carnival season, it was that wretched company you presented me with. Put your hand on your heart and confess that I was a model of

---

[1] The death of Verdi's first wife and both his children. The children had died in 1838 and 1839; Margherita Verdi died in 1840 while Verdi was at work on *Un giorno di regno*.

rare self-denial in not taking my score and going off in search of dogs, whose barking would have been preferable to the sounds of the singers you offered me. But *post factum*, after everything has happened etc. . . .

Excuse me, but I cannot write to Ricordi about reducing the hiring fees, as I am not used to taking part in this kind of thing. What is more, the amounts you offer for *Aroldo*, *Boccanegra* and *Un ballo in maschera* seem to me (however little value these operas may have) too modest. I don't know whether Ricordi will view it as I do; if he does, he will say what I say and what you too would say: do better elsewhere. If you should find that other people's requirements are also too high for you, then rummage about in the public domain and you can get out of it for a few farthings. Do you require three operas? Here they are: *Nina pazza* by Paisiello, *Armida* by Gluck and *Alceste* by Lully. Thus, besides being economical, you will save yourself from having to fight with the newspapers or anyone else. The music is beautiful, the composers are dead, everyone has spoken well of them for a century or two, and will continue to do so, if only so that they can continue to speak unfavourably of those who have not yet performed the foolish action of dying.

Farewell, my dear Jacovacci. Let's not think about new operas.

[113]

*To Countess Maffei*                                        *Busseto, 23 June, 1859*

[In an article in Bulletin No. 6 of the Institute of Verdi Studies, Frank Walker points out that this letter is printed in the *Copialettere* 'in two detached fragments, printed in the wrong order'. The present editor has followed Walker's reading insofar as the order of the excerpts is concerned, and has joined them together. But he has not translated any sentences not to be found in the *Copialettere*. Walker's text contains an additional sentence in the middle of the final paragraph as printed here, an additional sentence at the end of that paragraph, and three more whole paragraphs. His text is taken from the autograph in the library at Brera.]

Dear Clarina,

I have been wanting to write to you for ten or twelve days, but since those most illustrious persons blew up the forts at Piacenza, so much has happened and is happening, even in this remote place, so many alarms, so much news both true and false, that one never has a quiet hour. At last they have gone away, or at least have moved off somewhat, and I hope that our kindly star will drive them even further, until, pursued beyond the alps, they may go and enjoy their own climate, their own sky, which I trust will be even more beautiful, limpid and splendid than ours. What things have happened in a few days! It seems hardly true! And who would have believed our allies could be so generous? For myself, I confess, and say 'mea grandissima culpa', for I didn't believe the French would come to Italy, or, if they did, that they would shed their blood for us, without some thought of conquest. On the first point, I was wrong, and I hope and desire to be wrong on the second, and that Napoleon will not repudiate the proclamation of Milan. Then I shall adore him as I adored Washington, and even more so. Blessing that great nation, I shall even willingly put up with all their *blague*, their insolent *politesse*, and the scorn they have for everything that is not French.

The day before yesterday, a poor priest (the only right-thinking one in the whole of the district) brought me greetings from Montanelli[1] whom he had met at Piacenza, a private soldier in the volunteers. The old professor of law, setting such a noble example! That's beautiful and sublime. Oh, if only my health were better, and I could be with him! I say this to you, as a close secret. I wouldn't say it to others, for I should not like to be thought of as a brave armchair soldier. But what could I do, who am not capable of marching three miles, whose head can't stand the sun for five minutes, and who is sent to bed, sometimes for weeks, by a little wind or a little humidity? What a wretched nature I have. Good for nothing!

[114]

*To Countess Maffei*                    *Busseto, 14 July, 1859*

Dear Clarina,

Instead of singing a hymn of praise, it would seem to me more suitable today to raise a cry of lament for our eternally unfortunate country.

Together with your letter I received a bulletin of the 12th which said, 'The Emperor to the Empress . . . Peace is declared . . . Venice remains under Austria'!!

And where is the long hoped for and promised independence of Italy? What does the Proclamation of Milan mean? Or is Venice not

---

[1] See *Personalia*.

Italy? After such a victory, what a result! What blood spilled for
nothing! How our poor young men have been deluded! And Garibaldi, who has even made a sacrifice of his old and constant convictions
in favour of a king, has still not achieved his wishes. It's enough to
drive one mad. I am writing while still in a state of great anger, and I
don't know what you will think of me. It's really true then, that we
can never hope for anything from any foreigner of whatever nation!
What do you think? Perhaps I'm wrong again? Would that I were. . . . .
Farewell, farewell.


[115]

*To the Mayor of Busseto*                          *Sant'Agata, 5 September, 1859*

Dear Mr. Mayor,
  The honour which my fellow citizens have conferred upon me in
nominating me as their representative at the Assembly of the provinces
of Parma makes me both proud and extremely grateful. Though my
meagre talents, my studies and the art which I profess do not make me
very suitable for this kind of office, I hope I shall be fortified by the
great love I bear, and have always borne, our noble and unhappy Italy.
  Needless to say, in the names of my fellow citizens and myself, I shall
join in proclaiming:

  the fall of the Bourbon dynasty;
  annexation to Piedmont;
  the leadership of that illustrious Italian, Luigi Carlo Farini.[1]

  The future greatness and the regeneration of our province depend on
our annexation to Piedmont. Whoever feels Italian blood coursing in
his own veins must strive constantly and vigorously for this. Then for
us the day will come in which we can say we are part of a great and
noble nation.

          [1] Luigi Carlo Farini had been elected ruler of Emilia.

[116]

*To Angelo Mariani* *Busseto, 25 October, 1859*

[Angelo Mariani (1822–1873), conductor and composer, began his conducting career with Pacini's *Saffo* in 1844 at Messina. A patriot, he fought for Italian freedom in 1848 as a volunteer. He could have had a distinguished international career but preferred to work in Italy, apart from brief periods in Copenhagen and Constantinople. In 1871 he introduced *Lohengrin* to Italy. His compositions include orchestral pieces, songs, and two patriotic cantatas.

By 1846 he had already begun to acquire a reputation as a conductor of Verdi, and the composer would like to have had him conduct *Macbeth* in 1847.]

I have received your very kind letter, and the *Movimento*, and although your letter sounds so desolate, I shall not throw myself into a state of desperation yet. We shall see! Meanwhile, let's talk of something else. You know that in Turin Sir Hudson [sic][1] gave me a letter from Signor Clemente Corte, an officer under Garibaldi, to direct me where I could find some guns. Signor Corte accepted the commission in a very kind letter on 28th September, and at the same time forwarded to me a telegram about it that he had received from the firm of Danovaro in Genoa: '6,000 of various qualities possibly available now, mostly English, price 23 to 30 francs. 2,500 carbines, 60 muskets etc.'

After receiving both letter and telegram, I wrote to Corte on 2nd October to order, for the time being, 100 rifles. In another letter on 18th October, I ordered another 72, all to be sent to the Castle San Giovanni, where I would have sent someone to accept delivery of them, and would either have paid the station master or sent a cheque to Genoa, whichever the seller preferred.

I received no answer, either to my letter of 2nd October or my second one of the 18th. I'm on pins and needles about it, because the Mayor of my district keeps asking me about them. Tomorrow I shall send my foreman to Modena to see whether this Corte is alive or dead. Meanwhile, I should like to know:

1. Whether first 100, then 72 rifles, were ordered from the firm of Danovaro.

2. Whether they were sent, and, if Corte has not carried out the commission, whether the guns are available and at the price indicated in the telegram.

[1] Sir James Hudson, British Minister to the Court of Piedmont, was a friend of Mariani. Verdi required the rifles for the National Guard of Busseto.

3. Whether you, Signor Angelo Mariani, would be willing, if necessary, to order these rifles, and others later should the need arise, inspect them yourself, and have them examined by someone knowledgeable to see if they will serve our purpose. You would be performing a holy and meritorious deed.

Reply to me immediately, and carry out this commission with the common sense I know you to possess. Farewell, farewell.


[117]

*To Count Cavour*                                    *Busseto, 21 November, 1859*

[Verdi's visit to Cavour had been arranged through Sir James Hudson, with the help of Angelo Mariani.]

Your Excellency,

I trust that your Excellency will forgive my boldness and any annoyance I may cause you with these few lines. I had desired for a long time to know personally the Prometheus of our people, and did not despair of finding an occasion to satisfy this great desire of mine.

What, however, I had not dared to hope for was the frank and kindly reception with which Your Excellency deigned to honour me.

When I left you I felt deeply moved! I shall never forget your estate of Leri where I had the honour to shake hands with our great statesman, our most important citizen, he whom every Italian will call the father of our country. May your Excellency be kind enough to accept these sincere words from a poor artist who has no other merit than that of loving, and having always loved, his own country.


[118]

*To Angelo Mariani*                                    *Busseto, 21 March, 1860*

Dear Mariani,

When you were only a musician, I would not have dared write you a letter like this one, but now that you have become a capitalist, a speculator and a usurer, I am giving you several commissions for which I shall reimburse you in a few days (only a few days), on which you will have to spend a few hundred francs, which you will receive back with interest, broker's fee, discount charges and similar thieveries etc. etc.

First of all, go and get my portrait, and pay everything according to the terms of the letter I enclose.

Secondly, make Maestro Cambini take you to that particular gardener, and buy 10 Magnolia Grandiflora, about one and a half metres high, but in no case less than one metre. They are to be well packed in straw, but not until the day before departure.

Thirdly, go to Noledi and ask him if he will exchange my St Etienne rifle for his Liège, the one I like which is a 13–14 calibre. You know the one, and I'll also give him 4 gold napoleons. You can assure him that my rifle is as good as new, for I have only used it during part of December, and both the wood and the iron look as good as new. But if Noledi should wish to see it first, write to me immediately, so that I can put it in a little box and send it by train. I should like you, however, to try out the Liège rifle for me, and make sure that it shoots straight and doesn't kick. It will need to be tested with bullets five or six times.

The snow has all gone. However, if you wait a few days more, the ground will have dried and we can go into the woods.

Bring everything with you, and put it all on the train as luggage. You will take a ticket to Piacenza, and then from Piacenza to Borgo San Donnino. You will leave at ten in the morning, and arrive at Piacenza about three, wait half an hour at Piacenza and be in Borgo after four. You will find a carriage for Busseto, but, as this waits for the coach from Parma, it thus leaves Borgo very late. You can wait for the Borgo coach, or take an express carriage which will bring you to Sant'Agata, or write to me the day before and I shall come to Borgo, or send my horses. You understand?

Please take care with everything. Particularly the rifle, and if, when you test it, it seems to be really superior, don't worry about spending a little more money on it.


[119]

*To Angelo Mariani*                 *Busseto, 25 November, 1860*

Dear Mariani,

My carpenter has a nephew who is called to do his military service, but, due to a fall, he has a spinal inflammation in his foot, which makes it impossible for him to march. He has been examined, but the regimental doctors have referred his case to the doctors in Turin. He goes

to Turin at the beginning of the month, but he should have someone
there to look after him. Is there anyone there to whom you could
recommend him? But it should be a good man, not an Ambassador or
a Minister. You would be performing a deed of mercy. Write to me.

[120]

*To Angelo Mariani*                               *Busseto, 3 January, 1861*

Many many thanks for having found someone to help this poor
protégé of mine. His name is Angelo Allegri, born in 1840. It would be
best if the person writing to Turin prepares the letter which you should
send here, for me to give to the same Allegri to deliver in Turin to the
person to whom it is addressed. All this as soon as possible, as he may
have to leave on the 8th.

[121]

*To Dr Giuseppe Chiarpa*          *Sant'Agata di Villanova, 6 January, 1861*

[Dr Chiarpa was Mayor of Borgo San Donnino, and President of the group
of local authorities Verdi was to represent.]

Mr President,
    The honour spontaneously offered to me by the electorate of Borgo
San Donnino moves me deeply. It indicates to me that I enjoy the esteem
of honest and independent men, and that is dearer to me than the little
fame and fortune I owe to my art.
    I thank you, therefore, Mr President, and beg you to thank warmly
for me all the voters who have entrusted me with this honourable
office. Please assure them at the same time that, although it is not given
to me to bring to Parliament the splendour of eloquent speech, I shall
take with me my independence of character, my conscientiousness and
my strong desire to strive with all my might for the well-being, the
good name and the unification of our country for so long a time
divided and torn by civil discord.
    May our long and so far fruitless desire to see our country united
now be realized, and may fortune send us a King who loves his people.
Let us then gather around him, and, if he is soon acclaimed the first

King of Italy, perhaps he will be the only one who has really loved the Italians more than the throne.

[122]

*To Giovanni Minghelli-Vaini*    *Sant'Agata, 23 January, 1861*

[Giovanni Minghelli-Vaini, member of a liberal family from Modena, a solicitor and politically experienced, had announced that he wished to represent Busseto and the surrounding district, electorally known as Borgo San Donnino, in the elections for the first national Parliament. There were several suggestions that Verdi should stand, but he resisted them. When Cavour wrote personally to him, Verdi went to see him in Turin to explain his reluctance. While he was away, Minghelli-Vaini wrote to Sant'Agata to enquire if Verdi intended to stand, and was assured by Giuseppina Strepponi that Verdi had no intention of doing so. Verdi, however, had been persuaded by Cavour, whom he revered, that it was his duty to stand. Minghelli-Vaini sought an explanation, and Verdi replied with this letter.

When Minghelli-Vaini wrote again to say he did not consider Verdi responsible for the political intrigue against him, Verdi took offence, and replied at some length (letter 123.)

Verdi was elected, attended the sessions of Parliament in Turin regularly, and always voted the same way as Cavour.

See letter 136 for Verdi's account of his life as a Deputy from 1861 to 1865.]

Dear Minghelli-Vaini,

It was not between one glass and the next, but at that time when one drinks at most a cup of coffee, that the business, unsought by me, of my nomination to Parliament was discussed. My journey to Turin had no other purpose than my desire to free myself of it, which you know. I did not succeed, and I am most desolate, particularly since you are so much more used to parliamentary battles than an artist who has nothing in his favour but his poor name.

I proposed you, and spoke warmly for you in Busseto, in the knowledge that I would be procuring for my country a real Italian, an honest man, and a Deputy whose enlightenment would help our good cause. I have not put myself forward, I shall not put myself forward, nor make any move to have myself nominated. Although the sacrifice will be a heavy one for me, I shall, however, accept if I am nominated, and you know the reasons that force me to do so. I have definitely decided however, to resign as soon as I can. This letter, which I authorize you to show to anyone who dares to cast injurious aspersions upon you, must suffice to justify you, and to restore you to a state of perfect calm. As for the remedy suggested to me, that I should get myself nominated in another electoral district, forgive me, but this is against my principles. If I were to do that, I should be *putting myself forward* for election, and I repeat for the hundredth time, *I may be forced to accept* but I will not put myself forward or offer myself to another district.

If you succeed in winning a majority of votes over me, becoming nominated and thus freeing me of this imposition, I shall not be able to find words sufficient to thank you for this welcome service, and you will be a great acquisition for the Chamber, will give yourself pleasure and give the very greatest pleasure to

G. Verdi

[123]

*To Giovanni Minghelli-Vaini*                          *Busseto, 29 January, 1861*

Dear Minghelli,

I quote from your letter: 'I do not need to tell you that I am convinced you have nothing to do with, indeed that you abhor, the intrigues operating against me.' The word 'intrigue' does not exist in my dictionary, and I defy the entire world to prove otherwise.

Quite the contrary: if I had intrigued, the article in the *Gazetta di Parma* of the 22nd would not have appeared; if I had intrigued, the Parma Committee would not have advertised your candidacy on walls all over the district; if I had intrigued, that other article in the *Patriota* on the 28th would not have appeared. Nor do I now need to intrigue, because, if I had wanted to amuse myself by becoming a Deputy, there was nothing to stop me from accepting the candidacy from the beginning. On the 21st I told you frankly the reasons why I shall be forced to accept, if I am elected. But your acquaintance with me is too slight for you to know that my sense of dignity is almost akin to pride, and that my scorn for certain underhand dealings verges on disgust. I have never studied for a career in politics, and have neither the competence for such a career nor the desire for it. I have said, and I repeat for the hundredth time: I shall accept, against my will, if I am nominated, but I shall not say or do anything to bring this about. Let this serve to conclude a correspondence between us which should never have been opened.

Greetings to your wife, also from Peppina and believe me yours

[124]

*To Opprandino Arrivabene*                    Busseto, *14 June, 1861*

[Count Opprandino Arrivabene (1807–1886), an old and devoted friend of Verdi, was also his fellow-Deputy in Parliament. Verdi, at his own expense, organized in Busseto a memorial service for the great statesman, Count Camillo Benso di Cavour who had died on 6 June.]

The service for Cavour was held on Tuesday with all the pomp that could be expected of this little country town. The clergy officiated *gratis* and that's saying something.

I attended the funeral ceremony in deep mourning, but my heart was in even deeper mourning. Between you and me, I couldn't hold my tears back, and I wept like a child. Poor Cavour!........and poor us.

[125]

*To the Busseto Town Council*                    [*c. 1861*]

Fulfilling my duty as a Deputy, I add to it my petition as a citizen.

Italy is in serious danger, not from the threats of an enemy or from municipal dissension or the acts of any faction, for nowadays they are impotent, but from lack of funds. Heaven forbid that history should one day register that Italy was destroyed through lack of money when she possesses such rich territory, and at a time in which her cities are being embellished, and theatres and monuments are being erected everywhere. Even Busseto is building a theatre, and I don't want you to think I oppose this project, even though it seems a vain and useless thing to me. This is not the moment to discuss that, but to think about higher and more important matters, and this is why I return to the Council with the exhortation that this work be suspended, and that the noble example of Brescia and many other cities be followed by using the money to restore our country's economy.

I have done my duty as a Deputy. As a citizen I repeat my plea most

E

ardently. Perhaps this is unnecessary, for I am certain that the feelings I express are shared by all.


[126]


*To Tito Ricordi*                              *Busseto-Sant'Agata, 22 October, 1862*

Dear Ricordi,

Rain, rain and more rain!! Farewell, country; farewell, walks; farewell beautiful sun, which from now on we shall only see looking pale and sickly. Farewell, beautiful blue sky; farewell, infinite space; farewell to our desires and hopes of going to Como! Four walls will take the place of the infinite, and we'll have a fire instead of the sun, and boredom instead of pleasure! So be it, we shall make music in order to . . . to do what everyone else does: bore themselves to death with the greater part of so-called classical music, with the difference, however, that when I am bored I say 'I'm bored', while others pretend to be ecstatic at beauties that don't exist, or at least exist just as much in our music of today. At least it's true that the present age talks a great deal, moves about restlessly, expends a great deal of energy, produces little, and tries to invent a new music out of powder and the bones of the dead. If, however, there's a little sun in it, then three cheers for the new music. So, in order to do just what the others are doing, I ask you to be so kind as to send me the work you are now printing (I can't remember the title), music for piano by ancient and modern composers. But let's understand each other properly: I have resolved never to pay even a penny in future for pieces of music, nor to have anything more to do with theatrical agents. So if you, on your part, have resolved never to give away a piece of music again, you would have acted wisely, and you should then not send me the above mentioned work, and we'll be better friends than ever.

I'm going to Turin where I shall stay for eight or ten days. Make haste and write to me there.


[127]


*To Countess Maffei*                            *St Petersburg, 17 November, 1862*

[Verdi had gone to St Petersburg to stage *La forza del destino* which he had written for the Imperial Theatre. The opera had its successful première on 10 November 1862 (or 29 October according to the Russian Calendar).]

I'm leaving Petersburg in a few days, and have just time to squeeze your hands, and say that I'm as fond of you as always.

From Paris I shall write to you at length, and tell you about Russia and its high society. You'll be amazed, amazed! In these two months I've been frequenting salons, then there were suppers, parties etc. I've met both important and humble people, men and women of great amiability and a really exquisite politesse, quite different from the impertinent Parisian *politesse*. . . .

[128]

*To Vincenzo Luccardi*                                      *Madrid, 13 January, 1863*

[Verdi had gone to Madrid to stage *La forza del destino*. After the first performances, he and Giuseppina took the opportunity to spend some weeks sight-seeing in Spain. At the same time, the opera was being produced in Rome, and it is of the Rome production that Verdi demands news from Luccardi.]

If you always address your letters so badly, no wonder I never receive them. This one has reached me, only because it fortunately went to Sant'Agata, and my steward has sent it on to me.

I have been in Madrid for two days now, and I'm here to stage *La forza del destino*. I can't tell you anything about this city yet, but I shall write to you about the works of art I see, and about my opera. You, however, shall write to me frequently about this opera, the rehearsals and the performance. For the rest, I'm not worried about the musical performance, but about the various changes that have been made in the libretto. It's an opera of huge dimensions, and it needs great care. Enough, we shall see. I shall write in any case, and the plain, unadulterated truth.

And what are you doing? Working? Going to the theatre? Tell me all, and send me your news frequently, you know how much I want to hear from you. Write to Madrid where I shall stay for at least a month.

[129]

*To Vincenzo Luccardi*                              *Madrid, 17 February, 1863*

Many thanks for the telegram you sent me, and for the letter I have just this moment received. The opera went well enough in Rome, but it could have gone a thousand times better if Jacovacci had for once got it into his head that, to have a success, you need both operas suited to the singers and singers suited to the operas. It's true that, in *La forza del destino*, the singers don't have to know how to do *solfeggi*, but they must have soul, and understand the words and express their meaning. I'm sure that, with a sensitive soprano, the duet in the first act, the aria in the second, the romance in the fourth act and, in particular the duet with the Father Superior in the second act, would all have been successful. There you have four numbers spoiled in performance. And four numbers are quite a lot, and can affect the fate of an opera! The rôle of Melitone makes its effect from the first word to the last. Jacovacci has now seen the need to replace this singer, but as an old impresario he should have seen it from the beginning. For the rest, let's thank our good fortune that the singers and, in particular, the impresario, didn't completely ruin the opera by their shortcomings. I thank you, too, for your affectionate friendship and for the solicitude you have shown in sending me your comments.

The opera will be produced here on Saturday, and on Sunday morning I shall send you news of it. Rehearsals are going reasonably well.

I shall leave immediately afterwards for a little tour through Andalusia, then I shall go to Paris, where I shall stay for some time.

[130]

*To Countess Maffei*                                 *Busseto, 13 December, 1863*

[Franco Faccio (1840–1891) who was also a composer, was to become the finest Italian opera conductor of his time. He conducted the first European performances of *Aida* in 1872, and the première of *Otello* in 1887, both at La Scala, Milan. He was a friend of Boito, and in 1866 they were to fight side by side in Garibaldi's army. On 11 November, 1863, at the age of twenty-three, Faccio had an opera, *I profughi fiamminghi*, produced at La Scala. In

1865, his Shakespeare opera, *Amleto*, with libretto by Boito, was produced in Genoa.

The quotation, 'as ugly as the stink of a whore-house' is from an Ode to Italian Art, declaimed some weeks previously by its author Boito, at a dinner to honour his colleague Faccio. The Ode was subsequently published. It contains the lines

> Forse già necque chi sovra l'altare
> Rizzerà l'arte, verecondo e puro
> Su quel' altar bruttato come un muro
> Di lupanare.

(Perhaps the man is already born who, modest and pure, will restore art to its altar stained like a brothel wall.)

The inference was that the stain on the altar, like that of urine on the outside wall of a brothel, was caused by the music of Verdi, and that the saviour of Italian music was to be Faccio. Embarrassed, Faccio had written expressing his admiration for Verdi, and had also asked the Countess Maffei to write to the composer on his behalf.]

Dear Clarina,

For a fortnight, I've been whirling about here and there like a lunatic, doing nothing as usual, simply for the sake of boring myself and wearying any friend I came across, and this is why I've replied neither to your letter nor to Faccio's. Moreover, I can say to you with my customary frankness that Faccio's letter has caused me some embarrassment. How can I reply to it? A word of encouragement, as you have done, perhaps; but a word of this kind given by me would be made known to the public. The matter, however, is already discussed in public, so any word would be useless. I know there has been much talk of this opera, too much in my opinion, and I have read a newspaper article in which I found such big words as Art, Aesthetics, Revelations, the Past, the Future etc. etc. I confess that (great ignoramus that I am!) I understood none of it. On the other hand, I am acquainted with neither Faccio's talent nor his opera. And I don't want to know it, so that I can avoid discussing and giving judgment, things which I detest because they are the most useless in the world. Discussions do not convince anyone, and judgments are usually wrong. Finally, if Faccio, as his friends say, has found new paths, if Faccio is destined to restore art, currently 'as ugly as the stink of a whore-house', to its altar, so much the better for him, and for the public. If he is led astray, as others assert, then let him put himself back on the right road, if he believes in it, and if it seems right for him.

Ah, you have read Escudier's extravagant words[1] about me! There is a lot of truth in it, but he exaggerates everything to make it read better. It's a business matter and nothing more.

[131]

*To Opprandino Arrivabene*                                        *4 April, 1864*

. . . You've guessed it. Ricordi no longer sends me music, because he knows that, during the ten or twelve long years I lived in Milan, I never once went to consult his musical archives. I don't understand music by taking it in through my eyes, and, if you thought that the two compositions, because they are by Rossini, could perform the miracle of opening my mind to comprehend the beauties and treasures of harmony so praised by D'Arcais and Filippi, you were greatly mistaken. Nevertheless, I thank you for your good intentions, and say to you from my heart, farewell.

[132]

*To Léon Escudier*                                            *24 October, 1864*

[Léon Escudier, Verdi's French publisher, had suggested that *Macbeth*, which had had its première eighteen years earlier in Florence, should be translated into French for production in Paris. Escudier asked Verdi to revise the opera and add the obligatory ballet sequence.]

Your last letter to me contained so many nice things that, although I have been rummaging in my little sack of amiability for a month, I haven't been able to find anything to equal them. So I say nothing, and you must use your imagination and guess at what I want and ought to say.

I have glanced through *Macbeth* in order to do the ballet music, but alas! I have found a few things in it that must be changed. In short, there are certain numbers which are weak, or even worse, lacking in character. This is what will have to be done:

---

[1] In Léon Escudier's memoirs, *Mes Souvenirs*, published in 1863.

1. Write an aria for Lady Macbeth in Act II
2. Various cuts to be reconsidered in the vision scene of Act III
3. Completely re-do Macbeth's aria
4. Touch up the first scenes of Act IV
5. Do a new last act finale, deleting Macbeth's death scene.

To do all this, as well as the ballet, will take time, and you must try to convince Carvalho[1] to renounce any thought of producing *Macbeth* this winter. Discuss this with him, and then reply to me. I am leaving tomorrow for Turin where I shall stay for eight or ten days.


[133]


*To Francesco Piave*                        *Sant'Agata, 20 December, 1864*


[This letter is a fine example of Verdi's harrowing technique with librettists. The opera Piave was working on was a revision of *La forza del destino*. For the Scala production of 1869, further changes were made, but by then Piave had suffered a stroke, which left him completely paralysed for the remaining eight years of his life. The revisions to the libretto in 1869 were made by Antonio Ghislanzoni, who later wrote the Italian libretto of *Aida*.]


Dear Piave,

I have received your verses and, if I may say so, I don't like them. You talk to me about 100 syllables!! And it's obvious that 100 syllables aren't enough when you take 25 to say the sun is setting!!! The line 'Duopo e sia l'opra truce compita' is too hard, and even worse is 'Un Requiem, un Pater . . . e tutto ha fin'. First of all, this 'tutto ha fin' rhymes with 'Eh via prendila Morolin'. It neither sounds well nor makes sense. Why this 'Requiem'? Finally, you don't say the Lord's Prayer at a death bed. You will say I put it in my scenario, but you know that I only intend these scenarios as a guide to you.

Then, the seven-syllabled lines!!! For the love of God, don't end lines with 'che', 'piu' and 'ancor'.

Now then, can't you do better, retaining as far as possible the words I sent you, but turning them into better rhymes?


[1] Léon Carvalho was Director of the Théâtre Lyrique, Paris, where the revised *Macbeth* was produced on 21 April, 1865.

[134]

*To Léon Escudier*                                                    *January, 1865*

A short time ago you received the first two acts of *Macbeth*. And the day before yesterday I sent the third to Ricordi from whom you will receive it in two or three days. With the exceptions of part of the first chorus and part of the dance of the sylphs when Macbeth faints, all of this third act is new. I finish the act with a duet for Macbeth and Lady Macbeth. It doesn't seem illogical to me that Lady Macbeth, always intent on looking after her husband, should have discovered where he is: it makes a better end to the act. The stage machinist and the director will enjoy themselves in this act. You will see that in the ballet there is a certain amount of action which fits very well with the rest of the drama. The apparition of Hecate, Goddess of Night, is appropriate, because she interrupts all the witches' dances with her calm and severe adagio. I don't need to tell you that Hecate must never dance, but simply mime. Also, needless to say, this adagio must be played by the *clarone* or bass clarinet (as is indicated), so that in unison with cello and bassoon it will produce a dark, hollow and severe tone in keeping with the situation. Please also ask the conductor to keep an eye on the dance rehearsals from time to time, to ensure that the dances remain at the tempi I have asked for. You know that dancers always alter the tempo. (At your Opéra, for example, they say the Tarantella can't be danced as I want it. But a child from the streets of Sorrento or Capua could dance it very well at my tempo.) If the tempi are altered, the witches' ballet will lose all its character, and will not produce the effect of which I think it capable. Another thing to draw to the attention of Signor Deloffre:[1] at the moment of the apparition of the eight kings, he must be sure to have the players in the little orchestra all under the stage. This little orchestra of two oboes, six clarinets in A, two bassoons and one contra-bassoon, produces a sonority which is strange and mysterious, yet at the same time calm and quiet, something which different instrumentation would not achieve. They must be under the stage, but under an open trap-door large enough for the sound to escape and spread through the theatre, but in a mysterious manner and as though from a great distance.

Another observation on the banquet scene in the second act of *Macbeth*: I've seen *Macbeth* performed many times in France, in England, and in Italy, and everywhere Banquo's ghost was made to

---

[1] Conductor of the orchestra at the Théâtre Lyrique.

appear from the wings. It came forward, moved restlessly, railed at Macbeth and then returned quietly into the wings. This, in my opinion, produces no illusion, inspires no terror, and no one can understand whether it's a ghost or a man. When I produced *Macbeth* in Florence, I made Banquo appear (with a huge wound on his forehead) from below the ground, by means of a trap-door, right in front of the chair intended for Macbeth. He made no movement, except to shake his head at the proper moment. This is what the stage looked like:

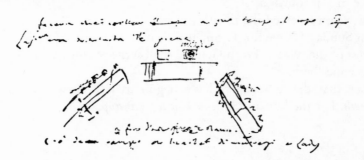

Thus Macbeth is able to move about, and Lady Macbeth can always stay close to him to utter, in asides, the words required by the situation.

Is it true that Duprez[1] is no longer to do the translation of *Macbeth?* I am sorry, because it will be difficult to find someone who is himself a musician, who understands singing, and who knows Italian as well as he. Incidentally, in the first act duet between Lady Macbeth and Macbeth, it is the first part that makes the most effect, and in it there is a phrase containing the words 'folie, folie che sperdono i primi rai del di'. The French translator must retain the words 'follie, follie', for it is perhaps in this word and in Lady Macbeth's secret derision that the whole secret of the effect of this piece lies.

[135]

*To Léon Escudier* *3 February, 1865*

Today I have sent to Ricordi the last act of *Macbeth*, absolutely complete. The whole of the chorus which opens the fourth act is new. The tenor aria is revised and re-orchestrated. Then all the scenes after the baritone's *romanza* to the end are new, i.e. the description of the battle

---

[1] Edouard Duprez, brother of the famous tenor Gilbert Duprez who had created the rôle of Gaston in Verdi's *Jérusalem* at the Opéra in 1847.

and the final hymn. You will laugh when you hear that, for the battle, I have written a fugue!!! I, who detest all that reeks of the academy. But I can assure you in this instance that particular form works well. The racing about of subjects and counter-subjects and the dissonant clashes can express the idea of battle very well. Ah, if you only had our trumpets, which sound so bright and full-toned. Your *trompettes à pistons* are neither one thing nor the other. Nevertheless, the orchestra will enjoy itself. As soon as possible I shall send you my notes on the whole of this fourth act.

Have you received the third?

On Sunday I leave for Turin, and then Genoa where I shall stay for the rest of the winter. From Genoa I shall write at length, and you can answer me there.

I see that the newspapers have begun to talk already about this *Macbeth*. For the love of God, *ne blaguez pas trop*.


[136]

*To Francesco Piave*                                            *8 February, 1865*

You ask me for news and information about my public life. My public life does not exist. It's true I'm a Deputy, but only by mistake. Nevertheless, I'll tell you the story of my Deputyship. In September 1860 I was in Turin. I had never seen Count Cavour and was most anxious to get to know him. I asked the English Ambassador there to introduce me. Since the treaty of Villafranca the Count had been living on one of his country estates, far removed from public affairs. I think it was at Vercellese, and one fine morning we visited him there. After that time, I had occasion to write to him and to receive a few letters from him, in one of which he exhorted me to accept the candidacy for a Deputyship, which my fellow citizens had offered me and which I had refused. His letter was most amiable, so much so that I did not see how I could answer it simply by saying 'no'. I decided to go to Turin; I visited him one day in December at 6 o'clock in the morning, in 12 or 14 degrees of frost. I had prepared my speech which seemed to me to be a master-piece, and I said everything that was in my mind. He listened to me attentively; and, when I described my ineptitude for the position of Deputy, and my outbursts of impatience at the long speeches you have to put up with occasionally in the Chamber, I did so in such a bizarre fashion that he uttered a great roar of laugher. Then he began to refute my reasons, one by one, and said to me things which seemed to make sense. So I said 'Very well, dear Count, I accept, but on condition that I can resign after a few months.' He was agreeable so long as I informed him first. I became a Deputy, and at first I frequented the Chamber. Then came that solemn sitting in which Rome was proclaimed capital of Italy. I voted, then approached the Count and said to him, 'Now it seems to me time to say farewell to these benches.' 'No,' he replied, 'wait until we go to Rome.'

'Are we going there?'

'Yes.'

'When?'

'Oh, when, when !'

'Well, meanwhile I'm going to the country.'

'Farewell, take care of yourself. Farewell.'

These were the last words he spoke to me. A few weeks later he died . . . After a few months I left for Russia, then went to London, from there to Paris and back to Russia, then to Madrid, then travelled through Andalusia and returned to Paris where I stayed a few months for business reasons. I stayed away from the Chamber for more than two years, and after that I attended on very few occasions. Several times I tried to offer my resignation, but on one occasion they said it was not a good time to have new elections, at other times there were other reasons, so I'm still a Deputy, without the slightest desire or taste for it, with no aptitude or talent for it, and completely lacking in the patience which is so necessary there. That's all. I repeat, if anyone needed to write about my career as a member of Parliament he would only have to print in the centre of a beautiful piece of paper, 'The 450 are really only 449, for Verdi as a Deputy doesn't exist.'

[137]

*To Countess Maffei*                      *Sant'Agata, 30 January, 1867*

[Verdi's old benefactor, Antonio Barezzi, was seriously ill. He lingered on until the summer, and died on 21 July, 1867. When the end came, Verdi and Giuseppina were with him. Barezzi was in bed, weak, and hardly able to speak, but he raised his eyes longingly to the piano which stood in a corner of his room. Verdi understood that the old man was asking for his favourite tune from *Nabucco*, so he sat and began to play 'Va, pensiero'. Barezzi raised a hand, murmured 'Oh, my Verdi', and died peacefully.]

Thank you, my gracious and kindest Clarina, for your affectionate letter.

Oh, this loss will be extremely sad for me. He has been better for three or four days, but I well realize that it is only a respite which may prolong his life for a few days, and no more! Poor old man, who has been so good to me! And poor me, who will see him for only a little while, and then never again!!!

You know that I owe him everything, everything, everything. And him alone, not others as people would have you believe. I still seem to see him (and this was many years ago), the day I had finished my studies at school in Busseto, and my father declared to me that he could not afford to maintain me at the University of Parma. I had decided, therefore, to go back to the village I came from. That good old man, knowing this, said to me, 'You were born for something better than selling salt or working on the land. Ask the Monte di Pietà for a small grant of 25 francs a month for four years, and I'll make up the rest. You will go to the Conservatorium in Milan and, when you are able to, you can pay me back any money I've spent on you.'

That's how it was. You see what generosity, what heart and what virtue he had. I've known many men, but none better! He loved me as much as his own sons, and I loved him like a father.

[138]

*To Vincenzo Luccardi*                                  *Busseto, 23 July, 1867*

Dear Luccardi,

A great misfortune has fallen upon us!

Poor Signor Antonio is dead!! He died in our arms, recognizing us almost until the last moment!

You know what he was like, what he was to me, and I to him. I leave you to imagine how great my sorrow is!!

I haven't the heart to go on. Farewell, farewell.

[139]

*To Paolo Marenghi*                                  *Torino, 15 August, 1867*

[Paolo Marenghi was Verdi's foreman in charge of the farm at Sant'Agata.]

Why did you use the machine, when I gave instructions it was not to be touched until my return? I should like to know once and for all whether my orders are going to be obeyed! . . . . You will never learn how to give orders or to take them!! . . . It's time that all this disorder came to an end, and I am absolutely determined that it shall.

You were wrong, and Guerino was also wrong, to let go of the keys to the workshop, which I had entrusted to him.

I am leaving for Paris, and you should direct your letters to: Monsieur Verdi, Poste restante, Paris, and nothing more.

[140]

*To Paolo Marenghi*                                        *Turin, 16 August, 1867*

When I told you to settle the accounts, if you had had a word with Spagna he would have told you about the bill for the timber. But the trouble is everyone sticks to his own little job, there is no co-operation, and so the administration suffers.

I am leaving tomorrow evening for Paris, and I repeat my orders again, to see if just once I can be understood and obeyed.

1. Apart from your usual inspection, you are to supervise the horses and the coachman whom I hardly trust to carry out my orders. He is to exercise the horses every two days, without going to Busseto.

2. Tell Guerino that he was wrong to give up the key to the machine, and tell him to clean it now, and keep it locked until he hears from me.

3. Repeat to the gardener what I have already told him. The garden is to be closed: no one may enter, and no one from the house may leave except the coachman, for a short time, to exercise the horses. If anyone goes out, then he can stay out for ever.

Please note that I am not joking, and that from now on I intend to be the master in my own house.

[141]

*To Paolo Marenghi*                                     *Paris, 4 September, 1867*

Permit me to say now to you in private that, instead of such meaning-less letters, it would be better for you not to write at all: nevertheless, a week is a long time. You say to me, for example, that the expenses amount to 518·06 lire, and that you need 276 lire. But, for heaven's sake, tell me how and why you incurred these expenses, and why you need exactly 276 lire.

Then you don't tell me anything about my house and about my servants. Are they all dead, perhaps? And how is the coachman? And what is he doing? Is it true that my old coachman, Carlo, has died at Piacenza? And, by the way, what about the cholera in our district? It seems to me that these are important matters, and that I can expect to know about them. I am leaving Paris immediately. Write to me as soon as you receive this letter, and give me an answer to everything I have asked you about.

[142]

*To Vincenzo Torelli*                                    *Genoa, 23 December, 1867*

[Achille Torelli, Vincenzo's son, was a writer of comic plays.]

Thank you for your portrait, and that of your Achille. But you have both written on them words which would make me blush if the country sun and air had not already turned my skin to tanned leather. However, I thank you, and if I do not send you mine, the reason is very simple: I have none!

I greatly, very greatly, approve of Achille's refusing the pension. If there is anything in life to be appreciated, it is the bread earned with the sweat of one's own brow. He is young, he can work. If his health is not robust, he should work moderately, but work. He should imitate nobody, least of all the great. Now, and only now (if the scholars will forgive me) can he dispense with studying them. Let him put his hand on his heart, and study that, and, if he really has the temperament to be an artist, that will tell him everything. He shouldn't be made conceited by praise or intimidated by blame. When confronted by criticism, even the most honest criticism, he should continue to go straight ahead. Criticism has its own job to do, it must judge, and judge according to rules and forms already laid down. The artist must look into the future, see new worlds among the chaos, and if, right at the end of his long road, he discerns a tiny light, he should not fear the darkness that surrounds him. Let him go straight on, and if sometimes he stumbles and falls, he must get up, and go straight on. It's a good thing that, sometimes, even the leader of a school can fall. . . . . But what the devil am I chattering on like this for!! . . . . . I am saying things that your Achille knows better than I do. Forgive me, and put it down to my desire and hope that he will become one of the greatest glories of Italy. Farewell, farewell. A happy new year to all, and Peppina joins me in this wish with all her heart. Farewell.


[143]


*To Tito Ricordi*                                    *Sant'Agata, 17 November, 1868*

[Verdi wrote this letter to Tito Ricordi, four days after the death of Rossini. It was published in the Milan *Gazzetta Musicale*. 'An organizing committee was set up in Milan to carry out Verdi's suggestion, and the composers, chosen by lot from a selected list, were Antonio Bazzini, Raimondo Boucheron, Antonio Buzzola, Antonio Cagnoni, Carlo Coccia, Gaetano Gaspari, Teodulo Mabellini, Alessandro Nini, Carlo Pedrotti, Enrico Petrella, Pietro Platania, Federico Ricci and, fortunately, Giuseppe Verdi. Most, if not all, of these composers submitted their finished movements in good time. Verdi certainly completed the "Libera me" which it had fallen to him to contribute. But, incredibly, difficulties in organizing a chorus proved insuperable. The Committee suggested postponing the performance, Verdi refused to consider this, and finally the composers received their manuscripts back.' (Osborne: *The Complete Operas of Verdi*, pp. 371–2.) See also letter 148.]


Dearest Ricordi,

To honour the memory of Rossini, I should like to ask the most distinguished Italian composers (Mercadante above all, if only with a few bars) to compose a Requiem Mass to be performed on the anniversary of his death.

I should like not only the composers but also the performers to give their services free and also contribute a small amount towards the expenses.

I want no foreigner, or anyone outside the world of music, to help in this, however powerful they may be. Otherwise, I should immediately dissociate myself from the project.

The Mass should be performed in the church of San Patronio in the city of Bologna, which was Rossini's real musical home.

This Mass should be an object neither of curiosity nor of speculation. After the performance, it should be sealed, and placed in the archives of the Music Academy of that city, whence it should never be removed.

Perhaps an exception could be made for future anniversaries of his death, should posterity wish to celebrate them.

If I were in the good books of the Holy Father, I should beg him on this occasion to allow the music to be performed by women's voices as well as men's. But since I am not, it will be necessary to find someone else to bring this about.

It would be a good idea to set up a Committee of intelligent men to arrange the details of this performance and, above all, to choose the composers, decide who will write what parts, and supervise the general form of the work.

However good its individual parts may be, this composition will necessarily lack musical unity, but, even so, it will still demonstrate how great is the veneration that all of us feel for this man, whose loss the entire world laments.

Farewell, and believe me yours affectionately

[144]

*To Léon Escudier*                                    *Sant'Agata, 2 December, 1868*

Dear Léon Escudier,

After so many years in which you have accustomed me to receiving news of you and information about interesting things in Paris (especially in the world of art), if you wished to terminate this correspondence which perhaps was becoming tedious to you, or even if you wished to bring our business relationship to an end, you had every right to do so. But that you should do it at the moment in which Rossini had departed from the world, this has surprised and upset me very much. With everyone talking and writing to satiety of his death, couldn't you have found a little piece of paper on which to write to me: 'Rossini is dead'!? . . . No, I cannot believe you acted like this without a very strong motive. I can't imagine you were merely reacting to some petty lack of etiquette of mine. Well then, if there is such a motive, tell me openly and frankly what it is. Your reply will indicate to me how I should conduct myself in future. Meanwhile, farewell, and believe me yours affectionately

[145]

*To Tito Ricordi*                    *Milan, 15 December, 1868*

[The revised version of *La forza del destino* was performed at La Scala, Milan, on 20 February, 1869. The tenor Mario Tiberini (1826–1880) sang Alvaro. Pietro Mongini (tenor, 1830–1874) was to sing Radames in the Cairo première of *Aida* in 1871.]

Dear Tito Ricordi,

I am coming myself to Milan to conduct what rehearsals I think necessary for *La forza del destino* and I am changing the last finale and various other numbers here and there throughout the opera.

I do not wish to have anything to do with the management of La Scala, I do not want my name put on the poster, and I shall not stay for the first performance, which cannot be given without my permission. I am not obliged to write to Tiberini whom I don't know, but if Mongini shows himself to disadvantage, or doesn't please in Milan, these obligations of mine will be null and void.

You will retain the rights to the new pieces, with the sole proviso that you must give a copy of them to the Management of the Opera in St. Petersburg if they ask for them.

In compensation for all this, you will give me:

1. Author's rights according to law, and as was done with *Don Carlos*.

2. A payment of fifteen thousand lire.

If these proposals are agreeable to you, that's fine; if not, don't stand on ceremony, but write me a word, and everything will be finished.

Farewell for now, and believe me affectionately yours

[146]

*To Senator Piroli*                    *Genoa, 1 March, 1869*

[Senator Giuseppe Piroli was an old friend of Verdi. Born in Busseto in 1815, he represented Parma in the Assembly which elected Farini ruler of Emilia. From 1866 to 1878 he was a Deputy for the constituency of San Donnino. He died in 1890.]

I returned yesterday from Milan at midnight. As you will know by now, *La forza del destino* had a decided success. Excellent performance.

Stolz and Tiberini superb, the others good. Orchestra and chorus divine. What fire and enthusiasm they all had. It's a shame, a shame that the Government ruthlessly refuses help to this art, and to this theatre which still has so many good aspects. You may ask why they can't get on without government help. It's not possible. La Scala Opera House has never been as well attended and as active as it is this year, but, despite this, if the management cannot achieve fifteen performances of *Forza* with nightly receipts of over 5,000 lire, they are lost. I don't believe it will be possible for them to give so many performances, so they will have to close the theatre with a deficit before the season is over. A shame, a shame!

[147]

*To Filippo Filippi*                                                          *Genoa, 4 March, 1869*

[Filippo Filippi (1830–1887), lawyer, music critic and composer, was Editor of the Milan *Gazzetta musicale* and, from 1859, critic of *La Perseveranza*. An admirer of the music of Verdi, he was also an apologist for Wagner. He had detected, in Leonora's aria '*Pace, pace, mio dio*' in *La forza del destino* a similarity to Schubert's 'Ave Maria'.]

Dear Signor Filippi,

I have no reason to take the article in the *Perseveranza* on *La forza del destino* in bad part. If, in the middle of a great deal of praise, you wanted to offer a little criticism, you had every right to do so, and you have done it well. Besides, you know I never complain about hostile articles, just as I never say thank you (perhaps I am wrong not to) for favourable ones. I am fond of retaining my independence in all matters, and I have the greatest respect for that of others. The fact is that I am extremely grateful to you for your reserve during my stay in Milan; for, since you had to write an article about my opera, it was a good thing not to allow yourself to be influenced either by a shake of the hand or a visit made or received. On the subject of this article I can say, since you ask me, that it didn't displease me, nor could it.

I know nothing of what passed between you and Ricordi, but it may be that Giulio, who, if I am not mistaken, prefers Leonora's *cantabile* to many other pieces, was a little upset when he saw it accused of being an imitation of Schubert. If it is, then I am as surprised as Giulio because, in my great musical ignorance, I don't know how many years it is since I last heard Schubert's *Ave*, so it would have been difficult for me to imitate it. Don't think that, when I speak of 'great musical ignorance', I'm just spreading a little *blague*. No, it's pure truth. In my house there is hardly any music. I never go to musical libraries, or to a publishing house, to look at a piece. I keep up to date with some of the better contemporary operas, not in the study, but by hearing them occasionally in the theatre. In all this, I have a purpose which you will understand. So I repeat to you that, of all composers of the past or present, I am the least erudite. Let's understand each other well, and again this is no mere *blague*: I'm speaking of erudition, and not musical knowledge. As far as that's concerned, I should be lying if I said that in my youth I had not indulged in lengthy and severe studies. That's why my hand is strong enough to make the notes go the way I want them to, and secure enough for me generally to succeed in obtaining the effects I have in mind. And when I write something that sounds irregular, it is because the regular is not what I want, and because I don't really believe that all the rules and regulations adopted up to now are correct. The counterpoint textbooks need to be revised.

What a lot of words! And, what's worse, so many useless ones. Please excuse me, and accept my sincere compliments.

[148]

*To Angelo Mariani*            *Genoa, 19 August, 1869*

[Verdi had hoped to use a chorus from Pesaro, conducted by Mariani, in the performance of the Mass for Rossini, but Mariani proved unco-operative. See also letters 151, 152 and 154.]

Sleep on in peace, for I have already replied that I cannot come to Pesaro.

I return to your letter of yesterday, because there are two phrases in it that I don't completely understand: 'What will the Milan Commission do?' and, further on: 'If I can be of service to you, let me know'. Do you mean to say we mustn't ask you to let us have your Pesaro chorus? First of all, you should have understood from the beginning that I, personally, am not involved in this, and that I am now just a pen which will write a few notes as well as possible and a hand to offer my 'widow's mite' towards bringing this patriotic celebration into being. Next, I must tell you that no one in this affair should ask, or be asked, for anything, because it is a duty which all artists should and must carry out.

I have never been able to ascertain whether the project of a Mass for Rossini has been fortunate enough to have your approval. When it is a matter not of personal interests but of an art, and of the fame and dignity of one's own country, a good deed requires no one's approval. So much the worse for anyone who doesn't recognize this! A man, a great artist who has made his mark on the age, dies: some individual or other invites his contemporary artists to honour that man, by honouring, through him, our art. A piece of music is composed for this purpose, and performed in the principal church in the town which was his musical home, and, so that this composition shall not feed miserable vanity and odious interests, it is to be locked away, after the ceremony, in the archives of a famous college. Musical history will one day have to record that 'at that time, when a famous man died, the entire world of Italian art united to perform in the church of San Petronio in Bologna, a Mass for the Dead, specially written by many composers, whose original manuscript is preserved under seal in the Bologna Liceo'. This becomes an historical fact, and not a piece of musical charlatanism. What does it matter, then, if the composition lacks unity, or if this or that part of it is more beautiful or less? What does it matter, if neither the vanity of this composer nor the conceit of that performer is fed? Individuals have nothing to do with this: it is enough for the day to arrive, and the commemoration to take place, in short for the historical fact, understand, the *historical fact* to exist.

This accepted, it is for all of us to do what we can to bring this about, without expecting petitions before, or praise and thanks afterwards.

If this commemoration takes place, we shall undoubtedly have done something good, artistic and patriotic. If not, we shall have proved once more that we bestir ourselves only when our own interests and vanity are involved, when articles and biographies lavish shameless adulation upon us, when our names are proclaimed in the theatres and dragged through the streets like charlatans in a public square. But when our personalities have to submerge themselves under an idea and a noble and generous act, then we hide behind the cloak of our egotistical indifference, which is the scourge and the ruin of our country.

Forgive my useless chatter and believe me, yours

[149]

*To Antonio Gallo*                                    *Genoa, 17 August, 1869*

[Antonio Gallo was Ricordi's agent in Venice. The reference to the 'solo pieces and duets for Colini, Stolz and Fraschini' is to a performance of *La forza del destino* with these singers, conducted by Mariani in the summer of 1869.]

Thank you for your first letter, and now for this one containing that of Z. He's gone quite, quite mad. The solo pieces and duets for Colini, Stolz and Fraschini have gone to his head, and will end by putting him in hospital. Of the various genre-scenes which take up a half of the opera, and which really constitute the musical drama, he simply follows the public and says nothing at all. It's a curious thing, and at the same time discouraging! While everyone cries out 'Reform', 'Progress', the public generally refrains from applause, and the singers only know how to be effective in arias, romances and canzonettas! I know that they now also applaud scenes of action, but only in passing, as the frame of the picture. They've got it upside down. The frame has become the picture!!! In short, despite the praises you have all sung to me about the performance, I believe, and am convinced, that while the numbers for solo, or two or three voices, were sung marvellously, the opera, and understand me well, the *opera* or music-scenic drama, was only imperfectly performed. What do you say to that, friend Tony?

Meanwhile, I wish them all well. To me in particular it hardly matters, but the art of the future will have to think carefully about it. It can't go on like this. Either the composers must take a step backward, or everyone else must step forward. Farewell.


[150]

*To the Mayor of Busseto*                         *Sant'Agata, 10 October, 1869*

Dear Mr. Mayor,

It is my desire to place at public disposal the annual pension of six hundred lire which I shall receive as a Knight of the Savoy Order for Civil Merit, by royal decree of June 23rd, 1869, reserving to myself the right to make in time such permanent arrangements as experience may prove best. For the time being, I have decided to donate the afore-mentioned sum of six hundred lire for two prizes of three hundred lire each, to be awarded at the end of the next scholastic year, 1869–70: the first to whichever poor youth shall have given the best proof of his intelligence and industry in the examinations of his last school year, according to the school regulations; and the second to that poor girl, who has shown the same aptitude in her examinations at the girls' school in Busseto.

In due course, I shall have this sum of six hundred lire paid into the treasury of the town of Busseto. The administration of this endowment I leave entirely to whichever conditions your Honour draws up, in consultation with the local school authority. I have the honour to sign myself your devoted servant

[151]

*To Giulio Ricordi*                      *Sant'Agata, 13 October, 1869*

Dear Giulio Ricordi,

Just as before I did not want to bring forward the date of performance of the Requiem Mass for Rossini, I now do not want to postpone it. This commemoration has no *raison d'être* other than the anniversary of his death. Otherwise, it just becomes one of the usual concerts. What's more, if it can't be done now, it will be even less possible in December. Orchestra and chorus in December?

Given the circumstances, there is, in my opinion, only one course the Committee can take. That is to announce to the public that the trouble taken to obtain the means to perform this Mass has proved to be in vain, and at the same time to give back to each composer his piece of music, with expressions of gratitude for the interest he has shown. The expenses incurred up to now by the Committee should be, as is only natural, my concern. Send me the bill and let's talk no more of it. Farewell, farewell.

[152]

*To Giulio Ricordi*                      *Sant'Agata, 27 October, 1869*

Dear Giulio,

It would be a good thing for the Committee to publish the reasons why the Mass for Rossini is not going to be performed in Bologna.

This would prevent useless gossip should this Mass later be performed somewhere else.

I am still of the same opinion. If the commemoration does not take place

        1. In Bologna
        2. On the anniversary of his death,

then it no longer has any meaning, and becomes just one of the usual concerts of music. This was, and still is, my opinion; but it should not be given any special consideration, becuse I am, after all, neither more nor less than one of many composers who have contributed pieces of music. The Committee, therefore, has every right to arrange matters as it thinks best.

Having said this, I should like to make a few observations, in semi-confidence. For example, if the Mass is performed in Milan, shall we find enough players capable of giving a really impressive performance? The usual theatre chorus lacks musical knowledge. (I am not speaking of style, which depends on the conductor.) A fugue cannot be performed as easily as the 'Rataplan' in *La forza del destino*. In Bologna, it would have been easy to find the necessary elements, thanks to the choir in that town, and those of the neighbouring towns. Mariani could have been immensely useful in this, but he has failed in his duty both as a friend and as an artist. Besides, who will conduct in Milan? Mariani cannot, nor should he any longer be asked to. In addition, the other aspects, which for the sake of brevity I shan't go into, make this performance an extremely difficult one. We, and I most of all, have had a fiasco at Bologna (a fiasco of which no one need be ashamed) but let's not take the risk of having a second one in Milan.

Farewell for now, and believe me yours

[153]

*To Camille du Locle*                           *Genoa, 7 December, 1869*

[Camille du Locle, with Joseph Méry, had written the libretto of *Don Carlos* which was first performed at the Paris Opéra on 11 March, 1867. He was also to write the French libretto of *Aida* for Ghislanzoni to translate.]

My dear Du Locle,

Thanks for *Froufrou*, which I read in one go. If, as the *Revue* says, all of it had been as distinguished and original as the first three acts, this play would be extraordinarily fine; but the last two, although they are greatly effective, fall into the commonplace. But, however good *Froufrou* may be, if I had to write for Paris I should prefer a cuisine, as you call it, finer and more piquant than that of Meilhac and Halévy. Sardou, for instance, with Du Locle to write the verses. But, alas, it's neither the fatigue of writing an opera nor the judgment of the Parisian public that prevents me; it's the certainty of never being able to have my music performed in Paris as I want it. It's very strange that a composer must always see his ideas altered and his concepts misrepresented. In your opera houses there are too many wise men (that is not meant to be an epigram). Everyone wants to pass judgment according to his own ideas, his own taste, and, which is worst of all, according to a system, without taking into account the character and individuality of the composer. Everyone wants to give an opinion or express a doubt; and, if a composer lives for too long in this atmosphere of doubt, he cannot escape having his convictions shaken a little, and begins to correct and adjust, or, to put it better, to look askance at his own work. Thus, in the end, you have not a work in one piece, but a mosaic. That may be fine, if you like it, but it's still a mosaic. You may reply that the Opéra has produced a string of masterpieces in this manner. They may be masterpieces, but allow me to say that they would be even more perfect if this pieced-together feeling and these adjustments were not so obvious at every point. No one, surely, will deny the genius of Rossini. All right, but, despite all his genius, his *Guillaume Tell* has about it this fatal atmosphere of the Opéra; and sometimes, although more rarely than in the work of other composers, you feel there's too much here, not enough there, and that it doesn't move with the honesty and security of *Il barbiere*. By this, I don't mean to disapprove of the way you work; I only mean to say that I really can't crawl once again under the Caudine yoke of your theatres, when I know it's impossible for me to have a real success unless I write as I feel, free from other influences, and without having to remember that I'm writing for Paris and not for the world of the moon. What is more, the singers would need to perform not in their fashion but in mine. The chorus, which certainly is very capable, would have to do likewise. In short, I would have to control everything. One will alone would have to prevail: mine. That may seem somewhat tyrannical to you, and perhaps it is. But if the opera is one whole, then the idea is a unity, and everything must work together to form this unity. Perhaps you will say that there is nothing in Paris to impede one from achieving this. No. In Italy, it can be done, at least I can always do it, but in France, no. For example, if I arrive in the foyer of an Italian theatre with a new opera, no one would dare to express an opinion of it, or a judgment, before having understood it properly, nor would anyone make silly requests. The work and the composer are respected, and judgment is left to the public. In the foyer of the Opéra, on the contrary, after four chords you hear everyone whispering, 'Olà ce ne'est pas bon . . . c'est commun, n'est pas de bon goût . . . . ça n'ira pas à Paris!' What do such poor words as 'commun', 'bon goût', 'Paris' signify if you are dealing with a real work of art which should be universal?

The conclusion of all this is that I am not a composer for Paris. I don't know whether I have any talent or not, but I know for certain that my ideas of art are quite different from yours.

I believe in inspiration, while you believe in construction. For the purpose of discussion, I admit your criterion, but I require the enthusiasm that you lack in feeling and in judgment. I want *art* in whatever form it is manifest, not *entertainment*, *artifice* and *the system* which is what you prefer. Am I wrong? Am I right? Whatever the answer, I am right to say that my ideas are quite different to yours and, what's more, that my backbone isn't pliable enough for me to be able to give way and deny my profound convictions which are deeply rooted in me. Also, I should be extremely upset if I were to write for you, my dear Du Locle, an opera which you perhaps would have to withdraw after a dozen performances, as Perrin[1] did with *Don Carlos*. If I were twenty years younger, I would say to you: 'Let us see if, later, your theatrical affairs take a turn which will bring them closer to my ideas.' But time passes quickly, and at present it's not possible for us to understand each other, unless something unexpected occurs, which I can't imagine. If you come here, as you have led my wife to hope you will, we shall speak more of this at length. If you don't come, it's probable that I shall go to Paris at the end of February. If you come to Genoa, we shall not be able to offer you the ravioli again, for we no longer have our Genoese cook. Still, you won't die of hunger and, what is certain, you will find two friends who think well of you, and to whom your presence will be a real delight. . . . A thousand greetings from us both to your charming Maria, and a kiss for *petite* Claire. Farewell, farewell. Yours

---

[1] Emanuel Perrin was at that time Director of the Paris Opéra.

[154]

*To Giulio Ricordi*                                    *Genoa, 27 December, 1869*

Dear Giulio,

I am making every effort to persuade myself of the propriety of performing the Mass for Rossini, but I haven't succeeded. The same wretched question keeps occurring to me: 'Why perform it? For the sake of the justifiable *amour propre* of the composers? But why should they need that, when they are noted for so many other compositions? To make an important work known to the musical world? But let me ask you this, *sotto voce*: is this mass good enough to be compared with other famous Masses for the Dead, which are perhaps themselves not such masterpieces as the world affects to believe? If it is good enough, then I could resign myself to the idea of its being performed; not, however in the church of San Antonio or the Hall of the Conservatorium. You will never achieve performances of grandeur and solemnity in those halls. I detest the shrill acoustics of these places, where where you can get neither a *piano* nor a real *forte*. Everything sounds loud and empty. For these halls there should be an orchestra of 6 first violins, 6 seconds, 6 violas, 6 cellos, 4 double basses and wind instruments without trumpets or trombones. So if the work is of huge proportions, this size of orchestra is too small. If the instruments are adapted to the work, the effect will be gross rather than great. But if you still want to make this Mass known, think of something else . . . find some excuse . . . . a benefit performance . . . and give it . . . . at . . . . . La Scala!! 'Foolhardy creatures' cries the ghost of the composer of the *Stabat* and the *Petite Messe*!! Yes, sir, foolhardy if you like, but there's no other remedy. Either fight, or don't put yourself in the field. In other words (this too is *sotto voce*), can our Mass stand comparison with these two works of Rossini? I'm not thinking now of their religious character, nor of the contrapuntal expertise in the fugues. Believe what you like—I'm in fact rather dubious about it—but I do believe in the musical value of these two works and especially in the numbers for solo voices, the disposition and arrangement of which is great enough perhaps to place Rossini even above the old Italian composers.

Conclusion: can the new Mass stand comparison with those of Mozart, Cherubini etc. . . . with the *Stabat*, with the *Petite Messe*? If so, perform it. If not, then *pax vobis*.

Farewell, farewell, affectionately

[155]

To Camille du Locle                                        Sant'Agata, 2 June, 1870

Dear Du Locle,

Here I am to talk about the Egyptian business.[1] First of all, it's necessary for me to reserve time to compose the opera, because we're dealing with a work of vast proportions (as though it were for the Grande Boutique),[2] and because the Italian poet[3] must first discover the thoughts of the characters and then express them in verse. Assuming that all this can be done in time, here are my conditions:

1. I shall have the libretto done at my expense.

2. Also at my expense, I shall send someone to direct and conduct the opera in Cairo.

3. I shall send you a copy of the score, and give you exclusive rights in the libretto and the music, only in Egypt, retaining for myself ownership of libretto and music for all other parts of the world.

In compensation, I shall be paid the sum of 150,000 francs, payable in Paris at the Bank of Rothschild at the moment when I consign the score to you.

There's a letter for you, as sober and dry as a promissory note, but this is a business matter, and you will pardon me, my dear Du Locle, if for now I do not digress to other matters. Excuse me, and believe me yours affectionately


[156]

To Giulio Ricordi                                         Sant'Agata, 25 June, 1870


[The synopsis on which the libretto of *Aida* was written was the work of the Egyptologist, Auguste Mariette. The Khedive of Egypt desired to commission an opera on the subject, to be performed to celebrate the opening of the Suez Canal. Verdi was the Khedive's first choice of composer: Gounod and Wagner were second and third. By the time the synopsis came into Verdi's hands, however, the Suez Canal had been open for some months.]

---

[1] *Aida*.

[2] The Paris Opéra. The nickname was first used by its Director, Perrin.

[3] Antonio Ghislanzoni (1824–1893), journalist, novelist, and ex-baritone. Some months earlier, he had provided verses for the revised *Forza del destino*.

Dear Giulio,

Are you taking the waters at San Pellegrino? If you are not, can you delay going there for a few days, in order to come here with Ghislanzoni? Let me explain why.

At the end of last year, I was invited to write an opera for a far distant country. I said no. When I was in Paris, Du Locle was commissioned to talk to me about it again, and to offer me a huge sum. I still said no. A month later, he sent me a printed synopsis, saying that it had been written by a powerful personage (which I don't believe), that he thought it good, and that I should read it. I found it very good, and replied that I would set it to music on condition that etc. etc. Three days after my telegram, he replied, 'Accepted'. Du Locle immediately came here, and we agreed on terms, studied the synopsis together, and together made what modifications we thought necessary. Du Locle left with the draft conditions and modifications, to submit them to the powerful and unknown author. I continued to study the synopsis, and I made, and am still making, further changes. We need now to think of the libretto, or rather of versifying it, for all we need now are the verses. Can Ghislanzoni do this work for me, and would he want to? Explain to him clearly that he hasn't to produce an original work, merely to put this into verse, for which, you understand (or at any rate I'm telling you now), he will be paid very generously. Reply immediately, and be prepared to come here with Ghislanzoni as soon as M. Rogier, whom I'm expecting any day, has left Sant'Agata. I'll send you a telegram.

Meanwhile, study with Ghislanzoni the synopsis I'm sending you. Don't lose it, because only two copies exist: this one, and another in the possession of the author.

Don't say anything, because the contract has not yet been signed. Anyway, there's no point in talking about it now, we'll discuss it orally.

[157]

*To Antonio Ghislanzoni*                                    *Genoa, 12 August, 1870*

Sig. Ghislanzoni,

I have been in Genoa for two days, but I am returning home tomorrow, so, from now on, write to me at Sant'Agata.

Corticelli[1] has forwarded your letter here, but he has not sent me the poetry or the second act finale. Mariette has said that we can have as many priestesses as we like, so you can add them to the consecration scene. Of the changes suggested, I have adopted the following: the first recitative, the romanza 'Celeste Aida, forma divina' and the two stanzas of recitative between Amneris and Radames.

In the little trio which follows, it would be better, at least in the first lines, not to let Aida say too much. Also, I don't like Amneris's threats.

The hymn that follows is fine, as modified, except that I would like Radames and Amneris to take part in the scene, thus avoiding those two asides which are never effective. Radames needs to say only a few words. Amneris could carry a sword or a banner or some such devilry, and address herself to Radames, warm, loving, yet a warrior-maid. I think the scene would gain by this. Aida is fine as she is; she could not be otherwise.

There are a few lines in the aria which should be changed, but we can attend to this when you next favour us with a visit at Sant'Agata. I shall write again, as soon as I have read the other verses. Meanwhile, my greetings.

[158]

*To Antonio Ghislanzoni*                    *Sant'Agata, 14 August, 1870*

[This letter refers to Act I, Scene ii, of *Aida*.]

Sig. Ghislanzoni,

Returning home, I found your poetry on my desk. To give you my honest opinion, I don't think this consecration scene has the importance that I was expecting. The characters don't always say what they should say, and the priests are not priestly enough. It seems to me that the right theatrical phrase is missing, or if it's there it's buried under the rhyme or the verse, and thus it doesn't leap out at one as it should. I'll write tomorrow, when I have read it over again quietly, and will tell you what I think should be done. I am convinced that this scene must have as much weight and solemnity as possible.

I shan't talk about the rest, because I should like to have this act completely finished so that I can begin work on it.

---

[1] Mauro Corticelli had been a theatrical agent in Bologna. He became Verdi's agent at the Villa Sant'Agata.

[159]

*To Antonio Ghislanzoni*                    *Sant'Agata, 16 August, 1870*

[This refers to Act II, Scene i, of *Aida*.]

Sig. Ghislanzoni,
    I think for the time being it would be better to give up work on the consecration scene. You need to give more study to the characters before being able to get the proper effect in this scene. We want, not a cold anthem, but a real scene. I attach here a copy of the French synopsis so that you can see how important this scene is.
    Let's now both turn our attention to the second act. We haven't a moment to lose. The first chorus is cold and insignificant. I know there is no action, which makes things more difficult, but, if we address ourselves to the task, we shall succeed. There is no action, either, in *Don Carlos* when the Queen's ladies are awaiting her, under the trees outside the convent. Nevertheless, with that little chorus and that song which have so much colour in the original French, it was possible to make a really realistic scene. Here we must make a scene out of a good lyric chorus, with the maids who dress Amneris, and the dance of the Ethiopian boys.
    I can explain better by writing out the scene:
    An apartment etc. Maids are dressing Amneris. They bring her perfumes, and wave fans. Ethiopian boys are carrying vases, perfumes, bouquets etc. They dance. Meanwhile,

CHORUS

Chi è colui, chi è colui che arriva splendente di gloria e bello come il Dio delle battaglie? (Verse) Vieni Radames, Radames: le figlie d'Egitto t'attendono ed intuonano per te inni di gloria, inni d'amor (Verse)
(Amneris, in an aside) Oh vieni, Radames. Te sol sospira, te sol ama la figlia del re (Two lines)

CHORUS

Dov'è, dov'è il feroce invasor? Egli resister non potè all'urto del guerrier. Ei fu disperso come il vento disperde la nebbia.
Vieni, Radames; le figlie d'Egitto ti attendono ed
intuonano per te inni di gloria, inni d'amor. . . .
(Amneris, as before) Vieni, Radames. . . .

There should be two couplets of ten lines each. The first stanza of four lines of warlike character, the second of four lines more loving in tone, and two voluptuous lines for Amneris. The second couplet the same.

And, without searching for strange rhythms, write seven-syllabled lines twice, then, if you have no objection, write some lines with masculine endings, which can be made to sound very effective in music sometimes. The tune in *La traviata*—'Di Provenza'—would be less tolerable if the lines had had feminine endings.

Tomorrow I shall write to you about the duet. In the meantime, please get to work quickly on this little scene.

[160]

*To Antonio Ghislanzoni*                                    *Sant'Agata, 17 August, 1870*

[This refers to the Aida–Amneris duet in Act II, scene i.]

Sig. Ghislanzoni,

There are some good things at the beginning and end of the duet, which is nevertheless too lengthy and distended; it seems to me that the recitative could be managed in fewer lines. The verses are fine until 'A te in cor destò'. But then, when the action warms up, I feel it lacks the 'theatrical word'. I don't know if I can explain what I mean by 'theatrical word' but I think I mean the word that most clearly and neatly brings the stage situation to life.

For example, the lines

> In volto gli occhi affisami
> E menti ancor se l'osi:
> Radames vive . . .

are less theatrical than the words

> . . . con una parola
> strapperò il tuo segreto.
> Guardami t'ho ingannata:
> Radames vive . . .

although these may be uglier.

Similarly, the lines

> Per Radames d'amore
> Ardo e mi sei rivale
> —Che? voi l'amate?—Io l'amo
> E figlia son d'un re

seem to me less theatrical than the words, 'Tu l'ami? ma l'amo anch'io intendi? La figlia dei Faraoni è tua rivale'. Aida: 'Mia rivale? E sia: anch'io son figlia etc.'

I realize that you will say to me, 'But what about the verse, the rhyme, the stanzas?' I don't know what to say, except that, if the action calls for it, I would immediately abandon rhythm, rhyme and stanza. I would use blank verse in order to be able to say clearly and distinctly what the action requires. Unfortunately, it is sometimes necessary in the theatre for poets and composers to have the talent not to write either poetry or music.

The duet ends with one of the usual cabalettas, which I think is too long for the situation. Anyway, we shall see what can be done with the music. Aida's words, however,

> Questo amore che t'irrita
> Di scordare lo tenterò

don't seem very effective to me.

Send me this re-worded duet as soon as possible, with the finale which follows, because I shall have to work on it if I am to finish in time.

[161]

*To Antonio Ghislanzoni*                                     *Sant'Agata, 22 August, 1870*

Signor Ghislanzoni,

I received the finale yesterday, and today the duet: the duet is fine, except for the recitative, which, in my opinion (forgive me) could be said with still fewer words. But, I repeat, it can very well stand as it is.

This isn't the time to write to Mariette, but I have already thought of something for the consecration scene. If it doesn't seem right to you, we can try again. But, in the meantime, it seems to me that we could make a rather effective musical scene of this. The piece would consist of a litany intoned by the priestesses, to which the priests respond; a sacred dance to slow and sad music; a short recitative, powerful and solemn like a biblical psalm; and a prayer in two stanzas, sung by the priest and repeated by all. I should like it to have a sad, quiet character, particularly the first stanza, to avoid similarity with the other choruses in the finale of the introduction and in the finale to the second act, which both sound a little like the Marseillaise.

Maria Waldmann as
Amneris in *Aida*

Franco Faccio

Tito Ricordi, from a
drawing by Mancastropa

Giulio Ricordi, from a
drawing by
Mancastropa

It seems to me that the litanies (and, for the thousandth time, forgive my boldness) should be in short stanzas of one long line and one five-syllabled line, or—and perhaps this would be better, in order to get everything said—two eight-syllabled lines. The five-syllabled line could be the *Ora pro nobis*. So there would be short stanzas of three lines each. That makes six, and that will be more than sufficient to make up one musical number.

Have no doubt, I am not averse to cabalettas; but I must have a situation that gives a reason for them. In the duet in *Un ballo in maschera*, there was a magnificent reason. After that entire scene, if I may say so, an outpouring of love was necessary.

[162]

*To Countess Maffei*                    *Sant'Agata, 30 September, 1870*

[The Franco-Prussian war, engineered by Bismarck, had broken out in July, 1870. Verdi was upset by the French defeats, and fearful of a victorious Prussia. At the battle of Sedan on 2 September, the Prussians captured most of the French army and the Emperor Napoleon III himself. This caused the bloodless uprising of 4 September in France, and the beginning of the Third Republic. On 20 September, Pope Pius IX and his troops were bombarded by the Italian army, in order, King Vittorio Emanuele had explained, to prevent a revolutionary uprising. This was the end of the Papal State, and it was a great day for most Italians.]

This French disaster fills my heart with despair as it does yours. . . . It's true that the *blague*, the impertinence, the presumption of the French was and is, despite all their misfortunes, insupportable. Nevertheless, France gave liberty and civilization to the modern world; and, if she falls, let us not delude ourselves, the liberty and the civilization of us all will fall. Our men of letters and our politicians may praise the knowledge, the science, and even (God forbid them) the art of these conquerors, but, if only they would look a little below the surface, they would see that the old blood of the Goths still flows in their veins, that they are terribly proud, hard, intolerant, scornful of everything that is not German, and of a rapacity without limit. Men of intellect, but lacking in heart, a strong race but uncivilized. And that king who is always talking about God and Providence, with the aid of whom he is destroying the greater part of Europe![1] He believes himself destined to reform

[1] William I of Prussia.

the customs and punish the vices of the modern world!!! What a splendid missionary!

The old Attila (another such missionary) stopped before the majesty of the capital of the antique world, but this one is about to bombard the capital of the modern world. And, now that Bismarck wants to make us believe Paris will be spared, I fear more than ever that it will be at least partly destroyed. Why? . . . I don't know how to say it. Perhaps so that there will no longer exist so beautiful a capital: for they will never be able to create its equal. Poor Paris, which I saw looking so gay, so beautiful, so splendid last April!

And now? . . . I should have liked a more generous policy and one which repaid a debt of gratitude. A hundred thousand of our men could perhaps have saved France. In any case, I would have preferred to sign a peace, having been conquered with France, than to have remained inert. We will be despised one day for this attitude of ours. We shall not escape the European war, and it will devour us. It will not happen tomorrow, but it will happen. A pretext is suddenly found. Perhaps Rome . . . the Mediterranean . . . And then why not the Adriatic, which has already been proclaimed a German sea?

The business in Rome is a great event, but it leaves me cold: perhaps because I fear it could lead to both external and internal disaster, because I cannot reconcile Parliament with the College of Cardinals, liberty of the press with the Inquisition, civil law with the Syllabus, and because I am frightened when I see that our Government continues haphazardly to hope that time will be on its side. If tomorrow there should appear a shrewd, astute Pope, a real schemer such as Rome has often had, everything would be ruined. Pope and King of Italy: I cannot envisage them together even in this letter.

I have no more paper. Forgive this tirade, I'm just letting off steam. Everything seems very black to me, and I haven't told you even half of what I think and fear. Farewell.


[163]

*To Antonio Ghislanzoni*                                          *8 October, 1870*

[This refers to Act III of *Aida*.]

Dear Ghislanzoni,

Let me say once and for all that I never intend to criticize your verses which are always good; I am only giving my opinion on the scenic effect. The duet between Radames and Aida has, in my opinion, turned out to be greatly inferior to the other one between father and daughter. That may be due to the situation or, perhaps, to the form, which is more ordinary than that of the preceding duet. It's certain that this row of cantabile passages of eight lines each, sung by one and repeated by the other, are not such as to keep the dialogue moving. What's more, the interludes between these cantabile passages are rather cold.

At the beginning of this duet, I still prefer the first lines to this recitative, which is too dry. For example, I would change the first eight lines of verse (I don't know if you can change the form) up to:

> D'uno spergiuro non ti macchiar.

Then the recitative, from 'Prode t'amai, benchè . . . nemico; non t'amerei spergiuro' as far as the whole of Radames's solo. After that, the lines

> D'Amneris l'odio fatal saria
> Insiem col padre dovrei morir.

are not theatrical, that is to say they don't give the singer a chance to act. The audience's attention is not held, and the situation flounders. There should be greater development, and the words should go something like this:

A. And do you not fear the anger of Amneris? Do you not know that her vengeance would fall like a thunderbolt on me, on my father, on all of us?

R. I shall defend you.

A. In vain . . . you could not! But if you love me, there is still one way for us to escape.

R. What?

A. To flee.

You may say, 'But this is nonsense, my lines say the same thing'. Very true, it is nonsense, if you like; but I am sure that phrases like 'Will fall on me, on my father, on us all. . . . In vain . . . You could not' etc. etc., if they are well delivered, will always hold the audience's attention, and can sometimes produce great effects.

Aida's eight lines, 'Fuggiam', and the first four for Radames are good. But, in the four now added, I don't like the idea of the bride very much. Would it not be better to say, as in the synopsis, 'Here, where I was born, and lived, and became the saviour of my country'? You have omitted Aida's outburst:

> My gods shall be yours,
> One's country is where one loves;

which must be said, either in the lines already done, or in recitative if you prefer.

Then we need to give greater prominence to the interlude which follows:

Aida: Go! You do not love me.
Radames: I not love you? Never have men on earth or gods in heaven loved more ardently.
(Whether these or other words doesn't matter, but it must be a theatrical phrase that grips you.)

Aida: Go, go. Amneris awaits you at the altar.
Radames: No, never.
Aida: Never, you say? Then fall etc. etc. (to the end of the duet).

Tomorrow, I shall write briefly about the rest.

[164]

*To Antonio Ghislanzoni*                                  *December, 1870*

*Saturday*

[This refers to the final scene in *Aida*: Act IV, Scene ii. Verdi wrote virtually the entire scene in prose, and dictated the metre he required.]

Dear Ghislanzoni,

Amneris's invective is stupendous. Now this piece is finished too. I shall not go to Genoa until the opera is completely finished. We haven't done the last piece, to put in the score, or the fourth act. Then the opera has to be orchestrated from beginning to end. It's a month's work at least. So, have patience; and arrange your affairs so that you can come to Sant'Agata, without being too rushed, for we must get the whole of the libretto in order.

Here, then, is the last scene, for which I shall need the following changes:

For the first recitative, which I agree with you seems a little messy, Radames would not be in the mood to utter phrases like

> I am separated from the living for ever . . .
> No more splendours will my sight behold . .
> I seem to hear a cry . . . etc. etc.

Then, Aida is there, and must be seen as soon as possible.

After the beautiful seven-syllabled lines for Aida, it's impossible to find anything for Radames to say. I should first write eight seven-syllabled lines for Radames, with this meaning: 'You will die! You, so innocent, so beautiful, so young. I cannot save you . . . Oh, agony. My fatal love ruined you' etc. etc.

At the end, I should like to avoid the usual death agonies, and not have words like 'I'm failing. I'm going before you. Wait for me. She is dead. I'm still alive' etc. etc. I should like something sweet, other-worldly, a very short duet, a farewell to life. Aida should then fall calmly into the arms of Radames. Immediately, Amneris kneeling on the stone of the vault, should sing a *Requiescant in pacem* etc. I shall write the scene down to explain myself better.

Final scene

[Radames] The fatal stone . . . . for ever.
          Here is my tomb. The light of day
          I never more shall see. I shall never see
             Aida again (Adjust this line)
          Aida, where are you? May you at least
          Live happily, and my dreadful fate
          Never discover! . . . What is that cry? Someone there.
                     A spirit?
          A vision? No, it's a human form.
          Heavens! Aida! . . . (These are just mixed up words to be worked into beautiful verses by you. Similarly the following:)
Aida:      It is I.
[Radames:] You here? But how?
Aida:      My heart guessed at your sentence.
          I have waited here for three days.
          And here, far from all human sight,
          Close to you, I shall die. (One more line)
Radames:  Die? you, so innocent,
          Die? You? (Eight beautiful seven-syllabled lines for
             singing)

Aida:        Do you see? The angel of death
             Radiant, approaches us
             To lead us to eternal bliss
             On his golden wings.
             Already I see the heavens opening,
             There all pain will cease,
             There will begin the ecstasy
             Of everlasting love.

Singing and dancing from the interior of the temple by the priests and priestesses.

Aida:        A sad song.
Radames:     The celebration of the priests.
Aida:        Our hymn of death.
Radames:     Nor can my strong arms
             Move you, o fatal stone.
Aida:        In vain. For us, all is over. Hope is lost.
             We must die.
Radames:     It's true. It's true.

Duet

O life farewell, earthly love            (Four beautiful twelve-syllabled
Farewell, sorrows and joys . . .         lines. But, to make them suit-
In infinity already I see the dawn,      able for singing, the accent
We shall be united for ever in heaven    must be on the fourth and eighth
                                         syllables.)

Aida dies in the arms of Radames. Then Amneris, in deep mourning, enters from the interior of the temple and kneels on the stone above the vault.

                    Rest in peace,
                    Beloved soul. . . . .

When you have arranged this scene for me, and have sent it, come to Sant'Agata two days later. By then, I shall have written the music and we can occupy ourselves exclusively with what little remains to be done on the scenes etc. etc.


[165]

*To Antonio Ghislanzoni*          [*No date—probably late December, 1870.*]

[The *Copialettere* appendix contains 33 letters from Verdi to Ghislanzoni on the subject of *Aida*, dating from August, 1870, to August, 1871.]

Dear Ghislanzoni,

I have received the verses which are beautiful, but they don't seem quite right for me. Since you were so late in sending them to me, I have written the piece already, in order not to lose time, using the monstrous verses I sent you.

Come quickly, even quicker than that: we shall adjust everything. Don't be frightened of the last scene, which doesn't yet scorch. It's cold steel!

[166]

*To Vincenzo Luccardi*          *Genoa, 30 December, 1870*

Thank you for your greetings, and here are mine in return, also to your wife and from Peppina.

My opera for Cairo is finished, but it can't be performed because the costumes and scenery are still held up in Paris.

It doesn't matter much. What does matter is this terrible war, and the advances these Prussians are making, which may be fatal for us later on. It's no longer a war of conquest, but of senseless ambition. It's a racial war, and it will last a long, long time. The Prussians are exhausted at the moment, but they will revive and return. It isn't a question of Rome, or the shrewdness of the priests that frightens me, it's the force of these new Goths that I'm afraid of.

Farewell for now. Stay healthy, and let us have faith in the stars that rule Italy's destiny, rather than the men.

[167]

*To Francesco Florimo*          *Genoa, 4 January, 1871*

[Francesco Florimo (1800–1888), author, librarian and composer, was the librarian of the Naples Conservatorium, the *Real Conservatorio*, whose library he built up into one of the finest in Europe. He had been a close friend of Bellini, and in 1885 was to publish a book, *Bellini: memorie e lettere*. Following the death of Mercadante on 17 December, 1870, Florimo and his colleagues agreed to invite Verdi to succeed him as Director of the Conservatorium.

The composer Alessandro Scarlatti (1660–1725) was traditionally thought to have taught at the Naples Conservatorio de' Poveri di Gesù Cristo, but there is no proof that he taught at this or any other Naples school. Francesco Durante (1684–1755) taught at the Conservatorio de' Poveri from 1728 to 1739. Leonardo Leo (1694–1744), however, taught at three other schools in Naples, one of them being the Conservatorio della Pietà de' Turchini, the last of the old Naples conservatories to close its doors, in 1808. The Real Conservatorio di Musica then came into existence, and its Directors included Zingarelli, Donizetti and Mercadante.]

Dear Florimo,

If anything could flatter my *amour propre*, it is this invitation to become Director of the Naples Conservatorium, forwarded to me, through you, by the teachers at that Conservatorium, and by other musicians of your city. I feel sad not to be able to reply to this honour as I should have liked to. But, given my various occupations, my habits, and my love of independence, it would be impossible for me to take on so important a task. You will say to me, 'What about art?' All very well, but I have done what I can, and if, from time to time, I am going to do more, I must keep myself free from other preoccupations. If that were not so, you can imagine how proud I would be to occupy a position once held by such founders of a school as A. Scarlatti, Durante and Leo. It would have been an honour for me to train the students in the important and lucid teachings of those great masters. I should have been able to stand, so to speak, with one foot in the past, and the other in the present and the future (for I have no fear of the 'music of the future'). I should have said to the young students: 'Practise the fugue constantly, tenaciously, to satiety, until your hands are strong enough to bend the notes to your will. Thus you will learn to compose with confidence, will dispose the parts well, and will modulate without affectation. Study Palestrina, and a few of his contemporaries. Then skip until you come to Marcello, and direct your attention especially to his recitatives. Go to very few performances of modern operas, and don't let yourself be fascinated by beauties of harmony and instrumentation, or the chord of the diminished seventh, that rock and refuge of all of us who don't know how to compose four bars without a half-dozen of these sevenths.'

When their studies had progressed, and they had achieved a broad literary culture, I would finally say to these students, 'Now put your hand on your heart and write. If you have the right artistic temperament, you will become composers. In any case, you will not add to the mob of imitators and sick men of our age, who seek and seek but, although they do occasional good things, never really find. For instruction in singing, I would combine study of the past with modern declamation.'

To put these few apparently easy maxims into practice one would need to supervise the teaching so assiduously that twelve months in the year would hardly be enough. I, who have a house, business interests, money . . . everything here, I ask you, how can I do it?

So, my dear Florimo, will you please express to your colleagues, and the other musicians in your beautiful Naples, my great sorrow at not being able to accept this invitation which does me such honour? I hope you will find a man who is, above all, learned and a strict teacher. Liberties and errors in counterpoint in the theatre can be allowed, and can sometimes even sound beautiful. But in the conservatorium, no. Let us turn to the past: that will be progress. Farewell, farewell. Believe me, always yours

[168]

*To Nicola de Giosa—Cairo*                    *Genoa, 5 January, 1871*

[Nicola de Giosa was the permanent conductor at the new opera house in Cairo. He had also composed a good many operas.

The standard pitch Verdi wished to propagate was one of 870 vibrations (i.e. 435 cycles per second), recognized in 1859 by a commission set up by the French Government, consisting of six eminent musicians, Auber, Berlioz, Halévy, Meyerbeer, Rossini, and Thomas, two distinguished scientists and four officials. Verdi had for some years propagated universal acceptance of this pitch. In 1885, an international conference on musical pitch was held in Vienna, at the invitation of the Austrian Government. It, too, recommended one single International Standard Musical Pitch of 870 single vibrations per second. Italy was represented in Vienna by Boito. Verdi wrote to Boito in Vienna, stating that, although ideally he considered the pitch of 864 vibrations used in Italian conservatories to be preferable, he thought it important, for the sake of unity, to agree to the Vienna resolution. (Great Britain was not represented at the Vienna conference, which is one of the reasons for the difference between English and continental pitch today.)]

I have received your letter of December 22nd, and, before answering it in detail, I should like to say that there cannot be any *misunderstanding* between us, because I have never been fortunate enough to have any dealings with you, except two years ago in Naples on the question of pitch; also because it is difficult to have *misunderstandings* with me because I occupy myself only with my own business, on which subject I always give my opinion openly, precisely to avoid misunderstandings. To return to the question of pitch, it's true that we did not find ourselves in agreement then, and I see that we still do not. I wanted to propagate a standard pitch, to be used, as far as possible, all over the world. You proposed a compromise which, as a remedy, was worse than the sickness. I wanted only one pitch in the musical world; you wanted to add another to the too many already existing.

It is certainly true that I have engaged Muzio to go to Cairo to produce *Aida* (in accordance with a clause in my contract), and I do not see how you can find his going there damaging to you. Permit me to say, Signor Maestro, that you see this purely as a personal matter, while I see it purely as an artistic one. Let me explain: you know better than I do that operas today are written with so many and various scenic and musical aspects that it is almost impossible to interpret them; and it seems to me that no one can take offence if the composer, for the first production of his work, sends someone who has studied the work closely under the direction of the composer himself. I confess that, if I had to conduct, for the first time, an opera by a colleague, I should not feel at all humiliated, but would be the first to seek to know the composer's intentions, whether from himself or from others.

You may still not agree with me on this occasion; but, for me, it's not simply an opinion but a profound conviction, arrived at after 28 years of experience.

Please believe me, dear Signor Maestro, with all esteem, your devoted servant.


[169]

*To His Excellency, Draneht Bey—Cairo*            *Genoa, 5 January, 1871*

[Draneht Bey was the Intendant of the Opera House in Cairo. Mariette Bey is Auguste Mariette (1821–1881). 'Bey' is a title of rank. It was conferred upon Mariette by the Khedive of Egypt.

This letter was written in French.]


Your Excellency,

It is true that I instructed Sig. Muzio to go to Cairo to conduct the rehearsals of *Aida*, and I was on the point of signing an agreement to give the same opera at La Scala during the month of February, with Signora Fricci, Tiberini etc.[1] I did not know then that Mariette Bey was detained in Paris, and with him the scenery and costumes etc. for *Aida*. As soon as this news was made known to me, I hastened to inform the management of La Scala, so that all preparations for the new opera could be suspended.

At the moment I am in Genoa, and I do not have the contract with Mariette Bey here, but this simply says (as I remember perfectly) that I am obliged to deliver the score of *Aida* in good time to be given in Cairo during January, 1871, and that if, through unforeseen circumstances beyond my control, the opera could not be given in Cairo during January, 1871, I had the right to have it produced elsewhere six months later. That is why I wrote to Cairo the letter Your Excellency knows about, in which I said that, having finished the opera, I was arranging to send it to Cairo during December, 1870, so that the first performance could take place during January, 1871.

Now, due to the position we have been placed in by the disastrous events which have swept France and Europe, Your Excellency can assure His Highness the Khedive that I would never have invoked my rights (even if I had any) at this moment, and that, although with great regret, I shall give up my desire to have my opera performed this season both at Cairo and at La Scala.

I must however point out to Your Excellency that the management of La Scala still intends to produce *Aida* during the coming Carnival season, 1871–72, and, with this end in view, has even engaged several artists recommended by me. Consequently, I should be grateful if Your Excellency would let me know what arrangements you intend to make for the performance of *Aida*, so that, for my part, I can look after its future and my own interests. I shall need to know, Your Excellency, when I should deliver the score, and when it will be performed in Cairo. Awaiting the favour of your reply, I have the honour to sign myself, Your Excellency's devoted servant.

PS. I believe it may be useful to remind Your Excellency that the performance of *Aida* requires two first-class female singers, one soprano, the other mezzo-soprano; a fine tenor, a baritone, two basses etc.

[1] The soprano Antonietta Fricci-Baraldi (1840–1912). Neither she nor the tenor Mario Tiberini (1826–1880) was to be in the first European production of *Aida* at La Scala, which eventually took place on 8 February, 1872.

[170]

*To Minister Correnti*                          *Genoa, 1 February, 1871*

[Cesare Correnti, Minister of Education, had invited Verdi to preside over a
Commission to consider the reform of the music schools. Verdi's letter
declining the invitation sounds final; but see letter 173.]

Your Excellency,

I do not know how to begin this letter, so great is my regret at not
being able to accept the invitation extended by Your Excellency to
preside over a Commission to reform musical studies. Please allow me,
Mr Minister, to speak now only of the Naples Conservatorium, on
which at the moment everyone's attention is focussed, and which is the
main reason why the reform of studies is being suggested. I am deeply
convinced that the reform can be carried out only by the musician who
is chosen to be Director. If he is a real musician, and dedicated to his
mission, there will be no need, in fact it could be inconvenient for him,
for a Commission to lay down rules of instruction. If he is not, then all
the studies and all the Commission's work will be useless. In support of
my statement, let me say that there were no fixed rules in the old Naples
Conservatorium, directed by Durante and by Leo. They themselves
created the path to be followed. Their paths diverged occasionally, but
both were good. And later, under Fenaroli, whose exercises are now
used by everyone, there were still no fixed rules. It was the same at the
Bologna Lycée in the time of Padre Martini, whose name is respected
by all, Italians and foreigners, among them Gluck and Mozart. The
Paris Conservatoire, on the other hand, has the finest of regulations,
despite which it has produced good results only when the Director was
a man of the greatest stature: Cherubini.

Convinced, as I had the honour of saying above, that reforms are
possible only when carried out by the Director, I ask you to excuse me,
Your Excellency, for not being able to accept the honour of presiding
over the Commission set up to reform our musical studies. I trust that
Your Excellency will not take too great account of my opinion. I may
be mistaken, and I hope, if it is for the good of art, that I am greatly
mistaken.

With the most profound esteem, I have the honour to sign myself,
Your Excellency's devoted servant

[171]

*To Alberto Mazzucato*                              *Genoa, 4 February, 1871*

[Alberto Mazzucato (1813–1877), violinist, teacher and composer, became
leader of the orchestra at La Scala in 1859. He taught the violin at the Milan
Conservatorium, of which he became Director in 1872. He also, for a time,
edited the Milan *Gazzetta Musicale*. He composed eight operas, including
*La fidanzata di Lammermoor*, based, like Donizetti's opera, on Sir Walter
Scott's novel. Another of his operas was an *Ernani* which disappeared from
the stage when Verdi wrote his opera on the same subject in 1844. Mazzucato had been a member of the committee to organize the communal
Requiem Mass for Rossini, which Verdi had suggested in 1868. On 2 February
1871, he wrote expressing his great admiration for the 'Libera me' which
Verdi had contributed to the abortive enterprise. ('You have written the
greatest, most beautiful and most immensely poetic pages imaginable.')
    When Mazzucato died six years later, the following extract from his diary
was sent to Verdi on the back of a photograph:

                                        'Monday February 6th. 1871
    'I had written to Verdi about the huge and profound impression made on
me when I read his "Libera me, Domine." He has replied in an expansive
letter: unusually expansive when one thinks of his habitual reluctance to
speak of his own affairs, or to embrace a critic. Verdi surprised me greatly
with his *Nabucco* and *I Lombardi*. I saw him descend to popular passions in
*Ernani*, *Il trovatore* etc. I saw him rise again with *Macbeth*, and increase his
stature with *Miller* and *Stiffelio*. He became insuperable with *Rigoletto*,
*Boccanegra* etc.
    'I adore this composer: and I wish him to know this, and so to know the
truth, kept from him by interested parties for over twenty-five years.'

    When Verdi came to compose his *Requiem Mass* for Manzoni, in 1873, he
was able to utilize parts of this 'Libera me'.]


If at my age one could still have the decency to blush, I should certainly
do so at the praise you have showered on my piece: praise which, I
don't deny it, coming from a composer and critic of your stature, is of
the greatest importance, and greatly flatters my *amour propre*. And, such
is a composer's ambition, your words arouse in me the desire, one day,
to write the entire Mass; particularly since, with a little further ex-
pansion, I would find I had already completed the Requiem and the
Dies irae, whose recapitualation I have composed in the Libera. Consider then, and be remorseful at the deplorable consequences your
praise might have! But stay calm after all: it's a temptation that will

pass, like many others. I am not fond of useless things. There are so
many, many, many Masses for the Dead. It would be pointless to add
one more.

I am most grateful for the courteous words you have spoken about
my piece of music, I thank you, and press your hand in greeting.

PS. My wife also thanks you, and joins me in greetings.


[172]

*To Dr Angiolo Carrara, Busseto*                   *Genoa, 7 Feburary, 1871*

[Angiolo Carrara, a notary at Busseto, was an old friend of Verdi. Four years
earlier, he had taken into his house, and informally adopted, Filomena Verdi,
a seven year old girl who was Verdi's second cousin, and who, in 1878, was
to marry Angiolo Carrara's son.]

Motivated by praiseworthy feeling, you wish to ignore everything that
has been said against me in Busseto for the last twenty years. Not to go
back too far, ask your cousin Leopoldo, who may be willing to divert
you with the story of the kindness I met with from him and others in
connection with the Workers' Society, before, on, and after the ninth
of October, 1870, a time in which the philharmonic branch of the
society was pleased to give some concerts as a tribute to me.

In Busseto (as you yourself will admit) there are some ignorant
people. Very well, they exist everywhere. There are some malicious
people. Their equals can also be found everywhere, and fortunately I
am even-tempered enough to be able to laugh at and rise above their
meanness. But no one who has any sense of dignity, and who is a friend
of mine, can advise me to accept ostentatious testimonials of respect
from a community in which the indecent slanders of a few could not
have been kept alive so tenaciously had they not been fed by the
approval of the many. For twenty years, I've heard the same refrain.
They may repeat it for another twenty years, and then begin all over
again. I can live very well without worrying about them. But it seems
to me that the more decent course for them to take would be to stop
occupying themselves with me at all, either for good or bad.

To conclude, let me add that you are aware I have never seen the
need for a theatre in Busseto. And I do not see now that the establish-
ment of a Philharmonic and Dramatic Society could be either possible

or durable. Being of this conviction, I cannot protect with my name a society in whose feasibility I do not believe. At best, I could become a contributing member, but never Honorary President. Believe me, yours

[173]

*To Giuseppe Piroli*                    *Genoa, 20 February, 1871*

[Verdi agreed, finally, to preside over the Commission. The letter to Florimo is no. 167.]

Dear Piroli,

In view of the musical conditions and tendencies of our day, this is what, in my opinion, a Commission called to reorganise training should suggest. These are general ideas which I have often put to you, both orally and in writing, and which I also mentioned in my letter to Florimo.

I shall speak only of composition and of singing, because I believe that on the instrumental side (which has always produced good results) there is little need for reform. So, then, I should like to see young composers doing very long and thorough studies in all branches of counterpoint. Study of old compositions, both sacred and profane. It must be noted, however, that not everything among these works of the past is beautiful, and so it will be necessary to choose.

*No study of the moderns!* That will seem strange to many. But when I hear and see so many works today, constructed the way bad tailors make clothes based on a model, I cannot change my opinion. I know well that one can find many modern works which are as worthwhile as those of the past, but what does that prove? When a young man has undergone strict training, when he has found his own style and has confidence in his own powers, he can then, if he thinks it useful, study these works somewhat, and there will be no danger of his turning into an imitator. You may object: 'Who will teach this young man instrumentation? Who will teach him the theory of composition?' His own head and his own heart, if he has any.

For singing, I should like the students to have a wide knowledge of music; exercises in voice production; very long courses in solfeggi, as in the past; exercises for singing and speaking with clear and perfect enunciation. Then, without having any teacher perfect him in vocal style, I should like the young student, who by now should have a strong knowledge of music and a well-trained voice, to sing, guided only by his own feelings. This will be singing, not of such-and-such a school, but of inspiration. The artist will be an individual. He will be himself, or, better still, he will be the character he has to represent in the opera.

I don't need to say that these musical studies must be combined with a broad literary education.

Those are my ideas. Would they be approved by a Commission? If so, then the Minister has only to command me. If not, then it's better for me to return to Sant'Agata.

Farewell, farewell, yours affectionately


[174]

*To Draneht Bey*                                             *Genoa, 1 March, 1871*

Your Excellency,

I am just as confused as you are, and cannot, for the moment, think which tenor to recommend. Fraschini would certainly not agree to go to Cairo. After him, the best are Capponi and Fancelli, but both are, I believe, engaged for La Scala. At one time, I would have said Nicolini, but I have not heard him for a long time, and do not know if he has kept his voice.

The rôle of Aida is also very important and I should be much obliged to Your Excellency to learn whether Signora Giovannoni[1] has been re-engaged for the next season, or if another artist is being thought of. Also I should very much like to know if Sig. De Giosa has been re-engaged as conductor.

Please excuse all these tedious questions, Your Excellency.


[175]

*To Draneht Bey*                                           *Genoa, 30 March, 1871*

[Verdi wrote this and the preceding letter in French.]

As soon as I returned to Genoa I hastened to speak to Mariani, but I did not find him disposed to come to Cairo. Unless he changes his mind (a

---

[1] The soprano Gianetta Giovannoni was a member of the Cairo company in 1870–1871. None of the singers mentioned in this letter was to be in the Cairo première of *Aida*.

strong possibility) one cannot count on him. Before you choose a conductor let me take the liberty of asking you to wait just a little longer, as I have someone very capable to propose to you.

For the tenor, Nicolini would be the best. I heard Pozzoni at Florence. She has talent, a great deal of feeling and she is an extremely beautiful woman, which does no harm.[1] There is also another young woman: Signorina De Giuli, who made her début at Rome this year with great success.[2] I have not heard her, but everybody says very good things about her. As far as looks are concerned either would be perfectly good as Aida.

[176]

*To Draneht Bey*                                       *Genoa, 14 April, 1871*

[This letter was in French.]

If, as you say, you want a conductor of *recognized* and certain talent, there is absolutely no-one but Mariani. Believe me, there isn't much to choose between any of the others and, if you haven't been satisfied by your experience of the past two years, you won't be with the next two either, as you will find virtually the same qualities and defects in all the conductors likely to be engaged. All the same, if you are not in too much of a hurry, Mariani may change his mind. In any case, you'll always find a conductor.

Signora Stolz is engaged for Milan, and I think that you should now try to get Signora Pozzoni. I have also mentioned Signorina De Giuli, of whom people speak very well, though I have not heard her.

I fear that the rôle of Amneris, which is for a mezzo-soprano, is a little too high for Signorina Grossi. Medini is very good. Who will the baritone be? Perhaps you would let me know about that?[3]

---

[1] Antonietta Pozzoni-Anastasi was chosen to sing Aida.

[2] This was the daughter of Teresa de Giuli-Borsi.

[3] Despite Verdi's reservation, Eleonora Grossi was chosen to sing Amneris in Cairo. The bass Paolo Medini sang Ramfis. The other principals were Antonietta Pozzoni-Anastasi (Aida), Pietro Mongini (Radames), Francesco Steller (Amonasro) and Tommaso Costa (King of Egypt).

[177]

*To Draneht Bey*                                    *Sant'Agata, 28 April, 1871*

[Verdi wrote this letter in French.]

I am quite certain that it is useless to hope you will get Mariani to conduct. Engage, therefore, whomever you think *best*, even though the *best* may be extremely difficult to find. I should very much have liked to discuss the choice of conductor with you, but if you cannot wait, do whatever is necessary in your own interests.

   I live in the country in a little *hovel* where I hardly dare invite you, nevertheless I should be most happy to receive you, and I am always at your disposal should you need to speak to me. Only, as I often travel about in the country nearby, it would be wise to advise me of the day you intend honouring me with a visit, so that you will be sure to find me at home.

[178]

*To Giulio Ricordi*                                 *Sant'Agata, 10 July, 1871*

   [Verdi and Ricordi were trying to find an Amneris for the Scala production of *Aida* in February, 1872. Waldmann is Maria Waldmann (1844–1920), the Viennese mezzo-soprano, who was chosen for the rôle. Verdi later wrote for her the mezzo-soprano part in his Requiem.]

You know the libretto of *Aida*, and you know that the rôle of Amneris requires an artist of great dramatic feeling who can really hold the stage. How can one hope to find this quality in someone who is almost a newcomer. Voice alone, however beautiful (and that's difficult to judge in an empty room or theatre), is not enough for this rôle. So-called vocal finesse means little to me. I like to have rôles sung the way I want them, but I can't provide the voice, the temperament, the 'je ne sais quoi' that one might call the spark. It's what is usually understood by the phrase, 'to be possessed by the devil.'

   I wrote to you yesterday, giving my opinion of Waldmann, and today I can only confirm what I said. I know perfectly well that it will not be easy to find an Amneris, but we can talk about that in Genoa. That, however, is not all, and you have yet to tell me if the conditions I indicated in my various letters are acceptable.

   Keep in mind, my dear Giulio, that if I come to Milan, it will not be out of vanity at having an opera of mine performed: it will be to obtain a really artistic performance. To achieve that, we must have all the necessary elements. So please answer me categorically whether, in addition to the company of singers,

1. the conductor has been chosen
2. the chorus has been engaged as I indicated
3. the orchestra will be composed also as I have indicated
4. the timpani and bass drum are being changed for bigger instruments than those of two years ago
4a. the standard pitch is being retained
5. the orchestra has adopted this pitch, in order to avoid the out-of-tune playing I have heard at times
6. the instruments of the orchestra will be arranged as indicated in a kind of sketch I made in Genoa last winter.

This arrangement of the orchestra is much more important than is usually believed, for the instrumental colouring, for the sonority and for the effect. These small improvements will open the way to other innovations that will certainly come one day. One of them will be the removal of the spectators' boxes from the stage, thus enabling the curtain to come right up to the footlights. Another improvement would be to make the orchestra invisible. This idea is not mine, but Wagner's, and it's a very good one. It's incredible nowadays that we should tolerate seeing horrid white ties and tails, for example, between us and the costumes of Egyptians, Assyrians or Druids etc. etc. and, in addition, see the whole of the orchestra, which should be part of a fictitious world, almost in the middle of the stalls among the crowd as it hisses or applauds. Add to all this the annoyance of seeing the tops of harps and contrabassoons as well as the flailing arms of the conductor waving about in the air.

Answer me, then, categorically and decisively, because if I cannot be given what I require, there is no point in continuing these negotiations.


[179]

*To Draneht Bey*                                        *Genoa, 20 July, 1871*

Your Excellency,
    Your letter of the 17th has been forwarded to me in Genoa.
    It seems to me that, before I send the libretto of *Aida*, we must

decide who is to play the rôle of Amneris. As I have already had the
honour of explaining to you, neither Sass nor Grossi will ever be mezzo-
sopranos. You say that Grossi sang *La favorita* and Fidès in *Le Prophète*.
For that matter, Alboni once played *La gazza ladra*, *La sonnambula*, I
believe, and even the rôle of Carlo V in *Ernani*!! What of that? It only
signifies that, on those occasions, singers and managements had no
scruples about mistreating their composers' works.

Let me tell you a little of the history of this *Aida*. I wrote the opera
for last season, and it is not my fault that it was not performed. I was
asked to postpone the performance for a year. Although this was not
entirely convenient for me, I agreed. As long ago as January 5th I
indicated that the rôle of Amneris was written for a mezzo-soprano.
Later, I asked you not to engage a conductor for the orchestra without
first consulting me. I had always hoped to have Mariani.

Even while I have been dealing with this, another conductor has
been engaged, yet no one has thought of engaging a mezzo-soprano.
Why? After all, the opera was written expressly for an occasion, and
every effort should have been made to ensure a success. It seems strange
to me that nothing has been done, and I must say, your Excellency, that
this is no way to obtain a fine performance or a success.

Yours very truly


[180]

*To Draneht Bey*                                        *Genoa, 2 August, 1871*

[In this letter, Verdi finally capitulates over Eleonora Grossi.]

Your Excellency,

Although certain notes in the rôle of Amneris may lie a little too high
for Grossi, I confirm what Signor Ricordi has told you orally: trust this
artist in the rôle of Amneris, rather than risk having a new singer. It
would be very difficult to find one good enough.

As I have already informed you, the libretto is in Paris, and at this
moment is in the hands of Mariette Bey.

Last year, I took the liberty of giving two instructions concerning
*Aida*, since there was no time to write to Cairo and receive a reply:

1. I instructed Signor Ricordi to get all the parts for singers, chorus
   and orchestra in *Aida* ready for Cairo.

2. I ordered from Pelitti six straight trumpets of the old Egyptian kind, which are no longer in use and which therefore had to be especially made.

If you agree that these orders can be confirmed, I shall pay the bills, and Your Excellency can repay me when we come to consider payment for the score. Otherwise, you can deal directly with Ricordi and Pelitti,[1] and settle the accounts with them.

I have the honour to sign myself, Your Excellency's devoted servant

[181]

*To Opprandino Arrivabene*        *Sant'Agata, 2 September, 1871*

[Verdi had completed the orchestration of *Aida*.]

I did not reply immediately to your last letter, because until this moment I have been very busy with the opera.

I revised, polished, corrected, and perhaps ruined it, and this very day I am sending the last section to Ricordi . . . Amen, then, and *à la grace de Dieu*!

You say the most sensible things in your last letter on the subject of the arts, and I agree with you completely, or almost completely. But in music one must not be exclusively a *melodist*. There is more in music than melody, or even than harmony. There is music! This may seem a riddle to you, but let me explain: Beethoven was not a melodist; Palestrina was not a melodist.

Let's be clear what I mean: a melodist in our sense. But I don't want to talk about these matters today because, as the Neapolitans say, my brain is out of tune. I'm tired.

[182]

*To Léon Escudier*        *Sant'Agata, 11 October, 1871*

Dear Léon,

I was very glad to have news of you and your country, which seems to be recovering little by little its former powers and splendour.

---

[1] Pelitti was a Milanese musical instrument maker.

Concerning *La traviata*, do whatever you think best. Perhaps, if well performed, it might succeed at the Opéra Comique.

Now for *Aida*. It's over a year since Ricordi asked me to sell him this opera, but, in view of the argument I had with him over France, I did not want to conclude anything, precisely because, your war being over, I thought you would contact me. Not having heard anything from you, I assumed you were not interested, perhaps because of the current state of your theatres and the likelihood that you would not be able to take advantage of *Aida*. So I agreed, about a month ago, to sell the opera to Ricordi.

I am very sorry about this, but as I am sure you will perfectly understand, I could not do otherwise. If you think there is anything I can do in the matter to be of any service to you, do not hesitate to tell me, and I shall make it my business to do everything I possibly can.

Greetings to all your family from Peppina and myself.

[183]

*To the Mayor of Milan*                              *Sant'Agata, 13 October, 1871*

Dear Mr Mayor,
A few days ago, I went to Milan to see whether the new disposition of the orchestra that we had proposed was working out well. Unfortunately, we, that is the members of the committee and the machinist of the theatre, found one serious inconvenience. The double-basses form a kind of barrier which, in certain places, prevents the spectator from having a good view of the performance. This is due to the way the old stalls were constructed. But it would be deplorable, and I should be particularly sorry, if we were forced to put the double-basses back in their old place. If this were done, it would spoil my plan to group the orchestra so that the sound is fuller, and weak and hesitant performances are thus avoided. We should have gone to a great deal of trouble, without having obtained any certain results.

There may be a remedy. When I examined the stalls, I saw, as did all the others, that the flooring is in so bad a condition that, in a little time, it will be beyond repair and will have to be completely replaced. Since this necessity will soon become imperative, and the expense will have to be undergone, would it not be possible, dear Mr Mayor, to put the work in hand immediately, lowering the floor so that, taking its height at the entrance as zero, it would be about fifty centimeters lower when it reaches the stage?

The orchestra would naturally be lowered, and the difficulty about the double-basses as I have indicated it would not exist.

The stage would be higher and, with the slope of the stalls which is *common to all theatres*, the spectators would get a better view of the performance.

In the midst of all your serious tasks, Mr Mayor, please try to take a moment to give some thought to my proposal. If it can be put into effect, you will have done a good deed for art, and rendered a great service to one who has the honour to call himself your devoted servant

[184]

*To Giulio Ricordi*                              *Turin, 12 November, 1871*

[The new chorus and *romanza* constitute the opening of Act III as we know it: the orchestral introduction, off-stage chorus of priests, arioso for Amneris and Ramfis, recitative ('Qui Radames verrà') and aria ('O patria mia') for Aida. These changes were made for the European première of *Aida* at La Scala on 8 February, 1872.]

I've escaped to Turin with my splendid bundle of music in my hand! Shame! If I had a piano and a metronome, I'd send you the third act this evening. As I wrote to you, I've substituted a chorus and a *romanza* for Aida for another four-part chorus worked out in imitation, in the manner of Palestrina. That might have earned me a 'bravo' from the big-wigs and made me aspire (but what would Faccio say?) to be given a post as teacher of counterpoint in some academy; but then I had an attack of scruples about working in the manner of Palestrina, about harmony, about Egyptian music! . . . . .

In short, that's my destiny . . . . I shall never be a musical savant, I shall always be a bungler!

[185]

*To Filippo Filippi*                              *Genoa, 8 December, 1871*

[Filippi (see note to letter 147) had written to Verdi informing him that he would be visiting Cairo for the première of *Aida*, at the invitation of the

Viceroy of Egypt, and offering to undertake commissions for Verdi or to be
at his disposal in any way required.]

What I am about to say to you will seem strange, very strange, but
forgive me if I cannot conceal all my feelings about this.

You in Cairo? That would be the most powerful publicity imaginable for *Aida*! It seems to me, however, that art treated in this fashion is
no longer art, but a trade, a pleasure-trip, a hunt, something which one
trails around after, something one wants to make, if not successful, at
least notorious at all costs! The feeling this inspires in me is one of
disgust and humiliation! I always remember joyfully my first years
when, almost without a single friend, without anyone to talk to me,
without preparations, without any kind of influence being exerted on
my behalf, I presented my operas to the public, ready to exchange shots,
and extremely happy if I managed to make an occasional favourable
impression. Nowadays, what an apparatus accompanies each opera!
Journalists, soloists, chorus, conductors, players etc. etc., all must carry
their stone to the edifice of publicity, to build up a framework of
wretched gossip which adds nothing to the merit of an opera, but
merely obscures its real value. This is deplorable, deeply deplorable!!

I thank you for your kind offers for Cairo, but I wrote yesterday to
Bottesini[1] about everything concerning *Aida*. All I want for that opera
is good and, above all, intelligent singing, playing and stage production.
For the rest, *à la grace de Dieu*. That's how I began my career, and that's
how I wish to end it.

Have a good journey, and believe me your devoted servant

[186]

*To Countess Maffei*                                              *11 December, 1871*

[Verdi refers to letter No. 185]

I wrote that letter (of which Giulio Ricordi has a copy) to Filippi with a
feeling of great sadness. In another letter I've now received, Filippi
tries to defend the idea of publicity in certain instances. Not I: it's
always humiliating and useless. At present, I'm somewhat indisposed,
and so irritated by all this theatrical nonsense that I'm capable of making

---

[1] Conductor of the first performance. (See note to letter 187).

the most serious resolutions. Oh, the years have not yet frozen my blood, and I still can't conceal my feelings whether cheerful or sad!! What a wretched nature mine is. Never, never an hour's peace!

[187]

*To Giovanni Bottesini* *Milan, 13 January, 1872*

[Giovanni Bottesini (1821–1889), who conducted the first performance of *Aida*, was also a composer and a celebrated double-bass player. His operas include *Ali Baba*, written for London where it was performed with considerable success in 1871.

Verdi decided against using the new Overture he had written for the Scala *Aida*. It is still in manuscript at Sant'Agata, unplayed since the Milan rehearsals, with the apparent exception of a broadcast performance by Toscanini in New York in 1940.]

First of all, I must thank you for the very great care you took over the performance of *Aida*, and congratulate you on your talent for interpretation. I am also very grateful to you for the remarks in your last two letters, which I shall certainly profit by. *Amen*, then, to this. I thank you again, and hope you will continue to be successful.

I have begun rehearsals here, but the devil has stuck his horns in and made Capponi[1] ill. We have had to replace him with Fancelli: it just couldn't be helped.

This year we have a good orchestra and chorus here. About 120 in the chorus, and 90 in the orchestra. The sound is big and full, and the trombones don't shriek. Our production won't be as lavish as yours in Cairo, but it will be all right. On the whole, so long as the devil doesn't continue to stick his horns in, we should have a success.

I have just written an overture for *Aida*. Would you kindly tell Draneht Bey that, if it proves to be effective, I shall make it my duty to send him a copy right away, so that it can be included in the Cairo performances.

When you have half an hour to spare, let me have news of you and of the opera.

[1] Giuseppe Capponi (1832–1889) sang the tenor part in the first performance of the Requiem in 1874.

[188]

*To Giulio Ricordi*                                    *Genoa, 31 March, 1872*

Dear Giulio,

For the record, I'll be at Sant'Agata tomorrow morning, and in Parma on April 3rd.

So this evening will be the last for *Aida*!! I can breathe again!! There'll be no more talk about it, or at least no more than a few final words. Perhaps some new insult, accusing me of Wagnerism, and then . . . . *Requiescant in pacem*!

And now, will you be kind enough to tell me what sacrifices this opera of mine has imposed upon the management? Don't be stupefied by the question: there must obviously have been sacrifices, since none of these gentlemen, despite all the work I have done and the thousands of lire I have expended, has said so much as 'Thank you, dog!' Or should I perhaps thank them for having accepted and produced this wretched *Aida*, whose twenty performances earned 165,000 lire, not counting the subscribers and the gallery? . . . Ah Shakespeare, Shakespeare . . . the great poet of the human heart! But I shall never learn!!

   Believe me always affectionately yours


[189]

*To Opprandino Arrivabene*                              *29 August, 1872*

I have tried to improve standards in our theatres, and to give reasonably good performances in them. In four theatres where for years they had fiasco after fiasco, and were simply unable to pay their way in the last quarter of the year, when I organized and directed the performances the crowds flocked and the receipts were tremendous. You will say 'What do the receipts matter to you?' But they do matter because they prove that the performance interested people, and they show us what to do in future. You know that in Milan and in Parma, I was present in person. In Padua, I wasn't, but I sent the same chorus from Parma, the same scene-painter, machinist, equipment, wardrobe as in Parma. I sent Faccio who had conducted the opera in Milan. We discussed everything in letters, daily, and the opera went well. Crowds at the theatre, and huge profits.

The impresario came here yesterday to thank me, and he was certainly under no obligation to do so.

That is what I have done now with *La forza del destino* in Brescia. Without moving from here, I supervised everything. . . . the same company, the same chorus as in Milan, etc. etc. And Faccio again. So, after the eighth performance, all the expenses were covered, and everything now is profit. Also large crowds and general enjoyment. Perhaps you will still say 'Other people can do that too'. No, and again, no. They don't know how to. If they knew how to, they would not put on such scandalously awful performances.

Now I shall occupy myself with Naples, which is a little more difficult. In Naples, as in Rome, because they have had Palestrina, Scarlatti, Pergolesi, they think they know better than anyone else. . . .

Nevertheless, they have lost their sense of direction, and now they know very little. They are a little like the French: 'We, we, we. . . .'

But forgive this chatter, which can't be very interesting. Still, I really wish our theatres would perk up a little. It could be done. . . .


[190]


*To Countess Maffei*                    *Naples, 29 December, 1872*


Good morning, and a happy new year, that's to say good health and a quiet life. Peace, it's the best thing in this world, and it's what I desire most at this moment. What devil ever put it into my head to get involved in theatrical matters again! I, who for several years had been enjoying the blissful life of a peasant. But now I'm at the ball I have to dance, and I can assure you the dancing is quite something here. I knew how disorganized this theatre was, but neither I nor anyone else could have imagined it to be like this. The ignorance, the inertia, the apathy, the disorder, the indifference of everyone to everything, is indescribable, and unbelievable. It almost makes me laugh when I think calmly of all the trouble I go to, of the agitation I suffer, of my obstinacy in doing things the way I want them done, at all costs. It seems to me that everyone watches me, laughing and saying: 'Is he mad?'

Oh, my vanity has been well punished, for I confess I really had a moment of vanity. I'll explain. When the Government withdrew its subsidy from the theatres, I said, well now, let's show this government it was wrong, and that we can do without its help. Then I came to Milan for *La forza del destino*. People found lots to criticize in the music, but the production and performance were, on the whole, impressive. This was what I wanted. I then went to stage *Aida*. The usual adverse comments on the music (by this time *La forza del destino* had become good) but again the production and performance were successful. A brilliant audience, and huge receipts. I went to Parma, and the outcome was again splendid: always a brilliant audience, and huge receipts. I kept an eye on Padua from afar, and, thanks to Faccio's efforts, again success and profits. I came to Naples in the hope of equal success, but here, whoosh, the earth falls from under my feet, and I can't find anything to hang on to.

It serves me right.

My vanity was well punished.

Now I am properly disillusioned,[1] and, if I hadn't been such an imbecile as to give my word to Giulio[2] on other contracts, I would have gone off even in the middle of the night, to dig my fields and completely forget about music and theatres.

For the rest, although I'm furious, I'm in good health.


[191]


*To Countess Maffei*                                            *Naples, 9 April, 1873*


On receiving the *Fanfulla* you sent me, I couldn't restrain a little smile, as I imagined to myself your enthusiasm on reading that article.

The success of *Aida*, as you know, was honest and decisive, and not poisoned by 'ifs' and 'buts' or crude remarks about 'Wagnerism', 'the future', 'the art of melody' etc. etc. The public abandoned itself to its feelings, and applauded. That's all! . . . . It applauded and even indulged in transports of feeling that I don't approve of. Still, it made its feelings known without reservations, and without *arrière-pensée*! And do you know why? Because here there were no critics acting as apostles; no crowd of composers who understand no more of music than they can study in the guidelines of Mendelssohn, Schumann, Wagner etc.; no aristocratic dilettantes who are carried away by what they don't understand, etc. etc. And do you know the result of all this? The aberration and confusion of mind of the youth of today. Let me

---

[1] Verdi uses the French word *dégrisé*.        [2] Giulio Ricordi.

explain. Imagine nowadays, for example, a young man of Bellini's temperament: not very certain of himself, irresolute because of his lack of training, guided only by his instincts. Harrassed by the Fillippis, the Wagnerites etc., he would end by losing faith in himself, and would probably give up. . . . Amen, Amen.

We are leaving this evening for Sant'Agata. By the time you receive this, we shall have arrived. And when are you coming? We await you with open arms.


[192]


*To Giulio Ricordi*                                    *Sant'Agata, 23 May, 1873*


[The famous poet and novelist, Alessandro Manzoni (1785–1873), author of *I promessi sposi*, had died on 22 May.

'Although violently anti-clerical in his extreme youth, he became converted to Catholicism at the age of twenty-five, wrote one or two volumes of Catholic apologetics, two verse tragedies on patriotic themes, an ode on the death of Napoleon, and then devoted his life to writing *I promessi sposi*. The effect of this novel, on its first publication in 1827, was extraordinary, and its success immediate. Manzoni continually revised it, as it went through edition after edition, until he produced his definitive version in 1840. It is still by far the most popular novel in the Italian language. From the beginning, it appealed not only to the educated classes, but to almost everyone who could read or be read to. Though it was not an overt propaganda novel, it spoke directly to emergent Italian patriotism. The huge response to *I promessi sposi* was undoubtedly extra-aesthetic, many people being inspired by it to attach themselves emotionally to the new liberal cause. The novel deals with events in Lombardy in the first half of the seventeenth century, at a time when the people were being oppressed by their Spanish overlords. But Manzoni's nineteenth-century readers were perfectly capable of making the transposition to the Italy of their own day, suffering under the Austrians. The local patriotism of the novel's submerged meaning worked on its public in the same way that Verdi's first operas did.

'Verdi revered Manzoni, but for years was too shy to meet him. When the Countess Maffei took Giuseppina Strepponi to meet Manzoni, a visit Verdi did not hear about till afterwards, he was both delighted and envious. The two men finally met in 1868 in Milan, and Verdi wrote to Clarina Maffei: "What can I say of Manzoni? How to describe the extraordinary, indefinable sensation the presence of that saint, as you call him, produced in me?"' (From Osborne: *The Complete Operas of Verdi*, pp. 397–8.)]

Dear Giulio,

I am deeply saddened by the death of our great man. But I shall not come to Milan tomorrow, for I haven't the heart to attend his funeral. I shall come in a little while to visit his grave, alone and without being seen, and perhaps (after further reflection, and after I have weighed up my strength) to propose some way of honouring his memory.

Keep this secret, and don't even say a word about my coming, because it's too distressing for me to read what the newspapers say of me: they report me as saying and doing things I have neither said nor done. Greetings to Clarina. Farewell.


[193]

*To Countess Maffei*                                            *29 May, 1873*

[Manzoni's funeral was held on 29 May.]

I myself was not present at the funeral, but there can have been this morning few people more sad and deeply moved than I, although I was far away. Now everything is finished! And with him ends the most pure, the most sacred, the highest of our glories. I have read many of the newspapers, and not one of them speaks of him as he should be spoken of. Many words, but none of them profoundly felt. No lack of stinging remarks, however. Even at him! .... Oh, what an ugly race we are!


[194]

*To Countess Maffei*                                            *2 June, 1873*

[On 2 June, Verdi travelled to Milan to visit Manzoni's tomb.]

I am in Milan, but I beg you to tell no one, no one. Where is the tomb of our saint? I shall visit you tomorrow, after ten. But be quiet about it, even to Giulio. I shall go to see him tomorrow, then to you. Farewell.

[195]

*To the Mayor of Milan* *Sant'Agata, 9 June, 1873*

[Within a few days of the funeral, Verdi had proposed to the Mayor and
Council of Milan that he should write a Requiem Mass to be performed on
the first anniversary of Manzoni's death. He himself would bear the expenses
of having the music printed, if the city would subsidize the first performance.
The Mayor agreed, and Verdi began work on the Mass during his summer
holiday in Paris with Giuseppina. The first performance was given in the
church of San Marco, Milan, on 22 May, 1874.]

I do not deserve any thanks either from you or from the Council for my
offer to write a Requiem Mass for the anniversary of Manzoni's death.
It was an impulse, or, to put it better, a need from my heart, to honour,
as best I could, this great man whom I held in such esteem as a writer,
and venerated as a man, and as a model of virtue and patriotism. When
my work on the music is sufficiently advanced, I shall not fail to let
you know what elements will be necessary to make the performance
worthy both of our country and of the man whose loss we lament.

[196]

*To the President of the Teatro Comunale, Trieste* *Paris, 5 September, 1873*

[Verdi had been invited to attend the first Trieste production of *Aida*, which
took place on 4 October, 1873, with Maddalena Mariani as Aida, Antonietta
Fricci-Baraldi (1840–1912) as Amneris, Giuseppe Capponi as Radames,
Francesco Pandolfini as Amonasro, and Armando Maini as Ramfis. The
conductor was Faccio.]

It was for artistic reasons that I thought it necessary to attend performances of *Aida* in two or three of the big opera houses, which I did
in Milan, Naples and Parma. In the case of the last-named town, I went
also because I am a native of the Province, and consequently almost a
fellow-citizen. Now *Aida* has gone on its way, and I have abandoned it
to its fate, hoping only that it will be performed with feeling and
intelligence, and, above all, in accord with my intentions.

I thank the Theatrical Management of Trieste for its courteous
invitation to attend the first performance, but, in addition to the fact
that my presence would be of no advantage to the performance of the

score, I prefer not to go to theatres purely and simply to be stared at as a curiosity.

I must ask you, therefore, to excuse me for not being able to comply with your wishes. I thank you once more, and have the honour, Signor President, of signing myself, Your Devoted Servant


[197]

*To Maria Waldmann*                                              *Paris, 23 October, 1873*


[Maria Waldmann (see note to letter 178) sang in the first performance of the Requiem.]


Dearest Maria,

Since it was about musical matters, my wife has handed me your letter for me to reply directly. So here I am, at your service, my dearest and kindest Maria.

Certainly it would give me great pleasure if you could take part in the Requiem Mass on the anniversary of Manzoni's death: 22nd May, 1874. You would gain neither reputation nor money from it; but since this is something that will make history, certainly not because of the merit of the music but because of the man to whom it is dedicated, I think it would be fine if, one day, history could say: 'On May 22nd there was a great Requiem Mass at . . . . for the anniversary of Manzoni's death, performed by Messrs. . . . . etc.' So try to be free at this time, and write to Ricordi to explain how matters are. For my part, I shall write to him tomorrow, so that the two letters will arrive together. It seems to me we shall merely have to postpone the Florence season.


[198]

*To Tito Ricordi*                                                  *Genoa, 1 March, 1874*


[A poor performance of *Aida* at the San Carlo Theatre, Naples, had been forecast by Neapolitan journalists when the names of the principal singers had been announced: Gabriella Krauss, Signora E. Sanz, Enrico Barbacini, Luigi Colonnese and Signor Antonucci.]

Edoardo Mascheroni

Count Opprandino
Arrivabene

Giuseppe Verdi and Arrigo
Boito at Sant'Agata

Vincenzo Torelli, from a painting
by Domenico Morelli

Dear Tito,

Read this little article from the Naples *Pungolo*! .... How is it possible for *Aida* to be performed repeatedly in this manner without the firm of Ricordi showing any interest at all? And is your representative allowing things to continue in this fashion?

I ask formally, by the terms of our contract, that a demand for damages be made to the Naples management, and that this should be done in the name of the composer. The proprietor, having received the fees, has suffered nothing. It is art that has been treated with contempt, and I feel it my duty to vindicate it.

No concessions, no compromise in this affair! I end by repeating that I am still stupefied to think that Ricordi's representative could have allowed such a shameful business.

A hasty farewell, yours

[199]

*To Léon Escudier*              *Genoa, 7 March, 1874*

[*La forza del destino* had more than once been announced for production at the Théâtre Italien, only to be postponed.]

Dear Léon,

The business of *Aida* and *La forza* is a most delicate one, and I must first of all tell you frankly that, both for musical and theatrical reasons, neither of these operas is suitable for the Théâtre Italien in Paris. For the Théâtre Italien, one needs works easier to stage, very dependent on the singing, and with a small orchestra. Furthermore, between ourselves, I haven't a very high opinion of the business talents of the two partners. If this year was anything to go by, they are awful. You will tell me they can do nothing other than select from the new artists available, because it's impossible to find great singers. That is so, but an impresario who was less of a speculator and more of an artist could have done better. You yourself have in the past made many comments and been most critical. It may be that the majority of the operas are all right under Vianesi, and it may well be, as you say, that there is no better conductor today; nevertheless, for my operas I would prefer one of the young conductors we have here. But this is a vain wish which has no chance of being fulfilled.

As far as the singers are concerned, I believe it's now too late, but I have nothing to say either way about this. I don't want the responsibility of engaging singers, because I cannot come to Paris to attend the productions of these operas. I am tired, and I don't want to have to fight new battles in your country. I must abstain from imposing any conditions about this.

Ricordi owns the score. The management should contact him, and he will know how best to order things to ensure a success, though I myself haven't much faith in the outcome.

To conclude, then: I am not opposed to this, but I don't want to be involved in it. Do whatever you think best.

One day soon, when you have replied, we shall speak seriously about the Mass. Farewell.


[200]


*To Tito Ricordi*                                          *Genoa, 11 March, 1874*


Dear Tito,

I understand nothing, absolutely nothing, of all this Naples business.

What's it all about? Can the contract with Musella[1] have been drawn up in so slovenly a fashion that he has been able to find a way to do what he has done?

And, further, have you also accepted an affidavit from Musella?

But what about me? What do I become then? A workhand, a daily labourer who brings his goods to the publishing house, and whom the publishing house exploits as it pleases! But that is not what I want. I have said before that, if I had wanted to become a business man, no one could have stopped me, after *La traviata*, from writing an opera a year, and making myself a fortune three times as big as I have. But I had other artistic intentions (as is proved by the pains I have taken with my recent operas), and I should have achieved something, too, if I had not encountered opposition, or at least indifference, in everything and everyone!

I want to distinguish Tito Ricordi from the Publisher, and for this reason I ask Tito Ricordi to tell me frankly how things stand. If the managers of the publishing house have not looked after my interests, I shall still not want to subject Tito Ricordi to the embarrassment of

[1] Musella was the impresario of the San Carlo Opera House, Naples, where *Aida* had been unsatisfactorily performed.

litigation. But permit me to say once again that the publishing house has treated me without any consideration whatsoever.

Farewell, farewell.

[201]

*To Tito Ricordi*                                    *Genoa, 25 March, 1874*

[Verdi later presented the manuscript score of the Requiem to Teresa Stolz.]

Dear Tito,

I have received a reply from Léon Escudier, and we have agreed on the following:

1. Complete ownership of the Mass for France and Belgium.
2. Half ownership of the score for England, and the right for him to sell his edition along with yours. 50% of the hiring fees for English performance will go to the composer.
3. He will have the right to sell his edition in Spain.

The remaining ownership rights will remain with you. As far as the income from hiring is concerned, you will pay me 50% as for *Aida*. I shall retain the original score.

Please send me a fair copy of the score before 10 May, so that I can revise it and send it to Escudier.

You will pay me for your ownership of the work, 35,000 francs. Francs, not lire, because lire will not mix well with the francs Escudier is to pay me. Let me have a few words of contract, and then we need speak no more of it. Reply quickly. Yours ever.

P.S. Before the end of this month, I shall send the Requiem and the Dies Irae. The rest by April 10.

[202]

*To Countess Maffei*                                *Genoa, 11 March, 1875*

[*I Lituani* is an opera by Amilcare Ponchielli (1834–1886). With a libretto by Ghislanzoni, based on Mickiewicz's *Konrad Wallenrod*, it had first been produced at La Scala in March, 1874. Revised, and with some additional pieces composed for it, it was staged again at La Scala on 6 March, 1875. The only opera of Ponchielli's to survive in performance today is *La Gioconda*, for

which, under the anagrammatic pseudonym of Tobia Gorrio, Boito wrote
the libretto, which was based on Victor Hugo's *Angelo*.]

Dear Clarina,

I put a pound of sugar in my ink-pot this morning to reply to the
letters of your Senator friend from Bergamo. But time and again, stir
as I might, my letters are not completely sweet because they say only
no, no and again no.

What can you expect! He could not act any differently, and I simply
did what I could.

It will be very difficult for me to come now to Milan. I really must go
to my house in the country on very urgent business, and then return
here quickly on other business.

I heard with pleasure of I *Lituani;* so much the better for everyone.
The only one to be sorry for is he himself, because if he doesn't take
heart he'll see that kindness. . . .

Are you serious when you speak of my *conscience obliging me to
compose*?? No, no, you're joking, because you know better than I do
that the *scores are settled*. In other words I have always conscientiously
fulfilled the obligations I have undertaken, and the public has accepted
my works, with equal conscientiousness, with splendid hissing or
applause etc. No one, then, has any right to complain, and I say again:
'Score settled.'

Farewell, my dear Clarina. Peppina greets you, and I squeeze both
your hands.

[203]

*To Opprandino Arrivabene*                              *Sant'Agata, 14 July, 1875*

I've no idea how we are going to escape from this musical ferment.
Some want to be melodists like Bellini, some harmonists like Meyerbeer. I don't want to be one or the other, and I want the younger
composers of today not to think about being melodists, harmonists,
realists, idealists, futurists or any of these other devilish pedantries.
Melody and harmony should only be tools for music-making in the
hands of the artist; and, if ever the day comes in which people no longer
talk of melody, harmony, German and Italian schools, the past, the
future etc. etc., then perhaps the kingdom of art will begin. Another
evil of our time is that all the works of these young composers are born

out of *fear*. No one writes by instinct. When these youngsters compose, the thought that predominates in their minds is how not to annoy the public, or how to get into the critics' good books.

You tell me that I owe my success to the fusion of the two schools. *I never thought about it.* But this is an old story, which at a certain time everyone goes through.

However, my dear Arrivabene, keep calm. Art will not perish, and even the moderns have done some good things, you know.


[204]

*To Countess Maffei*                                    *Genoa, 30 January, 1876*

We have just arrived in Genoa, but I don't know how many months or weeks we shall remain. We shall certainly not stay here for very long, as I have to return to Sant'Agata for a few days before leaving for Paris. I am asked to tell you that Peppina is well now, and that next season she will put on again all the weight she has lost.

Yesterday, I went to *Il suicidio.*[1] A beautiful production which has blood, nerves and energy. From the newspaper accounts, I had expected something different, but when can you ever believe . . . . O devoted friends, o stupid enemies, o *poseurs*! On Monday, I'm going to see Torelli's *Color del tempo.*[2] For quite some time, everyone has been attacking poor Torelli, but I shouldn't be surprised if he were in the right. When an artist allows himself to have two or three successes while young, still under thirty, he can be sure that the public will then grow tired of him. They begin to resent having showered applause on such a whippersnapper, and take the slightest opportunity to demonstrate their contempt. If the artist has the strength to stand up to this turn of the tide and go ahead on his own path, he'll be safe by the time he's forty. Then the public no longer has contempt for him but puts on its grand airs, keeping a gun cocked, ready at any time to let him have a good burst of shot. The artist may have genius, talent, as much knowledge as you like, it doesn't matter. It's a struggle that ends only with

---

[1] *Il suicidio* was the latest play by Paolo Ferrari (1822–1889), one of the most interesting Italian dramatists of his time. He began as a writer of historical plays, and later progressed to plays with a thesis. It has been said that his dialogue curiously anticipates Pirandello.

[2] *Color del tempo* is a play by Achille Torelli, son of Vincenzo Torelli (see note to letter 142).

life itself (What fine consolation for an artist!). But he will not fall if he is armed with a heavy shield of indifference and conviction. Beware of fear. Fear is the ruin of our artists. Everything being produced now is born of fear. No one thinks nowadays of following their own inspiration, they're all preoccupied with not upsetting the nerves of the Filippis, the d'Arcais and all the others.[1]

I do beg your pardon . . . . . What the devil am I saying?

[205]

*To Opprandino Arrivabene*                          *Genoa, 5 February, 1876*

The best thing would be a repertory theatre, but I don't think it could be achieved. The examples of the Paris Opéra and Germany have very little value for me, because in all these theatres the performances are deplorable. At the Opéra, the productions are splendid, and their costumes, their good taste, are superior to all other theatres. But the musical side is awful, the singers are always the most mediocre (except for Faure a few years ago), the orchestra and chorus are lazy and lacking in discipline. I have attended hundreds of performances at this theatre, and I have still to hear a good musical performance. But in a city of 3,000,000 inhabitants, and at least a hundred thousand foreigners, there are always two thousand people to fill the hall, however bad the show.

In Germany, the orchestra and choruses are more attentive and conscientious. They play accurately and well, although I have seen some deplorable performances in Berlin. The orchestra is huge, but sounds merely gross. The chorus is not good, the productions lacking in character and taste. The singers . . . . oh, the singers are awful, absolutely awful. This year in Vienna I heard la Meslinger (I don't know if I'm spelling her name right), who passes for the Malibran of Germany. Almighty God! A miserable, tired voice, her singing baroque and awkward, her stage manner unbecoming. Our three or four prima donnas in the company are infinitely superior to her in voice and style of singing, and at least her equal as actresses.

In Vienna (which is now the leading German-speaking theatre), things are better in the case of chorus and orchestra (most excellent). I have attended various performances and have found the majority of them very good, though the productions are mediocre, and the singers

[1] Filippi (see note to letter 147) and D'Arcais were music critics.

worse than mediocre. But the performance usually costs very little to attend. The public, who are made to sit in the dark during the performance, are either asleep or bored, applaud a little at the end of each act, and go home at the end of the performance neither enthusiastic nor displeased. That may be all very well for those northern natures, but try to put on that kind of performance in one of our theatres, and see what a noise the public will make!

Our audiences are too excitable, and would not be contented with a prima donna who cost only 18 or 20 thousand florins a year, as in Germany. They want the prima donnas who go to Cairo, St Petersburg, Lisbon, London etc., for 25 or 30 thousand francs a month. But how are we to pay them? Look at this, for example: this year at La Scala they have a company whose betters couldn't be found. A prima donna with a beautiful voice, who sings well, is lively, young, beautiful, and, what's more, is one of us. A tenor who is perhaps the best there is, certainly one of the best. A baritone who has but one rival: Pandolfini. A bass who is unrivalled. And yet the theatre does poor business. Last year, they spoke well enough of Mariani.[1] This year, they began to say she was a little tired (which, incidentally, is not true), now they say she sings well but does not draw an audience, etc. etc. If she were to come next year, everyone would say, 'Oh, always the same woman. . . .'

I remember meeting in Milan someone called Villa, an old impresario from the days when Lalande, Rubini, Tamburini and Lablache sang at La Scala. He told me that, after their initial fanatical enthusiasm, the public ended by hissing Rubini, and by staying away from the theatre to the point where one evening the management sold only six tickets!! Incredible. . . .

Now I ask you whether, with our public, it would be possible to engage a standing company for at least three years! And then, do you know what a company such as the one now at La Scala would cost for a year? Mariani might just be willing to sing for a season at La Scala for 45 or 50 thousand francs, but, if she were offered a year's contract, she would naturally ask to be paid 15,000 francs a month, since at the moment she can earn 25 to 30,000 abroad. The same with the tenor, etc.

Oh, good Lord, what a long letter! I have so many other things to tell you, but from what I have said you will understand the rest.

[1] Maddalena Mariani, who had sung Aida in Trieste.

[206]

*To Maria Waldmann*                                    *Sant'Agata, 10 July, 1876*

[Maria Waldmann was retiring from the stage to marry the Duke Galeazzo
Massari of Ferrara on 6 September, 1876.

In a footnote to this letter, the editors of the *Copialettere* state (p. 523) that
Waldmann had been the first interpreter of Amneris in Cairo. This is not so.
The first Amneris, in Cairo on 24 December, 1871, was Eleonora Grossi.
Waldmann first sang the role in the Scala, Milan, production on 8 February,
1872.

Maria Waldmann's sister was called Betty.]

Dearest,
      You have been in Venice for several days now, calm and happy,
occupied only with rehearsals for the opera this season, which will be
the last one for you . . . The last! It's a sad word which calls up a world
of memories and embraces a life of excitements, some happy, some sad,
but always dear to those with the fibres of an artist. You, however, are
fortunate in that you will find great consolation in your change of
fortune. It's not so for others, to whom the word 'last' means 'Everything is over!'
      But why, my dear Maria, do I go on repeating these painful things
to you? I said almost the same things that last evening in Paris! I was
sorry then, and now I'm saying it all from the beginning! Please forgive me! And if I have no cheerful words to tell you about myself,
please tell me about your good fortune. You are young, beautiful and
are now at the height of your happiness. Write to me then, and not
only to tell me about *Aida* and the Mass, but to speak to me of yourself.
      We pass the time here tranquilly, and, if not joyfully, then well
enough. Peppina unites with me to send greetings to you and to your
sister.


[207]

*To Countess Maffei*                                  *Sant'Agata, 20 October, 1876*

[*Color del tempo* was a comedy by Achille Torelli. (See notes to letters 142
and 204.)]

I saw *Color del tempo* in Genoa. There are great things in it, above all a
quick-wittedness which is a particular gift of the French. But, *au fond*,

there's little there. To copy truth may be a good thing, but *to invent truth* is better, much better.

There may seem to be a contradiction in these three words 'to invent truth', but you ask Papa.[1] It may be that Papa found Falstaff just as he was, but it would have been difficult for him to find a villain as villain- ous as Iago, and never, never such angels as Cordelia, Imogene, Desde- mona, etc. etc. and yet they are so true!

To copy the truth is a fine thing, but it is photography, not painting.

What useless chatter. We are leaving today. Bon voyage, you say? I hope so. Wish me well, and farewell.


[208]


*To Tito Ricordi*                                        *Genoa, 10 March, 1877*


It is an old habit of the firm of Ricordi to embarrass me with matters which I shouldn't have to worry about. The contracts exist: to each his share.

I write the operas:

The firm administers them.

Thus the firm of Ricordi does not ask for my authorization to have *La forza del destino* performed now at La Scala (and they were acting within their rights). By the same token, they should not have given me the objectionable task of replying in the negative to a request from an old friend, whom I love and esteem, to perform the duet from *Aida* in a benefit concert in Ferrara.

Believe me yours ever


[209]


*To Giulio Ricordi*                                 *Sant'Agata, 6 October, 1877*

Dear Giulio,

I have read the letter you wrote to Corticelli, and am answering it myself. I don't understand what you write about Patti agreeing to sing Aida. If that is so, you can imagine how pleased I should be. Other- wise, not!

[1] Shakespeare.

A great success, then! It couldn't have been otherwise! You heard her ten years ago, and now you exclaim 'How she's changed'. You're wrong! Patti was then what she is now: perfectly organised. Perfect equilibrium between singer and actress, a born artist in every sense of the word.

When I heard her for the first time in London (she was eighteen), I was struck dumb not only by her marvellous technique but by certain dramatic traits in which she revealed herself as a great actress. I remember the chaste and modest demeanour with which, in *La sonnambula*, she lay on the soldier's bed, and how, in *Don Giovanni*, she left the libertine's room, corrupted. I remember a certain reaction of hers during Don Bartolo's aria in *Il barbiere* and, above all, in the recitative preceding the quartet in *Rigoletto*, when her father points out her lover in the tavern and says 'And you still love him?', and she replies 'I love him'. I cannot describe the sublime effect of those words as she sang them. All this, and more, she was able to say and do, over ten years ago. But many people couldn't admit it then, and you did as your public did. You wanted her to be baptized by yourself, as if the entire public in Europe who had gone mad about her knew absolutely nothing! But 'Nun sem nun . . . Milanes . . el prim teater del mond!'—doesn't it seem to you that all that bears too close a resemblance to the detested 'chez nous' of the French? And the leading theatre of the world? I know five or six such leading theatres, and really they're the ones where you frequently hear the worst music. What's more, between ourselves, admit it, what a mediocre orchestra, what a poor chorus you had six years ago. The worst kind of machinery, a horrible lighting system, impossible equipment. Stage production then was unheard-of . . . which was not such a bad thing! Today, things are a little better, but not much; in fact very little!

When you see Patti, give her fond greetings from my wife and myself. I am not sending her the usual congratulations, because it really seems to me that, for Patti, that would be the most pointless thing in the world. And she knows, and knows well, that I didn't wait for her Milan success, but that from the time I first heard her in London, when she was hardly more than a child, I considered her a marvellous singer and actress, and something exceptional in our art.

So greet her for me, and nothing more.

I press your hand and say farewell to you.

[210]

*To Countess Maffei*          *Genoa, 12 February, 1878*

[Pope Pius IX had died on 7 February, 1878.]

But, now everyone is dying! Everyone! Now the Pope! Poor Pope! It's true that I am not for the Pope of the Syllabus, but I am for the Pope of the amnesty and of the *Benedicite, Gran Dio*. Italy! Without him, who knows where we would be now?

They accused him of going back on his word, of having lacked courage and of not having been able to wield a sword like Julius II. How fortunate! If, in '48, he had been able to chase the Austrians out of Italy, what would we have now? A Government of priests! Probably anarchy and dismemberment . . . it's better as it is! Everything that he did, both good and bad, proved useful to our country. In the final resort, he was a good man and a good Italian: better than many others who shout nothing but country, country, and . . . . So may the poor Pope rest in peace!

[211]

*To Sig. Cav. Cavagnari, Mayor of Parma*     *Parma, 25 February, 1878*

[Verdi wrote his only String Quartet (in E minor) in March, 1873, while he was rehearsing a production of *Aida* in Naples. He claimed to have written it merely to pass the time when the *Aida* rehearsals were postponed due to the prima donna's illness. Some days after the first performance of the opera, he invited a few friends to his hotel to hear the Quartet played by musicians from the orchestra: the brothers Pinto (first and second violins), Salvadore (viola) and Giarritiello ('cello). His audience liked the work so well that it was immediately played a second time; Verdi, however, professed to consider it of no importance, and for some years forbade not only publication but also further performances. The Quartet is, in fact, a charming, if slight piece, written under the influence of the Viennese school. It combines something of Haydn's gracefulness with the vigour of the young Beethoven.]

I am truly sorry not to be able to agree to what you ask in your very kind letter.

I have not given any more thought to the Quartet, which I wrote simply to pass the time when I was in Naples a few years ago, and which was performed in my house in the presence of a few people who were usually there every evening. This is to tell you that I have never attached any importance to this piece, and that I do not wish, at least for the present, to have it brought to the public's attention in any way.

Please accept my apologies, and believe me, your devoted servant

[212]

*To Signor Bettòli*                                        *Parma, 27 February, 1878*

[Bettòli was probably an official of the Parma Chamber Music Society which wished to perform Verdi's Quartet. See note to letter 211.]

It is true that in Naples I wrote a Quartet, which was performed privately in my house. It is also true that I have had requests from a few societies, chief among them the Quartet Society of Milan, to perform this Quartet. I refused, because I did not want any importance attached to this piece, and because I believed then, and believe now (though perhaps I'm wrong), that in Italy the Quartet is a plant unsuited to our climate. I do not mean to say that this type of composition may not take root and become useful among us, but I should like to see our societies, schools, and conservatoria encouraging vocal quartets as well as string quartets, in order to perform Palestrina and his contemporaries, and Marcello.

To Sig. Cavagnari, who was kind enough to ask for this Quartet, I have replied that, for the moment, I have no intention of bringing it forward to the public. To you, I can only repeat the same thing, begging you to accept my apologies, and to believe me, your devoted servant

[213]

*To  ?*                                                              *[April, 1878]*

[This fragment of a letter to an unidentified correspondent is printed in the Appendix to the *Copialettere*, with a footnote stating that it was preserved among the papers of the Carrara-Verdi family.]

Without wishing to, we are all working for the ruin of our theatre.

Perhaps I, you etc. are all in it. And, if I wanted to say something that appeared to lack common sense, I would say that the main reason in Italy was the number of String Quartet Societies. A recent cause was the success of the performance of the Scala Orchestra (but not the works it played) in Paris. There, I've said it: don't throw stones at me . . . It would take too long to give you all the reasons. But why, in the devil's name, must we in Italy produce German art. Twelve or fifteen years ago, I don't remember whether it was in Milan or somewhere else, I was nominated President of a Quartet Society. I refused to accept, and said: 'Why not form a vocal quartet society? That's Italian art. The other is German art.' Perhaps that was thought as blasphemous then as it would be now, but a vocal quartet society would have enabled us to hear Palestrina, the best of his contemporaries, Marcello etc. etc., and would have kept alive our love of song which we express in opera. Now everything tends towards instrumentation, harmony. The alpha and omega is Beethoven's Ninth Symphony, whose first three movements are sublime, and whose last movement is very badly set. The greatness of the first movement can never be equalled, but it will be easy to imitate the awful setting of the verses in the last movement. They'll all point to the authority of Beethoven, and cry 'That's how to do it' . . . .

So be it, let them do so! It may even be better, but this 'better' means without a doubt the ruin of our opera. Art is universal; no one believes that more than I do. But it is created by individuals, and, since the Germans have different methods from us, their art is intrinsically different. We cannot, indeed I say we must not, write like the Germans, nor the Germans like us. Even though the Germans assimilate something of our quality, as Haydn and Mozart did in their time, they nevertheless remain composers of quartets. And though Rossini appropriated certain formal elements from Mozart, he is nevertheless still a melodist. But if, because of fashion, desire for novelty, or a pretended interest in science, we turn from our own instinctive art, our spontaneous, natural sensibility which is dazzlingly bright, that will be absurd and stupid.

[214]

*To Countess Maffei*                                        *Genoa, 21 February, 1879*

[The 'fracas over one opera' was over Massenet's *Le Roi de Lahore* which was produced at La Scala on 6 February, 1879, with such success that the city initiated a number of celebrations in honour of the composer.]

Thank you for the little book of poems by Professor Rizzi, which I shall read and then write to you about. Thanks, also, for the newspaper clippings you sent me. I had already seen these newspapers because someone, I don't know who, sent them to me directly from Milan. Among these papers was one which had some hard things to say about intrigues, cabals etc. I don't know if there is any truth in this, and I don't want to know; but I do know that all this bother, this fracas over one opera, all this praise and cheering make me think of the past (as you know, the old always praise their own times) when, without publicity, almost without knowing anyone, we presented ourselves to the public; and, whether they applauded us or not, we simply said 'Thank you', or, if they hissed us 'All right, see you another time'. I don't know if this was a good thing, but it was certainly more dignified. In one of the papers Corticelli showed me, there was something that gave me a huge laugh. This paper proposed having a commemoration stone at La Scala, with the inscription, 'In the year 1879, a foreign composer came here and was greeted with huge festivities and a banquet attended by the Prefect and the Mayor. In 1872, a certain Verdi came in person to produce his *Aida*, and was not even offered a glass of water.'

Far from a glass of water, I thought to myself, more like a whipping. Don't take that phrase literally: what I mean to say is that I had squabbles with everyone over *Aida*, and everyone scowled at me as though I were a wild animal. I hasten to say that the fault was mine, completely mine, because, to tell the truth, I am not very amiable in the theatre, or anywhere else; and because I have the misfortune never to understand what everyone else understands. And, because I don't understand, I never succeed in producing those sweet words, those phrases that send everybody into raptures. No, I shall never, for instance, know how to say to a singer, 'What talent! What expression! It couldn't have been sung better! What a divine voice! What a baritone, there hasn't been anything like it for fifty years . . . What a chorus! What an orchestra! It's the world's leading theatre.' That's where I find it difficult. Time and time again I have heard them say in Milan (even when I produced *La forza del destino* there, they all said it) 'La Scala is the world's leading theatre'. In Naples, 'The San Carlo is the world's leading theatre'. In Venice they used to say, 'La Fenice is the world's leading theatre'. In St. Petersburg, 'the world's leading theatre'. In Vienna, 'the world's leading theatre' (but in their case, it's true). In Paris, they think the Opéra is the leading theatre of two or three worlds.

So I stand with my head going round, my eyes wide open, my mouth agape, repeating that I, blockhead that I am, don't understand any of it.

And I end by saying that one second-leading theatre would be better than all these 'leading' ones.

But enough of these jokes, which would make me laugh much more if I didn't happen to be a composer. I hear with pleasure that you have been in good health recently.


[215]

*To Opprandino Arrivabene*           *20 March, 1879*

All of us, composers, critics, audiences, have done everything possible to renounce our national musical character. We've now achieved it. One more step, and we'll be Germanized in this, as we are in so many other things. What a consolation it is to see Quartet Societies, Orchestral Societies, Orchestras and Quartets, Quartets and Orchestras etc. etc., being founded everywhere to educate the public in 'great art', as Filippi calls it. But sometimes a very wicked thought comes to me, and I murmur to myself, 'But if, instead, we Italians were to form a vocal quartet to perform Palestrina and his contemporaries, Marcello etc. etc., wouldn't that, too, be "great art"'?

And it would be Italian art. . . . The other isn't. . . . but be quiet, lest someone should hear me.


[216]

*To the Scala Orchestral Society*       *Genoa, 4 April, 1879*

[The new Milan Orchestral Society had asked Verdi to become its President.]

Dear Sirs,

    I am sorry not to be able to accept the honourable title which you so kindly offer me. As is well known, I am by nature averse to this kind of thing, the more so, nowadays, because of the chaos of our ideas into which tendencies and studies contrary to our nature have plunged the art of Italian music. In this chaos, which may very well lead to a new world (though not ours), but is more likely to lead to nothing, I desire to take no part. I sincerely hope, therefore, that this orchestral branch of our art may thrive, but it is also my ardent desire that the other branch may be equally cultivated, in order one day to restore to Italy that art which was *ours*, as distinct from this *other*.

It is fine to educate the public, as the academics say, to great art, but it seems to me that the art of Palestrina and Marcello is also great art . . . and it is *ours*.

I do not mean by these words to pronounce judgment (heaven forbid), nor even to offer an opinion. My only purpose is to try in some way to justify my decision.

I beg you to accept my apologies, and in wishing a splendid success to the new institution, I sign myself, with all esteem, your devoted servant


[217]

*To Giulio Ricordi*                                    *Sant'Agata, 26 August, 1879*

[In an extract from his memoirs, printed in the *Gazzetta Musicale* (Vol. XXXIV, p. 294), the sculptor Giovanni Duprè had quoted a remark uttered by Rossini many years previously, to the effect that Verdi, a composer of melancholy cast of mind, would never be able to write a light work like Donizetti's *Linda di Chamounix*, much less an opera buffa like *L'elisir d'amore*.

Verdi's letter puzzled Ricordi, since the composer was thought to be considering only *Otello*. But Verdi may also at this time have still been considering Molière's *Tartuffe*, one of the projects he had discussed with Du Locle immediately prior to *Aida*.]


Dear Giulio,

I have read, in your Gazette, Duprè's words about our first meeting, and the sentence pronounced by Jupiter Rossini (as Meyerbeer called him). But just a moment!! For twenty years, I have been searching for an *opera buffa* libretto, and now that I can be said to have found one, you put into the public's head with this article a mad desire to hiss the opera even before it's written, thus damaging both my interests and yours.

But have no fear. If by chance, by misfortune, by some disaster, my evil genius should tempt me to write this *opera buffa* despite the Great Sentence, have no fear, I repeat . . . I shall ruin some other publisher! . . . Farewell, and believe me yours

[218]

*To Giulio Ricordi*                                    *[End of August, 1879]*

[Ricordi's reply to Verdi's letter (217) was conciliatory. In it he suggested that, in the first half of September, he and 'a friend' might visit Verdi at Sant' Agata. He and Boito were anxious to commit the composer to embarking upon *Otello*. Verdi's reply to this was a cautious one.

The draft of this letter in the *Copialettere* ends in mid-sentence.]

That extract from Duprè's book in your Gazette seemed to me to have no other purpose but to say to me: 'Take care, signor Maestro, never to write *opere buffe*'. And so I thought it my duty to say to you 'I shall ruin some other publisher.' However, if you want to ruin yourself by my writing this *opera buffa*, so much the worse for you.

It would be always agreeable to have a visit from you with a friend (who would be Boito, of course), but permit me to speak very plainly to you on this subject. A visit from him would commit me too greatly. You know how this chocolate project was born.[1] You and Faccio were dining with me. There was talk of *Otello*, and there was talk of Boito. The following day Faccio brought Boito to see me: three days later Boito brought me his synopsis of *Otello*. I read it, and I thought it good. I said 'Turn it into verse, it will be always good for you, for me, for someone else etc. etc.' If you come now with Boito, I shall have to read his libretto. If I think it completely good, you will leave it with me, and I shall find myself, to a certain extent, committed. If I still find it good, but suggest a few modifications which Boito accepts, I am even more committed. If I don't like it, it would be too difficult for me to give my opinion to him in person. No, no! You have already gone too far, and we must stop now before there is any gossip or unpleasantness. It seems to me that it would be better to send . . . . [*sic*]

---

[219]

*To Emanuele Muzio*                          *Sant'Agata, 7 October, 1879*

[During Halanzier's direction of the Paris Opéra, Verdi had refused to allow a performance there of *Aida*. Instead, he had given permission for a production

[1] 'Chocolate project' (progetto di cioccolatta) was the name by which Verdi and his friends referred to *Otello*.

in 1876 in Italian, at the Théâtre Italien. In July, 1879, Auguste Vaucorbeil
became Director of the Opéra. He visited Verdi, and persuaded him to
stage and conduct *Aida* in French, at the Opéra, in 1880. The first performance
was conducted by Verdi on 22 March, 1880, with a cast which included
Krauss, Block, Sellier, Victor Maurel and Buodoresque.

The Théâtre Italien, where Muzio had been engaged as conductor, closed
after several years of unsuccessful productions. Muzio was reduced to teaching singing in Paris.]


Dear Em,

As matters stood, even I saw that I could not have refused to let them
have *Aida*. But, between ourselves, I am not very happy about it. Either
I don't go to Paris, and the opera will be performed flabbily,
lifelessly, without any effect, or I go, and find my body and spirit
eaten up.

Escudier remains his own everlasting self. This last contract for *Aida*
is absolutely wretched. If only Heugel[1] had managed to acquire the
rights to *Aida*, I should have been rid of Escudier forever. This man
makes it even more difficult for me to go to Paris. After more than
thirty years' association between publisher and composer, it's difficult
to break it off. All those who are now saying what a rogue he is would
start screaming at me if I were to change publishers. That's the way of
the world!

The Italian newspapers will not approve of my giving way over
*Aida*. Only yesterday, the *Corriere della sera* said that, due to the
continuing rudenesses I had had to endure, I had not allowed them to do
*Aida*. God knows what they'll say when they find I have given my
permission. The beauty of it is that I really agree with them ten times
over. If Capponi, who has written to me about *Aida* in Paris, can think
of something to say, he could put something in *Fanfulla*, and in
*Perseveranza*, to say that for such and such reasons, I had no option but
to do what I did etc. etc.

Don't let this letter be printed. You may show it to whomever you
wish, but don't publish it, because in that case it would look as though
I wanted to beg favours from the gentlemen at the Opéra.

What a mess! What a bore! What a nuisance! But one can't remain
tranquil, even at Sant'Agata!!

Farewell, yours


[1] Jacques Léopold Heugel (1815–1883), founder of the French publishing house of
Heugel et Cie.

[220]

*To Domenico Morelli*            *Genoa, 6 January, 1880*

[The painter Domenico Morelli (1826–1901) had sent Verdi photographs of two of his works, a painting of the temptation of St Anthony, and a sketch of King Lear.]

Dear Morelli,

Thanks, a thousand thanks for the two photographs. I have kept other photographs, engravings etc., of your last masterpiece, but this that you have sent gives me a more complete idea of it. This picture of the temptation must be really beautiful! . . . What do you say? I have heard so much talk of it, and have read so much about it . . . that I can hardly wait to see it myself.

And what a beautiful sketch that is of King Lear! As distressing as its subject! How powerful the expression of that figure must be; old Kent, I imagine.

Why not do a scene from *Otello* as a companion to this sketch?

For example, when Otello smothers Desdemona. Or, better still, (it would be more original), when Otello, mad with jealousy, faints, and Iago looks at him with a devilish smile, saying 'Work on, my medicine, work . . .'

What a character Iago is!!!

Well, then, what do you say to it?

Write to me, work, which is even better, and give me a good clasp of your hand. I embrace you with the greatest admiration.

[221]

*To Domenico Morelli*            *Genoa, 7 February, 1880*

Dear Morelli,

Good, very good, superb, most superb! Iago with the mask of a gentleman!

You've hit it! I'm sure you have. I was certain you would. I seem to see this priest, who is Iago with the face of an honest man. Quickly then, with your four strokes of the pen, and then send me this scribbled sketch. On, on, . . . quickly, quickly, . . . . inspiration . . . just as it comes . . . don't do it as for painters, do it as for a musician!

Don't play the modest man and say it's nothing, because it's no use, I won't believe you. When a man has done what Domenico Morelli has done, he doesn't raise his voice, or speak like the average man: he looks within and tells himself, 'I am I, and always I'.

So quickly then with the scribble!

The scene of the brothers kneeling, the Virgin of the Angels etc., is beautiful, but it's a subject for opera. This Iago is Shakespeare, it's humanity, that's to say a part of humanity, the ugly part.

[222]

*To Giulio Ricordi*                                                *20 November, 1880*

[*Simon Boccanegra*, with a libretto by Piave based on the play by Antonio Garcia Gutiérrez, had been first performed at the Teatro Fenice, Venice, in 1857. In 1880, Verdi was persuaded by Giulio Ricordi to consider undertaking a revision.

Francesco Petrarca (in English, Petrarch) (1304–1374) was the great medieval Italian poet. Verdi's recollection of the two letters by Petrarch led eventually to the magnificent Council Chamber scene in the revised *Boccanegra*. The task of improving the libretto was entrusted to Boito who, in this scene, made appropriate use of the closing line of Petrarch's *Italia mia*,

I'vo gridando: Pace, pace, pace.

This becomes, in the opera, Boccanegra's

E vo gridando: pace,
E vo gridando: amor.]

The score as it stands will not do. It is too sad, too desolate. There is no need to touch anything in the first act or in the last, and nothing in the third, except a few bars here and there. But the whole of the second act needs to be re-done, and given relief, variety and more life. From a musical point of view, the cavatina for the woman could be retained, the duet with the tenor, and the other duet between father and daughter, despite the cabalettas!! (Open, o earth!) In any case, I don't have such a horror of cabalettas, and if a young composer were to appear tomorrow who could write any as worthwhile as, for example, 'Meco tu vieni, o misera' or 'Ah perchè non posso odiarti', I would listen to them with all my heart and renounce all the harmonic sophistries, all the affectations of our learned orchestrators. Ah, progress, science, realism. . . . ! Alas, alas! Be as real as you like, but . . . Shakespeare was a realist, though he did not know it. He was an inspired realist; we are planning and calculating realists. So taken all in all, system for system, the cabalettas are still better. The beauty of it is that, in the fury of progress, art is turning backwards. Art which lacks spontaneity, naturalness and simplicity is no longer art.

Let's turn to the second act. Who could re-do it? How can we find someone? I have said that, in general, what this act needs is something to bring variety and a little animation to a drama which is too gloomy. How? For instance, should we include a hunting scene? It wouldn't be theatrical. A festival? Too ordinary. A battle with African corsairs? Not entertaining enough. Preparations for war with Pisa or with Venice?

In this connection I remember two magnificent letters by Petrarch, one to the Doge Boccanegra, and the other to the Doge of Venice, telling them they were about to take part in a fratricidal war, and reminding them that they were sons of the same mother, Italy etc. etc. This feeling for a united country of Italy as that time was sublime. All this is political, not dramatic, but an ingenious writer could turn it into drama very well. For example, Boccanegra, struck by this thought, wishes to follow the poet's advice. He calls together the Senate or a Privy Council and expounds the letter and its feeling. Horror on the part of all, speeches, anger, the Doge is even accused of treason etc. etc. The argument is interrupted by the abduction of Amelia. . . . I'm talking just for the sake of it. Anyway, if you find a way to adjust and smooth over the difficulties I've listed, I am ready to re-write this act.

Think about it, and let me have your reply.

[223]

*To Arrigo Boito*                                    *Genoa, 11 December, 1880*

[Arrigo Boito (1842–1918), poet and composer, had agreed to help with the revision of *Simon Boccanegra*. He was later to provide Verdi with the libretti of *Otello* and *Falstaff*. His *Mefistofele*, first produced unsuccessfully at La Scala in 1868, fared much better when revived in Bologna in 1875.

Ponchielli's only new opera to be performed at the Scala in 1880 was *Il figliuol prodigo*, but it did not reach the stage until 26 December. Verdi was presumably referring to a revival of an earlier work.]

Dear Boito,
   Either the Senate, or the Church of St Siro, or nothing.
   To do nothing would be the best thing. But reasons, not very

interesting, but of, so to speak, professional concern, prevent me from abandoning the idea of revising this *Boccanegra*, without at least trying to think of something. Among other things, it's in the interests of us all that La Scala should survive. Alas, this year's programme is deplorable! Ponchielli's opera was spendid, but the rest. . . . Ye Gods! There is one opera which could arouse great interest on the part of the public, and I don't understand why neither composer nor publisher wants it to be performed. I'm speaking of *Mefistofele*. The moment is propitious, and you would be rendering a service to art and to all of us.

The act that you have sketched out to take place in the church of St. Siro is really superb in every way. Fine for novelty, fine for historical colour, fine in the scenic and musical aspects; but it would be too much of a chore for me, and I don't think I could tackle so big a job. So, regretfully giving up the idea of this act, let's consider the scene in the Senate which, as written by you, I've no doubt will be a great success. Your criticisms are just, but immersed as you are in much more elevated work, and having *Otello* in mind, you are aiming at a perfection it would be impossible to achieve. Setting my sights lower, I feel more optimistic than you, and I do not despair. I agree that the table is wobbly, but with minor adjustments to a leg or two, it can be made to stand. I agree, too, that there are no characters in this work (they're rare enough, anyway) to make you exclaim 'How true to life.' Nevertheless, it seems to me that we can get something out of the characters of Fiesco and Simone.

So let's agree, then, on this finale to the act, with the Tartar ambassador, the Petrarch letter, and so on. We are expert enough in the ways of the theatre to be able to make something of this. If you have time, start work immediately, and I shall try to collect up my notes, and patch them together. Then . . . we shall see.

With affection, yours

[224]

*To Opprandino Arrivabene*                                   *Milan, 25 March, 1881*

[The revised *Simon Boccanegra* was produced at La Scala on 24 March, 1881. The leading man was the French baritone Victor Maurel, later to create both Iago and Falstaff for Verdi. The other principal singers were Anna d'Angeri (Maria), Francesco Tamagno (Gabriele), Federico Salvati (Paolo) and Edouard de Reszke (Fiesco).]

Even before last night's performance, I could have told you, if I had had the time to write, that the broken legs of this old *Boccanegra* seemed to me to have been properly mended. The outcome of last night confirms me in my opinion. So, a very good performance on the part of everybody, and stupendous on the part of the leading man. A splendid success.

I shall stay here for the second and third performances, and on Monday I shall leave for Genoa. If the success diminishes in these two evenings, I shall write to you.

[225]

*To Opprandino Arrivabene*                                    *Genoa, 2 April, 1881*

Dear Arrivabene,

From what they write to me, it seems that *Boccanegra* on the fourth night got as much applause as on the others, if not more. And what particularly pleases me is that the theatre was even more crowded than for the second and third performances. Everyone was terrified there would be a disaster as at Nice.

Now, if you want to know, I can tell you that *Boccanegra* will be able to tour round the opera houses like its sisters, despite having so sad a subject.

It is sad because it has to be sad, but it is interesting. In the second act, the effect seems to diminish somewhat, but I should not be surprised if, in a different theatre, the finale of the first act were to go less successfully, and if this second act were to have a success like the others. That's the way of the world . . . or, rather, of the theatre! We shall see and, meanwhile, we shall hope.

[226]

*To Opprandino Arrivabene*                                         *27 May, 1881*

[Verdi refers to the French occupation of Tunis. Quintino Sella had been a fellow Deputy.]

Dear Arrivabene,

You've gone mad!! Put on *Boccanegra* in Paris?!! Do you think that, at this moment, I want to go to that country? Never! Not for all the money in the world! We have been dealt a heavy blow! Oh, it's true the fault is ours, completely ours! It's impossible to believe that there could ever have been, could be now, or could exist in the future a government so—— (supply your own epithet). I'm not talking about the Reds, the Whites or the Blacks . . . the type and the colour don't matter to me. I look at history, and I read about great deeds, great crimes, great virtues in governments by a king, or by priests, or even in republics. It makes little difference to me, I repeat. But what I do require is that those who are in charge of public affairs should be citizens of great ability and spotless integrity. So I despair when I see a man of the highest ability, strong-minded, of the greatest intelligence and unquestioned honesty, a man like Sella, ridiculed, lied about and insulted. I repeat that I despair of my country. I have a sad presentiment about our future! The Left will destroy Italy!

And it will be the French who give us the *coup de grâce*! The French have never liked us, and, since '70, they have detested us. They will easily find a pretext! . . Who will defend us then? the Cairolis? The followers of Garibaldi?

We have offended all the other nations. They will let anything happen to us, and simply laugh! . . .

Let's not talk any more of it. You can see I'm not in a cheerful mood, and I don't feel like talking about anything else . . . I will tell you, however, that I am and will always be yours


[227]


*To Domenico Morelli*                               *Sant'Agata, 24 September, 1881*


Dear Morelli,

'What do you say to it?' are the last words of your letter. I say that if my name were Domenico Morelli, and I wanted to do a scene from *Otello*, in particular that scene where Otello faints, I wouldn't rack my brains about the stage direction which says 'Before the fortress'. In the libretto which Boito has done for me, this scene takes place inside, and I'm very pleased with it. Inside or outside, it doesn't matter. You don't have to be so scrupulous about this, because in Shakespeare's time production was . . . left in the lap of the Gods! Nothing could be better than to have Iago dressed in black, just as his soul is black. But I don't understand why you should dress Otello as a Venetian! I know very

well that this general, who was in the service of the great city, and
known as Otello, was none other than a Venetian called Giacomo
Moor. But if Signor William wanted him to be moorish, that was the
way Signor William thought about it. You can hardly have Otello
dressed as a Turk, but why not have him dressed as an Ethiopian,
without the usual turban? The question of Iago's type of figure is more
serious. You would like him to be slight, with limbs (as you put it)
somewhat under-developed and, if I have understood you rightly, one
of those sly, malevolent, so-to-speak pointed faces. If that's how you see
him, then do him that way. But if I were an actor, and had to play
Iago, I would rather have a long, thin face, thin lips, small eyes close
to the nose like a monkey, a high, receding forehead, the head well
developed at the back. An absent-minded air, nonchalant, indifferent to
everything, sceptical, a cutting manner, speaking good and evil lightly
as though he were thinking of something else, so that, if anyone were to
say to him in reproof: 'What you say, what you propose, is monstrous', he could reply: 'Really . . . . I didn't think so . . . Let's talk
no more of it' . . . . Someone like that could deceive everybody, even,
up to a point, his own wife. But a malicious little fellow puts everyone
on his guard, and deceives no one! Amen. You can laugh, just as I am
laughing at all this chatter.! But whether Iago is short or tall, whether
Otello is Turk or Venetian, do as you want to, and it will be fine. Only
don't think too much about it. Get on with it, get on with it . . .
quickly . . Greetings from my wife and myself, and believe me yours
affectionately

[228]

*To Opprandino Arrivabene*                    *Genoa, 17 March, 1882*

[The phrase from Rossini's *Il barbiere di Siviglia* to which Verdi refers is:

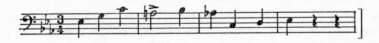

On the subject of musical opinions, we must be open-minded, and for
my part I am extremely tolerant. I admit the melodists, the harmonists, the boring, and those who desire at all costs to be bored for the
sake of good taste. I admit the past, the present, and I should admit

the future if I knew it and thought it good. In short, melody, harmony, declamation, a decorated vocal line, orchestral effects, local colour (a word used most frequently, but one which usually serves to cover up a lack of thought), these are only means. Make good music with these means, and I will admit everything and every genre. For example, in *Il barbiere*, the phrase, 'Signor giudizio per carità' is neither melody nor harmony. As declamation it is true and good, and so it is music. . . . Amen.

[229]

*To Opprandino Arrivabene*                                  *5 June, 1882*

[Berlioz had been dead since 1869.]

. . . . Berlioz was a poor, sick man, furious with everyone, bitter and malicious. His talent was very great and acute. He had a feeling for instrumentation, and he anticipated Wagner in many orchestral effects. (The Wagnerites don't admit it, but it is so.) He lacked moderation. He lacked the calm, and what I call the equilibrium, to produce complete works of art. He always went to extremes, even when he created something praiseworthy.

His success for the time being in Paris is in great part justified and merited, but reaction has even more to do with it. He was so badly treated when he was alive! Now he is dead! Hosanna!!

[230]

*To Baron von Hoffmann, General Intendant of the Hofoper, Vienna*
                                  *Sant'Agata, 31 October, 1882*

Greatly flattered by your esteemed letter, I make it my duty to confirm what Signor Ricordi has written to you. It is true that I am working on a revision of *Don Carlos*, reducing it to smaller proportions and to four acts. It is a tedious and rather lengthy job, but it will not be long before it is completely finished, and you can then have it performed whenever you think it opportune and convenient.

I should be extremely grateful for the telegram you promised me after the first performance of *Simon Boccanegra*.

Please accept, dear Baron, my respectful greetings, and believe me your devoted servant

[231]

*To Giulio Ricordi*                                         *14 February, 1883*

[Wagner died in Venice on 13 February, 1883.]

The card is very good, the first as much as the second. Perhaps better, the more subtle R.B., but take care in making the rule that the ink is not too dark.

----

Sad. Sad. Sad!
Wagner is dead!
When I read the news yesterday I was, so to speak, horrified! Let us not discuss it. It is a great individual who has disappeared! A name that leaves the most powerful imprint on the history of art!

[232]

*To Francesco Florimo*                                  *Genoa, March 12, 1883*

[Verdi is referring to letter 167.]

Dear Florimo,
    I have just this moment read in the Gazzetta Musicale published by Ricordi that you have a book coming out in April, which will include 'a letter from Giuseppe Verdi to Florimo concerning the Naples Conservatorium . . .'
    You know that I have never liked publicity, and this announcement has made me feel rather upset. I should be grateful if you would delete this letter from your book. If this is not possible, please be kind enough to add a note, making my own wishes clear in this matter.
    With best wishes for your health, yours sincerely

[233]

*To Giulio Ricordi*                                        *Genoa, 24 March, 1883*

Dear Giulio,

I read this morning in *Fanfulla*: 'Maurel has also told us that Verdi is preparing some greater surprises for the musical world, and some great lessons for the young musicians of the future with his Iago etc. etc.'

God save me from it!

It has never been, and it will never be, my intention to give lessons to anyone. I admire, without being prejudiced by schools, everything that pleases me. I do as I feel, and I leave everyone else to do as they wish.

For the rest, I have not yet written any of this *Iago*, or rather *Otello*, and I don't know what I shall do next.

Believe me always yours.

PS. Put together a little article to this effect, or publish my own words in some big newspaper as soon as possible.

[234]

*To Countess Maffei*                                    *Sant'Agata, 11 October, 1883*

[Carlo Tenca, for many years editor of the literary magazine, *Rivista Europea*, had died. The Countess Maffei's affair with Tenca had been one of the reasons for her separation from Andrea Maffei in 1846. The liaison lasted until Tenca's death.]

Dear Clarina,

I have heard about everything: I admired your courage, and can well understand, now that the first nervous agitation is past, how heavy you must feel in spirit. There are no words that can bring comfort in this kind of sorrow. And I will not utter to you that one stupid word, 'courage', a word which has always aroused my anger when directed at me. You don't need that. You will find comfort only in the strength of your soul and the firmness of your spirit.

My 'widow's mite' will not be lacking. I thank you.

I wish you good health in your mountains, and advise you to lay in a good provision of it to bring back with you to Milan.

Ah, good health, good health! I haven't thought about it for many years, but I don't know what it will be like in the future.

My years are really beginning to be too many, and I think. . . . I think that life is such a stupid thing, and, what is worse, a useless thing. What do we do? What shall we do? Taking it all together, there is only one answer, humiliating, and extremely sad:

NOTHING!

Farewell, my dear Clarina. Let us avoid and push as far away as possible all sad things, and let us keep as well as we can.


[235]

*To Giulio Ricordi*                    *Genoa, 13 December, 1883*

[Verdi's revised, four-act version of *Don Carlo* in Italian was first performed at La Scala, Milan, on 10 January, 1884. The cast included Abigaille Bruschi-Chiatti (Elizabeth), Giuseppina Pasqua (Eboli), Francesco Tamagno (Carlo), Paul Lhérie (Rodrigo), Alessandro Silvestri (Philip) and Francesco Navarrini (Inquisitor).]

Dear Giulio,

'Maestro Verdi will come to Milan to preside over the rehearsals of *Don Carlos* and, naturally, to attend, we hope, the first performance' etc. etc. These words in the *Corriere* place me under an obligation to the public which can now claim that I must go, for Heaven's sake, and make the usual *pirouettes* and display my beautiful face!! I wrote a pencilled note yesterday on a card from Fiorenzuola to have this *réclame* denied before I come to Milan. I repeat the same thing today. It is not possible, as you ask, to produce *Don Carlos* on the 2nd or the 3rd or . . . It's impossible to fix a date. Don't tell me the singers have been studying the opera, and that they know it. I don't believe any of it. Two things they certainly don't know: clear enunciation and how to keep in time, qualities essential in *Don Carlos*, more so than in any of my other operas.

Faccio can begin, or continue, to rehearse *Don Carlos*. I recommend, indeed I demand, that he insist above all on enunciation and keeping in time. This may be mere pedantry on my part, but what do you expect? The opera is written like that, and must be performed that way if you hope to have any success with it.

As soon as I have seen a denial of the aforementioned article, I shall come to Milan and, allow me to repeat it to you, *shall attend only a few rehearsals, principally of the new pieces.* Nothing else, nothing else! Absolutely *nothing else*!!! Farewell, farewell.

[236]


*To Giulio Ricordi*                                    *Genoa, 26 December, 1883*

You know as well as I do that there are people who have good sight,
and who like bold, strong and genuine colours. Others have a slight
cataract and prefer dirty, faded colours. They are in fashion, and I don't
disapprove of following fashion (because we must keep up with the
times), though I would prefer to see it accompanied always by a little
judgment and good sense. In other words, neither the 'past' nor the
'future'. It's true that I said 'Let us turn to the past', but I meant that
past which is our base, fundamental and solid. I meant that past which
has been forgotten by modern exuberance, and to which we are bound
to return sooner or later. For now, let's allow the tide to rise. The dams
can be built later.

Peppina thanks you for the piano pieces by Burgmein[1] that you sent.
And I thank you for the four Spanish songs which are beautiful and
characteristic. My compliments, stay healthy and have a good holiday.


[237]


*To Opprandino Arrivabene*                                    *12 February, 1884*

Good operas have always been rare at all times, but now they are almost
impossible. Why, you ask? Because we write too much music, because
we try too hard, because we search about in the dark, and neglect the
sun! Because we exaggerate the importance of mere trimmings!
Because we create *big* works rather than great works! And from the big
are born the small and the baroque! There we are. Farewell, and believe
me always yours


[238]


*To Franco Faccio*                                    *Genoa, 27 March, 1884*

[The 'chocolate project' almost came to grief when Verdi read a newspaper
article in which Boito was quoted as having said he regretted not being able

---

[1] Giulio Ricordi composed salon pieces under the pseudonym of Burgmein.

himself to set it to music. Over-sensitive and easily depressed, Verdi wrote to
Boito's friend, the composer and conductor, Franco Faccio.]

Dear Faccio,

Just a word or two to thank you for your very kind help to the
person I recommended to you, and a further word or two about something that concerns me personally.

The *Pungolo* reports this sentence from the Naples *Piccolo*: 'Concerning *Iago*, Boito says that he took on the subject almost against his will,
but that, when he had finished it, he was sorry not to be able to set it to
music himself...' Admittedly, one should not place great value on such
words, spoken at a banquet; but unfortunately they may give rise to
comment. It might be said, for example, that I had forced his hand in
choosing this subject. So far, little harm has been done, and, after all,
you know how things are. The worst of it is that Boito, in regretting
that he could not set it to music himself, naturally leads one to suppose
that he feels there is little chance of my setting it as he thinks it should be
done. I'm perfectly willing to admit this, I admit it completely, and this
is why I turn to you, as Boito's oldest and most faithful friend, and ask
you to tell him orally, not in writing, when he returns to Milan, that,
without the slightest resentment, without any suggestion of rancour, I
shall send his manuscript back to him intact. What's more, as this
libretto is my property, I offer it to him as a gift, if he should wish to
set it to music. If he accepts it, I shall be happy in the hope of having
contributed, and been of use, to the art we all love.

Forgive me for troubling you in this way, but it is a matter to be
treated confidentially, and there is no one better able to do so than
yourself.

Keep in good health, and believe me yours

[239]

*To Arrigo Boito*                               *Genoa, 26 April, 1884*

[Boito had apparently been misreported (see letter 238), and hastened to
reassure Verdi of his desire to collaborate with him: 'This theme and my
libretto are yours by right of conquest. You alone can set *Otello* to music.
All the dramatic creations you have given us proclaim this truth.' (Piero
Nardi: *Vita di Arrigo Boito*, p. 494.)

This letter is Verdi's reply to Boito. *Nerone* is the opera Boito had begun
work on in 1862. He spent the rest of his life trying to complete it, and it was

not until 12 October, 1916, that he was able to write the word 'end' at the
close of the fourth act, signing it 'Arrigo Boito and Chronos'. When he
died in 1918, his score still needed some revision. This was undertaken by
Toscanini who conducted the première of *Nerone* in 1924.

When Cesare and Luzio were editing the *Copialettere* for publication in
1913, Boito was still alive. They asked him for his comment on the 1884
newspaper report, and he made this reply: 'When *Mefistofele* was first performed in Naples at the San Carlo in 1884, the professors at the Conservatorium gave a banquet for me, at which, asked about the *Otello* libretto, I
expressed sentiments very different from those so grossly interpreted by the
*Piccolo*.']

Since you do not accept my offer, the letter I wrote to Faccio has no
longer any significance or purpose.

I read hastily, and I never believe anything I see in the newspapers. If
something strikes me, I stop, consider, and try to get to the bottom of
it and see it clearly. The question fired point-blank at you like that at
the Naples banquet was at the very least . . . a strange one, and no doubt
it contained hidden meanings that the words did not express. Perhaps
you could not have answered differently, I agree. But it is also true that
the overall effect of this interview could easily cause the kind of comment that I alluded to in my letter to Faccio.

But it is pointless now to talk about this at length, since you absolutely refuse to accept my offer, which, believe me, was made without
the slightest trace of irony.

You say 'Either I shall finish *Nerone* or I shall not finish it' . . . For my
part, I will repeat the same words concerning *Otello*. There has been
too much talk about it! Too much time has gone by! I am too old, and
I have seen too many *years of service*!! So there is no need for the
public to tell me too plainly that they have had enough!

My conclusion is that all this has led me to cool off somewhat on
*Otello*, and has stiffened the hand that had begun to sketch a few bars.

What will happen next? I don't know. Meanwhile, I am delighted
with this explanation we have had, which would perhaps have been
even better given immediately you had returned from Naples; I press
your hand affectionately, and send you greetings from Peppina. Yours

[240]

*To Opprandino Arrivabene*            *10 June, 1884*

[Puccini (1858–1924) had had his first opera, *Le villi*, produced at the Teatro dal Verme in Milan, on 31 May, 1884. Boito was one of the people on whose recommendation the opera was produced.]

I have heard the composer, Puccini, well spoken of. I have seen a letter in which he is highly praised. He follows the modern tendencies, which is natural, but he adheres to melody, which is neither modern nor antique. The symphonic element, however, appears to be predominant in him. Nothing wrong with that, but one needs to tread cautiously here. Opera is opera, and the symphony is the symphony and I do not believe it's a good thing to insert a piece of a symphony into an opera, simply for the pleasure of making the orchestra perform.

I say this just for the sake of talking, so don't consider it important. I'm not certain that what I've said is true, though I am certain I've said something that runs contrary to the modern tendencies. Every age has its own imprint.

History will tell us later which epoch was good, and which bad. Heaven knows how many people in the seventeenth century admired that sonnet of Achillini, 'Sudate, o fuochi', more than a canto of Dante![1]

Meanwhile, whatever is good or bad, keep healthy and good-humoured for a long time.

[241]

*To Countess Maffei*       *Sant'Agata, 2 September, 1884*

[Giulio Carcano had died on 13 August, 1884.]

Dear Clarina,

My dear Clarina, I had not expected to receive such very sad news. Peppina had known it for 24 hours and wanted to keep it from me, but

[1] Claudio Achillini is remembered today for one extravagantly bad line in a sonnet to Louis XIII:
'Sudate o fuochi a preparar metalli.'

H

the post brought me your letter yesterday, as well as the family announcement with black edges. Without my making a speech, you will understand how great is my sorrow at the loss of our saintly friend. When I saw him in Milan a few months ago, I found him greatly weakened, but I hoped he would recover and I might see him again. Poor Carcano! I remember his last words to me. It was a Sunday, and I went to see him at about one o'clock and found him preparing to go out. 'Don't stand on ceremony', I said, and he replied with adorable simplicity 'My dear Verdi, I am still one of those who go to Mass on Sunday'. Fine, fine, and I accompanied him right up to the door of the church. 'Until next time', and now I shall never see him again. Alas, alas!

You are quite right: when you get to our age, every day brings nothing but emptiness and, by the time you are resigned to that, you no longer have the strength of our last saint (really the last) to bear it without complaining . . . But don't let me upset you, my dear Clarina.

And so he is gone, and leaves his good wife and his daughter deeply afflicted. Oh, he will certainly be mourned for a long time by his fellow-citizens, as a distinguished and most elegant poet, but infinitely more by his friends and his family who know his immense goodness, and his public and private virtues.

My poor Carcano! Farewell!!

And you must keep calm and healthy. Take comfort in remembering that all your friends, near and far, all send their good wishes to you.


[242]


*To Countess Maffei*                                          *Genoa, 17 December, 1884*

Dear Clarina,

I am very happy to have your news, and I thank you for the poem by Maffei, to whom my greetings. His sonnet is beautiful and true, but the evil it deplores does not frighten me too much. Whatever happens had to happen. It's in the nature of things.

Dilettantism (inevitably fatal in all the arts), in its craze for novelty and fashion, chases after the vague and the odd, and pretends to be enthusiastic, when it is in fact bored by foreign music which it calls 'classical' and 'great music'. Why 'classical' and 'great music'? Who knows? And journalism (that other scourge of our times) praises this music in order to attract attention, and to make people think it understands what others do not understand, or understand less fully. The crowd, undecided and unsure of itself, remains silent and follows behind. Despite this, I repeat, I am not afraid, convinced as I am that this current art which is so artificial, and often intentionally odd, is not in conformity with our nature. We are positivists, and very largely sceptics. We don't believe much, and we can't continue to believe for long in the oddities of this foreign art which lacks naturalness and simplicity. After all, art which lacks naturalness and simplicity is simply not art. Inspiration is necessarily born of simplicity. Sooner or later, some youngster with genius will appear and get rid of all this, and give us back the music of our finest times, avoiding the faults but profiting from the discoveries of the moderns. By which I mean . . . the good discoveries!

Oh, what idle chatter! And to what purpose? Forgive me!

[243]

*To Sig. Frignani, Busseto*            *Genoa, 16 February, 1885*

[The Frignanis were a Busseto family. The architect was probably a son of the Dr Frignani who practised in Busseto.

The hospital referred to was the one Verdi had built at Villanova, near Sant'Agata. 'He himself was largely responsible for the simple design, carefully supervised the construction of the building, engaged the medical staff, and enlisted the aid of Giuseppina in choosing furniture and linen. The hospital had been badly needed in the district, and, after it opened on 6 November, 1887, all its beds were quickly filled. Verdi refused to have his name on the façade, which to this day has the single word "Ospedale" imprinted upon it. The hospital still serves the local community.' (Osborne: *The Complete Operas of Verdi*, p. 433.)]

Dear Frignani,

In yesterday's *Corriere della sera* I read, among a few lines on the hospital, this sentence: 'It is said that Verdi intends to restore the church of Sant'Agata, which is falling to ruins.'

I have never had any such intention, as you know. Nevertheless, I shall not contradict this sentence, although I consider it a piece of pressure to make me feel in some way obliged to do something I have no intention of doing.

I turn to you, as the architect of the church, so that you may warn those involved not to expect anything from me.

Believe me, always yours

[244]

*To Opprandino Arrivabene*                          Milan, 2 May, 1885

I have received the issue of *Ars nova* that you sent me. I have not had time to read it closely but, as far as I can see, it's one of the usual articles which don't discuss but simply pronounce sentence, with an incredible intolerance. On the last page, amongst other things, I read this sentence: 'If you believe that music is the expression of feelings of love, or sorrow etc., then give it up, it is not for you.'

And why should I not believe that music can express love, sorrow etc.?

The writer begins by citing as the *non plus ultra* of music Bach's Mass, Beethoven's Ninth Symphony and the Pope Marcellus Mass. For my part, I shouldn't be surprised if someone were to tell me that Bach's Mass, for example, is a trifle dry, that the Ninth Symphony is badly written at some points, that, among the nine symphonies, there are movements he prefers that are not in the Ninth, and that there are even better things in Palestrina than the Pope Marcellus Mass.

Why not? If someone is of this opinion, why can he not be one of the elect, and why must music not be for him?

For the rest, I'm not arguing. I don't know anything, and I don't want to know anything. I do know, however, that if the new man of *Ars nova* should be born amongst us, he will renounce many things from the past, and despise the pretentious utopias of the present, which do no more than substitute new defects and conventions for the defects and conventions of a time past, cloaking emptiness of thought in a baroque garment.

And now, keep well and happy, which is much more important to us than *Ars nova*.

[245]

*To Victor Maurel*                          Genoa, 30 December, 1885

[Victor Maurel, the distinguished French baritone (1848–1923), was renowned for his performances in Verdi and Wagner, as well as in the French repertoire. He had sung Boccanegra in the première of the revised version at La Scala of *Simon Boccanegra*, in 1881, and Verdi admired him sufficiently to promise, during one of the rehearsals, to write the rôle of Iago in *Otello* for him. Maurel wrote to Verdi from Paris on 22 December, 1885, to remind him of his promise, having read in the newspapers that 'Verdi a fini son Yago!'

Maurel did, in the event, create Iago, and later the title rôle in *Falstaff*.]

*Otello* is not yet completely finished, as has been said, but it is certainly well advanced. I am not in a hurry to complete the work, because I have not yet given any thought, nor am I giving thought now, to its being performed. The condition of our theatres is such that, even if one obtains a success, the cost of singers and production is so exorbitant that the impresario almost always has to face a loss. So I don't want the remorse of being, with my opera, the cause of anyone's ruin. Thus things remain suspended between heaven and earth like Mahomet's tomb, and I haven't come to any practical decision.

Before ending this letter, I should like to clear up and explain a misunderstanding. I do not believe I ever promised to write Iago for you. It is not my habit to promise a thing unless I am really sure I can fulfil it. But I may very likely have said that the rôle of Iago was one which perhaps no one would interpret better than you. If I said that, I'm willing to confirm what I said. That, however, does not include any promise; it is simply a desire, which may well be realized as long as no unforeseen circumstances arise.

For the present, then, let us not speak of *Otello*. Allow me, my dear Maurel, to send you my best wishes for the new year and to call myself your sincere admirer

[246]

*To Francesco Tamagno*                              *Genoa, 31 January, 1886*

[The tenor, Francesco Tamagno (1851–1915), who had sung Gabriele in the revised *Boccanegra* at La Scala in 1881, wrote to Verdi on 29 January, 1886, to stake his claim to the rôle of Otello. He was to create the rôle at La Scala in 1887.]

Dear Tamagno,

I am delighted to hear of the satisfaction it would give you to perform the rôle of Otello. At the same time, however, I cannot help but complain against people making promises in my name which they had no right to make.

I have not finished the opera, and, even if I had finished, I am not absolutely certain whether to have it performed. I have written it purely to please myself, without thoughts of publication, and at this moment neither I nor anyone else can say what is likely to happen. There is another difficulty and that is to find artists suited to the respective rôles. You know better than I do that, however fine an artist may be, he is not suited to every rôle, and I don't want to sacrifice anyone, least of all you! So then, my dear Tamagno, (but this must remain a secret between us), when you return from Madrid, let us meet in Genoa or somewhere, and then we can talk, and discuss it all frankly and honestly. For now, nothing is decided, particularly since, I repeat, I have neither finished nor formally promised to produce the opera.

I thank you for the very courteous letter you have written me, and take this opportunity of assuring you of my feelings of esteem and cordiality. Yours


[247]

*To Antonio Ghislanzoni*                                            *Sant'Agata, 22 July, 1886*

[The Countess Maffei died of meningitis in Milan on 13 July, 1887. Verdi hurried to her side, but she had already lost consciousness, and did not recognize him.]

Dear Ghislanzoni,

Thank you for your kind remembrance which is always dear to me, and for the book you sent me. It is something of yours, so I shall read it with the greatest pleasure. This kind of collection of humorous and satirical essays should make a splendid book. It is the sort of book that is rare nowadays.

You will have heard about poor Countess Maffei! I arrived in Milan in time to see her die! Poor Clarina! So kind, so considerate and so sensible. Oh, I shall certainly never forget her! We had been friends for 44 years!! Poor Clarina!!


[248]

*To Arrigo Boito*                                                        *1 November, 1886*

[Verdi sent this note to Boito the day he completed work on *Otello*.
The opera was given its première at La Scala, Milan, on 5 February, 1887,

with Romilda Pantaleoni (Desdemona), Francesco Tamagno (Otello), Victor Maurel (Iago), Francesco Navarrini (Montano) and Giovanni Paroli (Cassio). The conductor was Franco Faccio.]

Dear Boito,
  It's finished!
  Greetings to us . . (and also to Him!!)
  Farewell,

G. Verdi

[249]

*To the President of the International Circle of Art, Rome*
*Genoa, 7 March, 1887*

Various newspapers have announced that the 'International Circle of Art' is asking people to sign a petition to invite me to Rome for the first performance of *Otello*.

I do not know if this is true but, in case it is, allow me to warn you, Mr President, that I cannot, I must not go to Rome in these circumstances.

My presence, artistically speaking, would be perfectly useless. So why should I go to Rome? . . . . To display myself? To make them applaud?

My feeling is not one of modesty or of pride, it is a feeling of personal dignity, which it would be impossible for me to put aside.

If things are as people say, I request you, Mr President, to try to prevent this petition from being sent to me, in order to spare me the very great sorrow of having to refuse.

Please forgive me for bothering you with this letter, and believe me, with the greatest esteem for you, Mr President, Your devoted servant

[250]

*To Franco Faccio*                    *Sant'Agata, 19 August, 1887*

[Faccio was at the Teatro Grande, Brescia, where he conducted performances of *Otello* in the summer of 1887. Verdi refers ironically to Tamagno and Maurel, the Otello and Iago of the Scala première. Their rôles were sung in

Brescia by G. Oxilia (Otello) and Paul Lhérie (Iago). The Brescia Desdemona
was Adalgisa Gabbi.

In the *Copialettere* the date of this letter is misprinted as 1884. Verdi did not
finish composing and orchestrating *Otello* until December 1886.]

Thank you for your telegram and letter, and my apologies for not
having replied immediately. Although not writing operas, I am extremely busy putting things in order, my business affairs, so that I can
then . . . stay at rest if I can!

Well, then. *Otello* is making its way even without its *creators*?!!
I had got so used to hearing people proclaim the glories of those two
that I was almost persuaded they had written this *Otello*. Now you
deprive me of my illusions by telling me that the Moor is going well
without these stars! Can it be possible? I also hear, which consoles me
greatly, that in Brescia, as also in Venice, the first night audience was
sparse. 'Good', I said to myself. 'This is a progressive public'. It was
an act of distrust against a composer of the past, an act which revealed a
passionate and praiseworthy desire for the new and the beautiful.
All that was logical and just. But now, if they go to the theatre and
applaud, o dear, my arms drop to my side . . . It is I who lose all
faith! Finally, I can only congratulate both of us on having made this
crazy boat sail!

Farewell, my dearest Faccio! I greet you from Peppina, who is well,
and I press your hand affectionately.


[251]


*To Arrigo Boito*                              *Sant'Agata, 5 October, 1887*

[The Government was considering the foundation of a School of Choral
Singing, and Boito asked Verdi to suggest six names of composers, from
which one might be chosen as a name for the proposed school. As well as
such famous and fairly obvious choices as Palestrina, Victoria, Carissimi
etc., Verdi's list contained some lesser-known names. Luca Marenzio (1553–
1599) is one of the greatest Italian masters of the madrigal; Gregorio Allegri
(1592–1652) is chiefly known today for his famous Miserere, which the
fourteen-year-old Mozart is said to have copied down while the Sistine
Chapel choir was singing it; Antonio Lotti (1667–1740) wrote both church
music and operas; Leonardo Leo (1694–1744) is remembered both for his
sacred music and his comic operas; Niccolo Jomelli (1714–1774) was
primarily an opera composer, though he also wrote for the church. For

many years he was Kapellmeister to the Duke of Württemberg at Stuttgart. Niccolo Piccinni (1728–1800) worked for many years in Paris, where he was considered a great rival to Gluck. *La cecchina* may not have been 'the very first opera buffa', but, for years after its first performance in 1760, it was extraordinarily popular. Its libretto by Carlo Goldoni is based on Samuel Richardson's novel, *Pamela*. Pietro Alessandro Guglielmi (1728–1804) wrote more than 100 operas, as well as a few oratorios and cantatas.]

Dear Boito,

If you will promise neither to praise nor to blame me for it, I send you the first few names that have occurred to me. There are more than six, but there are so many good ones in that period that it was difficult to make a choice.

Sixteenth century: xPalestrina (*in primis et ante omnia*)
　　　　　　　　Victoria
　　　　　　　　Luca Marenzio (a very pure writer)
　　　　　　　　Allegri (of the *Miserere*)
　　　　　　　　and many other good composers in this century, with the exception of Monteverdi, who was not a good part-writer.

Beginning of the
seventeenth
century:　　　　　xCarissimi
　　　　　　　　Cavalli
Later:　　　　　Lotti
　　　　　xAlessandro Scarlatti (who is also
　　　　　　　　　　　　　wonderful harmonically)
　　　　　　　　xMarcello
　　　　　　　　Leo

Beginning of the
eighteenth
century:　　　　　xPergolesi
　　　　　　　　Jomelli
Later:　　　　　xPiccinni (the first, I believe, to write Quintets, Sextets etc. Composer of the very first opera buffa, *Cecchina*)

If you really want only six, the ones marked with x are those I prefer. In later times, we have Paisiello,
　　　　　　　　Cimarosa
　　　　　　　　Pietro Guglielmi etc. etc., then
　　　　　　　　Cherubini etc.

I wish you success; if you succeed you will have done good work, because the young (though not in the schools, which can be very good) are studying the wrong things. They've already gone off the tracks. If music is what you define it as (and it is), one needs really to know a little about prosody and declamation, and be cultured enough to know what one needs to know. If you really understand what you are setting to music, when you have to shape a character or portray a passion, you won't so easily be led astray by bizarre extravagances, whether vocal or instrumental.

Let me know how you are, what you are doing and have been doing. In haste, I press your hand. Peppina sends her greetings.


[252]

*To V. Rocchi*                                    *Genoa, 6 January, 1888*

[Sig. Rocchi wrote from Perugia on 5 January, 1888, tersely requesting Verdi to return a book he had sent the previous October. 'In my time,' said the offended author, 'such salutation was a courtesy, and a reply was obligatory.']

Sir,

You allow yourself to give me a lesson which I do not accept. I, on my part, ask you:

Why do you, who do not know me, send me one of your works? And why should I bother myself with it?

Do you know how many letters, pamphlets and compositions I receive every day from all parts of the world? And am I obliged to answer them all?

You say it's my *duty* to, but I say on the contrary that it's an absolute *tyranny* to expect me to waste my time replying to all the letters, and examining all the pamphlets and compositions, almost all of which are insipid and worthless.

PS. I don't remember your book very well; but, if it was sent in August, it will be at my house in the country, whence I shall have it sent to you as soon as I return there.

[253]

*To Giulio Ricordi*                                    *Sant'Agata, 9 November, 1888*

[The year 1889 marked the fiftieth anniversary of Verdi's first produced opera, *Oberto*, and newspapers had already begun to mention plans to honour the composer with a series of performances of his works. Despite Verdi's irritable letter to Ricordi, La Scala revived *Oberto* on the anniversary date, 17 November, 1889.]

Dear Giulio,

I see that the newspapers are talking about a jubilee!! Lord, have mercy on me! Of all the useless things in the world, this is the most useless, and I, although I've performed many useless deeds, detest them most of all. What's more, it's impracticable, and an imitation of foreign customs which encourages suppositions which are not true, cannot be true, and must not be true. In theatres organized on the repertory system, this jubilee, though still useless, would at least be feasible, but with us it can only result in something wretched and ridiculous. Ye Gods, they are even talking of singers! Uhmmm!! Patti, who is a true artist, might perhaps, in a moment of madness, say yes; but the others, although they wouldn't say no, would discover at a convenient moment other obligations, some of them in a world unknown. You, who are a man of good sense when you want to be, must write a line or two squashing this idea as useless and impracticable. As an authority on these matters, you will be believed. And, if you find it necessary to make some concession, why not suggest that the jubilee be held fifty days after my death. Three days are enough to consign men and things to oblivion! As the Great Poet says: 'O Heavens! died two months ago, and not forgotten yet?'[1]

I put my trust in the three days. Farewell.


[254]

*To Sig. Borrani, President of the Hospital at Villanova*
                                            *Genoa, 16 January, 1889*

[See note to letter 243.]

[1] *Hamlet*, Act III, Sc. ii.

I think it only right to let you know that I have received reports of the Hospital at Villanova, which I hope are not true. This is what is said:

1. That the food is sparse.

2. That the wine is even more sparse (yet the cellar is well stocked.)

3. That the milk costs more than it's worth, and that it is poor in quality.

4. That the oil is of the poorest kind, and so both food and lighting are affected.

5. That the management wanted to buy rice which was half rotten, and black, home-grown pasta.

6. That funeral expenses are being charged, even to people who haven't the means to pay.

7. Many other things which, for the sake of brevity, I shan't mention.

From far away, I can't comment on this, and I can neither believe nor disbelieve it. In any case, these reports distress me very much, and make me feel I have not achieved the purpose I had in mind when I decided to dedicate part of my wealth to endowing this charitable institution.

I believe the Hospital is well provided for, and that there should be no need to practise economies. But, to tell you the truth, rather than hear these complaints, I would prefer to close down the Hospital and say no more about it.

I hope, however, that none of this is true, and that you will be able to reassure me immediately with a few words.

With all esteem, Your devoted servant

[255]

*To Arrigo Boito*                                    *Genoa, 17 February, 1889*

[See note to letter 253.]

Dear Boito,

I am writing by chance in the hope that this letter will reach you.

I don't like disturbing you from your work, even for a few minutes, but I feel the need to talk to you about this . . . Jubilee, which I think is pointless, and which can't have any good result.

Putting aside my ego, my modesty, my pride and all the rest, I ask you, what are you going to do on this evening of November 17th? A concert of various opera excerpts?

Heavens above, what stinginess!

Performances of some of the operas?

But then, if the performances are to have any significance, you will have to put on at least three or four: the first, the last, and one of the others. The last two would not be difficult to perform, but the first would be difficult and expensive, as it has four leading rôles (which require good singers), would have to be newly produced, and would need as many rehearsals as a new opera. And the result? I ask you if our public, whose tastes are so different from those of fifty years ago, would have the patience to listen to the two long acts of *Oberto*! They would either sit in silence, politely bored (which is always humiliating) or make their disapproval known! In that case, it would no longer be a festival but a scandal!

As for the other idea of founding a perpetual endowment by national subscription, I ask you again: What amount do you think could be collected?

A small sum would only serve to give one of the usual competition prizes which are of no help either to art or to the prize-winner. A sum which would be really useful (but difficult to raise in these critical times) would have to be considerable, considerable enough for the capital to provide interest sufficient to help a young man with his first experiments in the theatre. And then, what difficulties we discover.

1. To guarantee to an impresario the worth of the opera.
2. To guarantee to the composer a decent performance.

To assure this, there is no other way but to appoint a committee or two, and I'm not even sure of that. One committee to judge libretti, the other to judge music. It will be easy to find the first, and I'll give you their names now: Boito and two others. The second is more difficult: Boito again . . . and who else? What's more, these committees would have to take on the thankless and difficult task of strictly supervising the production and the musical performance, so that the impresario was not able to put the opera on as a *pis aller*, for the sole purpose of pocketing the money.

And here another question arises. Where would the opera be performed? Milan? But if it is by national subscription why shouldn't the Romans, for example, demand it be in Rome, the Neapolitans in Naples, and so on?

So many difficulties! I've finished. I conclude by saying to you what I have been telling Giulio since the beginning of last November: that this Jubilee, beside being highly distasteful to me, is neither useful nor practical. If you are of my opinion, then at the first opportunity, since you can speak with greater authority than the others as both poet and composer, you should suggest that this is all quietly allowed to die down. Don't leave them any excuse to revive it. You would be doing a good deed.

Treat this letter as confidential. There is nothing in it that I could not say aloud, but there is no point in letting people hear my voice in this any further. I've wasted a little of your time, and I'm sorry for it. Forgive me. Farewell. Peppina greets you, and I press your hand. Affectionately yours

[256]

*To Arrigo Boito*                                           *Genoa, 11 March, 1889*

Dear Boito,

Thanks for having prepared the ground with Mr Edwards.[1] It will be easier for me now to reply in the negative. In Shakespeare's country we are reproved for having left out the first act. But they don't criticize your Iago's Creed. Anyway, you are the principal culprit who will have to do penance for that creed. Now the least you can do is set a Catholic creed to music, in four parts, in the style of Palestrina. But not until you have finished writing that . . . which I dare not name.[2]

[257]

*To Arrigo Boito*                                     *Montecatini, 7 July, 1889*

[Boito had sent Verdi the synopsis of a libretto on Shakespeare's *The Merry Wives of Windsor*, to be called *Falstaff*, and the composer was delighted with it. He wrote immediately to Boito with detailed comments, and the following day, 7 July, wrote again to express one or two doubts about the project.]

I said to you yesterday that I would write to you today, and I keep my word at the risk of annoying you.

[1] Mr Edwards is probably H. Sutherland Edwards (1829–1909), English writer on music, particularly Italian opera, whose books include *A History of the Opera (from Monteverdi to Verdi)*, *Rossini*, and *The Prima Donna*. For many years he was a music correspondent on the Continent, and was also for a time the music critic of the *St James's Gazette*.

[2] Boito's unfinished opera, *Nerone*.

As long as one is roaming freely in the world of ideas, all is well, but when one puts a foot on the ground in a practical act, doubts and discouragements arise.

In sketching out *Falstaff*, have you ever thought of the enormous number of my years? I know well that you will reply, exaggerating the state of my health, good, very good, robust. . . . And that may be; nevertheless you will agree with me that I could be accused of great temerity in taking on such a task. What if I were to become fatigued? What if I were not able to finish the music? Then you would have wasted time and labour in vain. I would not want that, for all the gold in the world. The idea is intolerable to me, and all the more intolerable if you, in writing *Falstaff*, should, I won't say abandon, but find yourself neglecting your *Nerone*, or postponing its production. I should be blamed for the postponement, and thunderbolts of public ill-will would fall on my shoulders!

Now, how could these obstacles be surmounted? Have you a good argument to oppose mine? I hope so, but I doubt if you have. So let's think about it (and take care to do nothing that would interfere with your own career), and if, on your side, you can find a reason, and I find some way of casting ten years from my shoulders, then . . . . what joy, to be able to say to the public:

> Here we are again!!
> Come and see us!

Farewell, farewell

[258]

*To Franco Faccio, Lyceum Theatre, London      Montecatini, 14 July, 1889*

[Faccio conducted the first performance in England of *Otello*, at the Lyceum Theatre, on 5 July, 1889.]

From telegrams, and from Muzio, I have had news of the London *Otello*. Now you confirm this news, and it pleases me, although, at my age and in the present condition of our musical world, a success means nothing. You speak of a 'triumph of Italian art'!! You deceive yourself! Our young Italian composers are not good patriots. If the Germans, stemming from Bach, arrive at Wagner, they are doing as good Germans should, and that is fine. But for us, descendents of Palestrina, to imitate Wagner is to commit a musical crime, and we are doing something useless, even harmful.

I know that many good things have been said of Boito, and this gives me the greatest pleasure, for praise of *Otello* in Shakespeare's country is worth a great deal. So then, a greeting; I am very happy, and I press your hand.


[259]


*To Giulio Ricordi*                              *Sant'Agata, 4 November, 1890*

[Muzio was seriously ill in a Paris nursing home. Knowing the end was near, he had written to Verdi asking his old friend to be his executor, and apologizing for the 'piccola noia'. 'I shall leave for another world shortly, full of love and friendship for you and for your dear, good wife.' He died on 27 November. See also note to letter 262.]

At the moment, my head is good for nothing, and I can hardly collect my thoughts. Poor Muzio wrote these precise words to me on October 25th: 'I have put my affairs in order.' I know he is an orderly man, and would certainly have thought of everything. Nevertheless, if there is anything lacking, please ask Sig. Pisa, in these sad circumstances, to do on my behalf anything that should be done, and in the most convenient manner.

Peppina and I are absolutely desolate. If I weren't 77 years old, and the season so cold . . . but I am 77!!!

Farewell.


[260]


*To M. Érard*                              *Busseto—Sant'Agata, 7 November, 1890*

[The Érards were an Alsatian family who established firms to manufacture musical instruments, particularly harps and pianos, both in London and Paris. The founder was Sebastien Érard (1752–1831).

Verdi wrote this letter in French.]

Some months ago, M. Bossola of Genoa was entrusted with sending to the House of Érard in Paris, on my behalf, one of my pianos which needed repairing.

I understand that this piano has been returned to Genoa, perfectly restored—Maestro Bossola has just written to me—and I know also that the House of Érard has refused to accept any compensation for its expenses or its labour. I am embarrassed, and at the same time deeply grateful, for this courteous act. The work was lengthy and not easy, and my gratitude to the House of Érard must be equally lively and constant.

Please accept this expression of my gratitude and respect.


[261]

*To Marquess Gino Monaldi*                    *Genoa, 3 December, 1890*

[Gino Monaldi was an art critic, and the author of several books on Verdi, among them *Verdi e le sue opere* (1887); *Verdi, 1839–1898* (1899); *Verdi nella vita e nell' arte* (1913); and *Il Maestro della rivoluzione italiana* (1913).]

What can I tell you? For forty years now I have wanted to write a comic opera, and for fifty years I have known *The Merry Wives of Windsor*. However, the usual 'buts' which pop up everywhere have always prevented me from doing what I wanted. Now Boito has swept away all the 'buts', and has written me a lyrical comedy which is unlike all others.

I am enjoying myself writing the music. I have no plans for it, and I don't even know if I shall finish it . . . I repeat, I'm enjoying myself . . .

Falstaff is a deplorable creature who does all kinds of bad things, but in a diverting manner. He's a real character. There are so many different characters! The opera is completely comic!

Amen. . . .


[262]

*To Maria Waldmann*                          *Genoa, 6 December, 1890*

[Giuseppe Piroli (see note to letter 146) and Emanuele Muzio (see note to letter 259) had both died in November, 1890, while Verdi was at work on *Falstaff*.]

Dear Maria,

Your letters, my dearest Maria, are always a consolation to me. But the last one was a cure, a balm, in this moment which is so sad for me. Within a fortnight, I have lost my two oldest friends!

Senator Piroli, a learned, frank, sincere man, of a rectitude not to be equalled. A constant friend, unchanging in sixty years! Dead!!

Emanuele Muzio whom you knew when he conducted the orchestra in Paris for *Aida*. A sincere friend, devoted to me for fifty years. Dead!!

And neither of them as old as I!! Everything is ending! Life is a sad business!

I leave you to imagine the sorrow I felt, and still feel! And that is why I am not very keen to continue writing an opera which I have begun, but not got very far with. Pay no attention to what you read in the newspapers. Will I finish it? Will I not finish it? Who knows? I am writing without a schedule, with no object in mind, other than to pass a few hours each day,

Peppina's health and mine are well enough, despite our years.


[263]

*To M. Roger*                                        *Genoa, 16 December, 1890*

[Roger was the Agent Général in Paris of the Société des Auteurs et Compositeurs Dramatiques. Verdi wrote to him in French.]

On the tenth of every month you normally send me my royalty statement through poor Muzio. Alas, poor Muzio, that fine man, that friend of my youth, whose loss I deplore, is unfortunately no longer with us!

I beg you, M. Roger, to send me the November statement. Address it simply to Maestro Verdi, Genoa, Italy.

Please accept my best compliments.


[264]

*To Giulio Ricordi*                                        *1 January, 1891*

And now we come to *Falstaff*. It really seems to me that all these plans are crazy, quite crazy! Let me explain. I began to write *Falstaff* purely to pass the time, without preconceived ideas, without plans. I repeat: *to pass the time*! Nothing else! But now the talk that is going on, and the proposals that are made, however vague, the words they extract from you, will all turn into obligations and undertakings which I absolutely refuse to accept. I said to you, and I repeat: 'I am writing to pass the time.' I told you that the music was about half finished, by which I meant to say, 'half sketched out'. By far the greater part of the work is still to be done, the assembling of the parts, revision and adjustment, as well as the instrumentation which will be extremely fatiguing. To cut a long story short, the whole of 1891 will be insufficient time to finish it. So then, why make plans and undertake obligations, however indeterminately worded? Furthermore, if I thought myself in any way bound, even in the slightest, I would no longer feel *à mon aise*, and wouldn't be able to work well. When I was young, despite ill-health I was able to stay at my desk for ten or twelve hours, working constantly. More than once, I set to work at four in the morning and continued until four in the afternoon, with only a cup of coffee to sustain me, working without a break. I can't do that now. In those days, I was in command of my health and my time. Now, alas, I am not. So, to conclude: the best thing to say now, and in the future, to everyone, is that I cannot and will not make the slightest suggestion of a promise in connection with *Falstaff*. If it is to be, it will be, and it will be as it is to be!

The *Perseveranza* said it was publishing a supplement on *Falstaff* on January 1st. This supplement hasn't arrived here. Would you be kind enough to send it to me? So much has already been said about this *Falstaff*, and not very well said. Who knows whether the *Perseveranza* may not have found something good to say?

[265]

*To Ambroise Thomas*                                      *Genoa, 23 January, 1891*

[The French composer Ambroise Thomas (1811–1896), whose operas *Mignon* and *Hamlet* are still occasionally performed, had been Director of the Paris Conservatoire since 1871.

Léo Delibes, successful French composer of opera and ballet (1836–1891), had died in Paris on 16 January. In 1881, he had become a professor of advanced composition at the Conservatoire.

Verdi wrote this letter in French.]

My dear Maestro,

Having been away from Genoa for a few days, it was not until I returned that I heard of the death of the much lamented Delibes.

As I know how interested you were in that valiant artist, I address myself to you, sir, to express to you my sincere condolences. The loss of this composer is doubly regrettable for, with his brilliant qualities, he greatly honoured French musical art.

Please accept, dear Maestro, as well as my regrets for poor Delibes, this expression of the great esteem in which I hold you, and of my feelings of devotion.

[266]

*To Countess Negroni-Prati*                                   *Genoa, 8 March, 1891*

[The Countess Giuseppina Negroni-Prati (1824–1909) (see note to letter 25) was a daughter of Emilia Morosini. She had married Count Negroni-Prati in 1851.]

Dear Signora Peppina,

We arrived yesterday evening fairly well. Peppina was suffering a great deal from very strong pain in the knees, but, with the cure prescribed by Todeschini, I hope the acute pain will go, and that she will be, at the very least, as well as she was before.

And you too are having your afflictions? I can only say that sorrows are the daily bread of life, but when you reach a certain age they multiply with surprising force. They say you must put up with it, and take courage; but at the moment I'm too well provided with them, and they are huge and serious. I shall have to re-read Job to find the strength to bear them, though even he cursed mightily.

Courage, then, and onward as long as we can.

[267]

*To Arrigo Boito*                                             *Genoa, 26 April, 1891*

[Boito had been asked by a committee of the Milan Council to advise on the choice of a new chief conductor for La Scala.]

Dear Boito,

I must leave at once for Sant'Agata on business, so I can't come to Milan now. Our bags are already being packed, tomorrow morning the servants will depart, and the day after tomorrow at seven in the morning we shall leave, in order to be at Sant'Agata by three in the afternoon.

In any case, I could not be of much use to you regarding the appointment of a conductor for the Scala orchestra. As I seldom go to the theatre, I don't know the best conductors. However, in my opinion you oughtn't to have a competition. A conductor should be judged *on the rostrum.* Those who are said to be the best are the two Mancinellis[1] and Mascheroni.[2]

I believe I told you that Luisa Cora came to visit Peppina one day, and told her that her husband would renounce all the riches of Madrid and London, if he could find a permanent, respectable, and well-paid position here.[3] We discovered later, however, that this was only Luisa's wish. Now then, if you can't have Luigi Mancinelli, the best would be Marino Mancinelli or Mascheroni. Of these last two, I should choose the second for many reasons, and above all because I'm told he is both a hard worker (and a worker is necessary for La Scala), and a conscientious man without particular sympathies and, better still, without antipathies.

But it isn't enough just to choose a conductor. He must be independent of the management, and he must assume complete musical responsibility in the eyes of the Committee, the management and the public.

Further, you need a good chorus master, who should always be subordinate to the musical director, and who not only is to look after the musical instruction, but also to concern himself with the staging, as though he were a régisseur. At all the performances, either the chorus master or his assistant should put on a costume and sing with the chorus.

Further, you need a stage manager, always subordinate to the conductor.

Finally, a clear and exact programme should be drawn up, so that the operas will not be selected haphazardly (as they have been in recent

---

[1] The two Mancinelli brothers, Luigi and Marino, were both conductors. Luigi (1848–1921) began his professional career as a cellist. He also composed operas and instrumental music.

[2] See note to letter 277.

[3] Luisa Cora's husband was the conductor, Egidio Cora.

years), nor the singers who perform them. Get the right singers for the operas, or the right operas for the singers.

Two permanent companies should be formed complete, for the entire season, and they should be engaged in time to have two operas ready at the opening of the season. Thus you avoid putting the public in a bad humour, which can sometimes last right through the season.

All this could go well, but . . . . there is always a 'but'. Everything depends on finding the MAN!

I shall write to you from Sant'Agata. Farewell from Peppina and myself.

Yours affectionately

[268]

*To Giulio Ricordi*                                                  *Sant'Agata, 9 June, 1891*

You're joking, my dear Giulio! I'm glad to know you're in such a good humour! What? Six or seven months ago no one was giving a thought to *Falstaff* or the Venerable Old Man of Sant'Agata. The theatre was carrying on as usual, with fiascos and successes (fewer of the latter), and now you come and tell me that the theatre would not be so badly off without a subvention!! Enough of these jokes. This is not the time to talk of *Falstaff*, which is coming along slowly, but I am more convinced than ever that the huge size of La Scala would ruin its effect. In writing *Falstaff*, I have given no thought to theatres and singers. I have written it on my own behalf to please myself, and I believe that, instead of La Scala, it ought to be put on at Sant'Agata.

I repeat, let's discuss it orally.

[269]

*To M. Bertrand*                                               *Sant'Agata, 27 October, 1891*

[Bertrand was, at this time, Director of the Paris Opéra.
  This letter was written in French.]

M. Bertrand

While feeling very honoured that you should ask me to produce *Otello* at the Opéra, I cannot give an immediate answer, as I do not know all the singers who would take part in the opera. You mention Mlle Melba who, I know, is an artist, but I do not believe that the rôle of Desdemona is right for her kind of talent.[1] And who would the Otello be? That is most important. For the rest, you tell me I could see M. Maurel here some time. In that case, I should be able to discuss the matter at some length with him. I shall be in Milan in a fortnight, and later in Genoa. In either of these two towns I am easy to find.

Meanwhile, please accept my best compliments

[270]

*To Giuseppe Gallignani*            *Milan, 15 November, 1891*

[Giuseppe Gallignani, choir-master at the Duomo in Milan, had recently been appointed Director of the Parma Conservatorium.]

Dear Gallignani,

I am sorry not to have been able to attend your concerts of sacred music. I know they were very successful, and I am glad to hear it. I am particularly glad that you performed the music of Palestrina, the true Prince of sacred music, and the Eternal Father of Italian Music.

Palestrina cannot compete with the very daring harmonic discoveries of modern music, but, if he were better known and studied, we might write in a more Italian manner, and might be better patriots (in music, I mean).

Continue in Parma with the good work you began here, and you will be performing an artist's task. Yours

[271]

*To Camille du Locle*            *Genoa, 9 December, 1891*

[Auguste Mariette, who wrote the synopsis on which *Aida* was based, had died in 1881. His brother Edouard published a posthumous biography of him, in which he claimed that the *Aida* plot had been plagiarised from a novel he, Edouard, had written, called *La fiancée du Nil*. The manuscript, according to Edouard, had lain on a table in the tent he shared with his brother for six

---

[1] The Australian soprano Nellie Melba (1861–1931) had made her Paris début at the Opéra in 1889, as Ophélie in Thomas's *Hamlet*.

weeks in Upper Egypt in 1886, during the time Auguste was sketching out
his *Aida* synopsis.]

Dear Du Locle,

On arriving here last night, I found your letter of 3rd December.

Ricordi has, in fact, mentioned to me this claim of Mariette's brother.
I'm struck with amazement!

You know the facts of the matter. I believe it was you yourself who
gave me those four little pages of print, bearing no author's name.
You told me the Khedive wanted an opera written on the subject
because it was Egyptian. At the time, I imagined that the author of those
pages was the Khedive himself. All I knew of Mariette Bey was that
he had undertaken to design the costumes etc. That was all. There is
nothing else I can say, and I don't know what kind of claim this Mariette can have.

And now here we are in the middle of winter, and I nourish the
hope of seeing you here sometime, whether passing through, or on a
visit. It would be a great pleasure to Peppina and myself to greet you
here. I hope we shall, and I press your hand affectionately.


[272]

*To Hans von Bülow*                                              *Genoa, 14 April, 1892*

[The German conductor Hans von Bülow (1830–1894) had been in Milan at
the time of the first performances of the Requiem, eighteen years earlier, and
had written scathingly of the work, without having heard it. On 7 April,
1892, von Bülow wrote to Verdi asking the composer to 'hear the confession
of a contrite sinner', and expressing his extreme admiration for 'the Wagner
of our dear allies!']

Illustrious Maestro Bülow,

There is no trace of sin in you, and there is no need to talk of repent-
ance and absolution!

If your earlier opinions were different from those you profess today,
you were very right to make them known; I would never have complained of it. Besides, who knows? . . . perhaps you were right then.

Nevertheless, your unexpected letter, coming from a musician of
your worth and importance in the artistic world, has given me great
pleasure! Not out of personal vanity, but because I am made to see

that really superior artists judge without being prejudiced by school, nationality or period.

If the artists of north and south exhibit different tendencies, it is good that they are different! They should all hold on to the character of their own nation, as Wagner very truly says.

You are fortunate in still being the sons of Bach! And we? We, on the other hand, sons of Palestrina, used to have a great tradition, and our own! Now it has become bastardized, and ruin threatens us.

If only we could go back to the beginning!

I am sorry not to be able to attend the Musical Exposition in Vienna, where I would have not only the good fortune to find myself among so many distinguished musicians, but also the particular pleasure of shaking your hand. I hope that my weight of years will be taken into account by the gentlemen who so kindly invited me, and that they will forgive my absence.

Your sincere admirer

[273]

*To Giulio Ricordi*                    *1892 [between April and September]*

Dear Giulio,

We are wasting our time writing letters and telegrams: I tell you none of you has a leg to stand on. I, on the other hand, am in my own house, and determined not to permit others to evict me from my property.

There is no point in pressing me to put on *Falstaff* to please others.

1. Do not pay exorbitant fees to the artists.
2. Do not pay for rehearsals.
3. I am not obliged to put on *Falstaff* wherever other people want me to.

For the first, I don't want the management to lose money on my new opera even though it's a success.

Second, paid rehearsals would set a disastrous precedent . . . . . created, really, by *Falstaff*.

Third, let us suppose that, for example, after the Scala performances I thought it useful to make a few changes. Could I allow a singer to come to me then, and say, 'But I have no time to wait, because I want to perform this opera in Madrid, or London etc. etc.'? Heavens above,

that would be too humiliating. I have told you that you haven't a leg
to stand on, and what's more, neither has Maurel.[1] Can't he see that, if
the libretto of *Falstaff* is good and the music tolerable, and he gives a
really first-rate performance in the rôle, he will gain the upper hand
without making demands that are useless to him and offensive to
others?

Madame Maurel, who is an intelligent enough woman, but a little
irritated at present, will say I am wrong, but in a month's time she will
say, 'Le Maitre avait raison'.

Let's keep things in their proper places. I only ask to remain in charge
of my own belongings, and not to ruin anyone. And let me add that, if
it came to a dilemma, if I had either to accept these conditions or burn
the score, I should light the fire immediately, and send Falstaff and his
fat belly to the stake myself. Farewell, Farewell, Yours

PS. These claims have already startled me sufficiently.


[274]

*To Giulio Ricordi*                          *Sant'Agata, 18 September, 1892*

Dear Giulio,

I am returning the vocal score with a few observations, and the
libretto.

There are a few mistakes in the score which I'd like you to note, so
that they can be corrected.

The libretto looks even more beautiful now that it's printed. On page
20, the verse 'Giungi in buon punto' is missing . . . . and it's in the vocal
score! On page 21, they have crossed out the word 't'offro' . . . perhaps
because I forgot to write it, but it should be there. Speak to Boito
about it.

You have some queries on the entrances and exits of the characters.
Nothing is easier or simpler than this production, if the designer
produces a set as I imagined it when I was writing the music. Nothing
more than a huge, real garden with paths, masses of bushes and plants
here and there, so that, as they want to or need to, people can hide,
appear and disappear, as the drama and the music require.

Thus, the men will have their own place, and, later on, can invade

[1] Maurel wanted the rôle of *Falstaff* to be his alone for a certain period after the first
performances in Milan.

that of the women, when the women are no longer on the stage. And the women, at the end of the act, can occupy the place where the men were. Don't say anything to anyone about these blotchy sketches of mine, not even Boito, but make sure that Hohenstein's ideas conform reasonably to mine.

Tito tells me that Hohenstein proposed putting the screen close to the wings, 'because it is natural and logical for a screen to lean against the wall'. Not at all. Here, we're dealing with a screen which, so to speak, takes part in the action, so it has to be put where the action requires it to be, particularly since, at one point, Alice says 'More this way, more that way, more open still' etc. etc.

For the second act finale, the stage must be completely empty, so that there is room for the action, and so that the principal groups can be distinctly seen: those round the screen, round the basket, and by the big window.

I repeat: don't say anything to anyone, because I don't want to impose on anyone, and I would rather that the others found something better . . . but on the other hand I shan't approve of anything unless I am persuaded by it completely and in every way.

18 September

I was about to post this, when I received your letter of the 17th. Both Peppina and I are truly grieved by the misfortune in your house, and we share your sorrow and that of your Giuditta. What can one say but 'Be patient and have courage'?

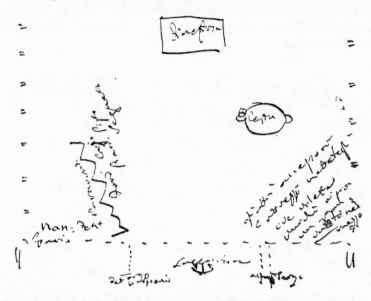

As for *Falstaff*, I don't want to put myself under an obligation to anyone, but I can promise the publishing firm of Ricordi to present *Falstaff* at La Scala during the carnival season of 1892–93, if the company we alluded to has been assembled, reserving to myself the right to replace anyone found unsatisfactory at rehearsals. The first performance of *Falstaff* can take place at the very beginning of February, if I have the theatre completely at my disposal from the 2nd January, 1893.

Concerning the rehearsals, everything must be done as on other occasions. The dress rehearsal alone must be managed differently from other times. I've never been able to get a dress rehearsal at La Scala conducted the way it ought to be in that theatre. This time I shall be inexorable. I shall not complain, but if anything goes wrong I shall immediately leave the theatre, and you will then have to withdraw the score.

Let's leave Paroli where he is. The rôle of Bardolph is perhaps more important than that of Caius.[1] With the flute it's simply a small matter: D flat with E flat. The bass clarinet in A is used in *Otello* as well. It's especially needed in *Falstaff* in the third act, when the women sing that kind of Litany: 'Domine fallo casto'. A hunting horn is required here also: an old hunting horn, without valves, with a low A

---

[1] Giovanni Paroli (tenor) sang Caius in the first performances of *Falstaff*.

flat. The instrument should have a rather full tone, so that it will sound more easily. That's enough for now.

Has Pasqua been engaged?[1]

And what about Cesari? . . . As far as I know, he won't be at La Scala this year.[2]

Let me know about a few of these matters. Farewell farewell, yours

PS. I am sending with this the vocal score of the first act, with a few changes. Please add these to the original score, so that I can correct what errors there are.


[275]

*To Giuseppina Pasqua*                    *Genoa, 5 November, 1892*

[The passage in Act II, Scene ii, to which Verdi refers is sung to the words:

'Infine, per farla spiccia, vi crede entrambe innamorate cotte delle bellezze sue. E lo vedrete . . .']

Dear Signora Pasqua,

As I promised, I am sending you the first proofs of *Falstaff*, which I should like you to return to me when you have read them.

In the second scene of act two, there is a solo which presents some difficulties to be cleared up before the music is printed. It has to be performed as quickly as possible, in a *mezza voce*, in one breath, enunciated clearly and distinctly. I send you these few bars: let me know what you think. My greetings to your husband.


[276]

*To Minister Ferdinando Martini*            [*Milan, 11 February, 1893*]

[Verdi's plea to the Minister was successful.]

I read in the *Perseveranza* an announcement that the title of Marquis is to be conferred upon me. I call on you as an artist to do all you can

---

[1] Giuseppina Pasqua (1855–1930), mezzo-soprano, sang Mistress Quickly.

[2] The comic bass Pietro Cesari was not engaged for the *Falstaff* première.

to prevent this. My gratitude will be much greater if I am not given the title.

*To Edoardo Mascheroni*                                *Genoa, 23 April, 1893*

[Edoardo Mascheroni (1857–1941), who was chosen to be the new conductor (see letter 267), and who conducted the first performance of *Falstaff* at La Scala in 1893, was a literary critic before he took up music as a profession. In his younger days he also composed a great deal. He was generally considered the leading Italian conductor of his day.

Mascheroni had lent Verdi 100 lire at the railway station in Rome, so that he could buy a ticket to Genoa. Verdi had forgotten to repay it.]


Dear Mascheroni,

'Ha! Ha! Ha! Ha! Ha! Ha!' I sang, just like the merry wives, when I read your letter!

Poor Farfarello . . . in addition to all that bother and fatigue, the danger of losing 100 lire as well!

Ha! Ha! Ha! Ha!

I sent a telegram to Giulio immediately, and he sent a telegram immediately to Nuti, who has perhaps already paid the debt. So that's it!

And you don't tell me anything about the internal happenings at the Argentina, not in the stalls but on the stage!!

Tell me about it next time!

A really wasted evening. That poor Piontelli will weep blood!!

Only 30 thousand lire!!!

And us? . . . And art . . . But what 'us' and what 'art'? We? We're poor extras with the job of beating the big drum until they say 'Quiet, there! . . .'

*Tutto nel mondo è burla.* . . .

*Ha! Ha! Ha! Ha!*

Giulio will send me the photographs and, just think, I shall send one immediately to Zanardelli, or, rather, I shall send it to you, if you are still in Rome.

My greetings to everyone on the stage who asks after me! You may not have to greet anyone!

I'm not going to pay you compliments (I've already done that), nor shall I say thanks, because I hope soon to be bothering you again!

[278]

*To Edoardo Mascheroni*                                    *Genoa, 27 April, 1893*

Dear Mascheroni,
    You are not the only privileged one! I made a huge blunder too.
    Don't laugh, because I am in danger of killing myself!
    Listen and be terrified!
    I wanted to be pleasant for once in my life, and I failed badly! . . .
I sent a portrait of myself to the proprietor of the Quirinale, and I
addressed it 'To Signor Bruni, proprietor of the Hotel Quirinale' etc.
etc. As Boito was leaving for Milan yesterday evening, he cried out in
a voice in F sharp, 'But it's Bruno, and he isn't the proprietor of the
Quirinale'. Ahhh!
    And who is? He didn't know! In a fury, I took a *revolver* (it was
made of chocolate) and fired it into my mouth!
    And I still live!!! Alas, alas!! AND I STILL LIVE!![1]

I throw myself into your arms. Save me, save me . . .
What can you do? . . . .
What must I do? . . . . .

[279]

*To Edoardo Mascheroni*                                   *Sant'Agata, 15 May, 1893*

Dear Mascheroni,
    Greetings, greetings and greetings again to you, *third* author of
*Falstaff*. Who will be the fourth? . . . Perhaps P.

[1] 'E vivo ancora' is a quotation from *Il trovatore*, but the present Editor has been
unable to trace the music.

And the fifth?

The merry wives.

Incidentally, I have received a most gracious and, what is more, very kind letter from Pasqua.

Thank her for me, and say that I shall answer her later, because I am now very busy putting the finishing touches to an opera in twelve acts plus a prologue and an overture which is as long as the nine symphonies of Beethoven put together. What's more, there is a prelude to each act in which all the violins, violas, cellos and double basses play a melody in octaves. Not like those in *Traviata, Rigoletto* etc. etc., but a modern melody, one of those beautiful ones with neither beginning nor end, which stay suspended in air like the tomb of Mahomet . . . I have no more time now to explain how the singers must perform the accompaniment, but I am hoping to find an inspiration and imitate the clashing of the cymbals with the singers' voices . . . I shall tell you about that another time. Farewell.

[280]

*To Edoardo Mascheroni*               *Busseto—Sant'Agata, 8 June, 1893*

Dear Mascheroni,

I declare that I did not receive your letters from Vienna. Your last one was from Trieste, and carried the date May 12th. After that, I heard almost nothing about *Falstaff,* and I'm not sorry about it. In the midst of my worries, I can imagine yours. As well as all the fatigue, the gossip, the whims, and the, as you say, the *insults*!! . . . . That is bad, very bad, but have no illusions. In the future, as well, you will find yourself in a similar atmosphere. The theatre is made that way, and has to be like that!

When the seasons are normal ones, they finish quickly. Some people go off to the right, others to the left, and so good-night. But, on a tour like this, the artists are together too much. They get to know each other too well. Everyone believes himself indispensable, everyone thinks in his turn that he has the sole right to applause. They become more and more excited, and end by believing themselves to be God knows what! There is no remedy for it! Perhaps, in moments of the greatest exaltation, one might try pouring a stream of cold water over their heads, inundating the stage, the boxes and everything else etc.

If you are waiting to come to Busseto until there is a performance of *La forza del destino*, you'll have quite a wait. The Bussetian finances do not run to theatrical performances. But even if we don't see each other at Montecatini, the house at Sant'Agata stands here immovable, and is always open to you.

[281]

*To Edoardo Mascheroni*                            *Genoa, 8 December, 1893*

Dear Mascheroni,

I have received the *Lombardia* you sent me, and in my view you were wrong to have written that letter.

Let them have their say, and then do what you want to do, to the best of your ability. An invisible orchestra! . . it's an idea so old that everyone, or almost everyone, has dreamed of it. I too would like an invisible orchestra in the theatre, but no half and half measures. I would want it *completely invisible.* To have the orchestra, which is part of an ideal poetic world etc. etc., playing in the middle of an audience which is applauding or hissing, seems to me the most ridiculous thing in the world. The tremendous advantages of an invisible orchestra would more than compensate for any inevitable lack of power and sonority, or the nasal, childish sound due to its playing, so to speak, with mutes.

But if a *completely invisible* orchestra is not possible, as has been demonstrated not only by the Opéra, but also by many German theatres, even Munich and Berlin (I repeat, *completely*), then any modifications you make will be puerile and will have no connection with art. And alas, I think that in thirty years from now, people will laugh at these discoveries of ours.

For my part, I don't believe your harmonic sounding-box under the orchestra will make any difference. Whether it's there or not, the sonority will remain the same.

I believe, too, that the orchestra, as it is now, is well placed and laid out. And I don't say this because I was guilty of having it set out thus for *Aida*, but because the instruments blend well, with the strings surrounding and enclosing the wind instruments in the middle, especially the brass. They would not blend so well if all the double-basses were to be put in a single row close to the stage. The brass would remain too exposed and would reverberate from the walls of the

I

theatre. If you leave the double-basses where they have been till now, you avoid the problem of their sticking out . . . But where would you put the harps which stick out even more?

And what about the conductor of the orchestra being so high up, with his stick always in motion, up, down, to the sides, all over the place?

You will have to dispose of the conductor of the orchestra!!!!

Holy Mother, fancy wasting time with these questions!

Indeed, there is but one sole and simple question. *Amen*! You devil, Farfarello, for making me waste half an hour writing this nonsense, which is quite useless.


[282]

*To Signora Zilli*                                              *Genoa, 15 December, 1893*

[The soprano Emma Zilli was the first Alice Ford in *Falstaff*.]

Dear Signora Zilli,

It's true, it's true!

A year has passed since the time we began studying *Falstaff*, first in my house, and then in a foyer at La Scala. A splendid time of enthusiasm, when we all breathed nothing but art! I remember our moments of joyful emotion, and also . . . . do you remember the third evening of *Falstaff*? I said my farewell to you all, and you were all a little moved, especially you and Pasqua. Imagine what that farewell was for me. It meant, 'We shall never meet again as artists!!!'

It is true that we did meet later, in Milan, in Genoa, in Rome. But memory always carried us back to that third evening, which meant: It's all over!

You are fortunate still to have so much of your career ahead of you, and I wish it may be always as splendid for you as you deserve.

Thank you for your good wishes for the holidays (good wishes a trifle premature, but they can be renewed later) which I reciprocate with all my heart.

[283]

*To Giuseppe Gallignani*                    *Genoa, 27 December, 1893*

[Gallignani (see note to letter 270) had asked Verdi to write a vocal piece on the occasion of the three hundredth anniversary of the death of Palestrina (1525–1594) which was to be commemorated in Parma.]

Do you mean it? No, no, you're joking. You must know well that I can't do anything else now, except to have myself sent off to the asylum. I'll just send you my widow's mite, and the rest is up to you.

I am very much in favour of the project to honour the everlasting father of Italian music.

I see that Count Lurani is one of the committee members. They say he is a passionate admirer of Bach, and of Bach alone! But they've been lying about him. If he's on the Palestrina committee, this proves he's a musician with an open mind, free from prejudice and bias. One can admire Bach and honour Palestrina, they are both the true and only fathers of the music of our age, from the 1600s till now. Everything derives from them.

And now, greetings, courage and good luck.


[284]

*To P. Gailhard*                            *Genoa, 31 January, 1894*

[Gailhard was the Director of the Paris Opéra. He had proposed to present *Otello* at the Opéra in Italian, with Eva Tetrazzini (Desdemona), Francesco Tamagno (Otello) and Giuseppe Kaschmann (Iago).

This letter was written in French.]

My dear M. Gailhard,

*Otello* at the Opéra, in Italian?!!! That surprises, indeed astonishes me!

I am not doubting your right to perform works at the Opéra in Italian. But, for me, when I think of the Opéra, your great National Theatre, I can't imagine having a work that is not French in this theatre! There is something astonishing, even shocking, in this association of the Opéra with an Italian work.

It's perfectly true that *Aida* was performed in Italian before it was done in French, but that's a different matter. When *Aida* was performed for the first time in Paris, it was in an exclusively Italian theatre.

If you are now to do *Otello* at the Opéra, I believe it should be done in a French translation.

I regret, my dear M. Gailhard, not being able to share your opinion, but that will not prevent you, I hope, from accepting my expressions of esteem and friendship.

[285]

*To Camille du Locle*                    *Genoa, 8 February, 1894*

[When *Otello* reached the stage of the Opéra on 12 October, 1894, it was in a French translation by Boito himself and Camille du Locle. The Otello was Albert Saléza.]

Dear Du Locle,

I am extremely embarrassed by our musical affairs in Paris. Affairs which concern not only me, but also my collaborators on *Otello* and *Falstaff*.

You know that *Falstaff* is shortly to be produced at the Opéra-Comique, and then later *Otello* at the Opéra. This is an important, and perhaps serious, matter, and we must not put a foot wrong.

In Paris they say that Carvalho is not the Carvalho he used to be, that his theatre is in a state of decadence, that his associates are distressed at his choice of operas, and at the slender receipts etc. etc. Some of this gossip has been echoed in the newspapers, which are spreading an atmosphere of gloom. You may say that all this is no concern of yours. For the moment that is true, but when they come to produce *Otello* it is in the interests of all, including you, that the atmosphere should not be black.

I no longer have any faithful friend in Paris who can give me truthful information about this situation. Nuitter is the person to whom I should turn, but I don't know him well enough, so I don't feel I have the right to question him on so delicate a matter. But you? You have for so many years been an intimate, sincere and faithful friend. Could you do it? Would you do it? If so, you would be doing me the greatest of favours, relieving me of much embarrassment, and making a decision that could not injure our artistic reputation or our personal dignity. Nuitter can

be assured of my word of honour, and of my silence and discretion.
I send you best wishes and greetings from Peppina.
Yours affectionately

PS. If you will do this, I recommend the greatest promptitude; there
is no time to lose.

[286]

*To Léon Carvalho    Opéra-Comique, Paris        Genoa, 11 February, 1894*

[Carvalho, Director of the Opéra-Comique, had written to Verdi on 5
February, 1894, announcing the names of the singers he had engaged for his
production of *Falstaff* in French, and suggesting Mlle L. Grandjean (soprano)
for the rôle of Alice. In a letter to Verdi written from Lisbon on 16 February,
Maurel, who was to sing Falstaff, gave his opinion of her:
'A sympathetic voice, especially in the upper register. The lower notes a
little weak. Vocally and musically already quite good, and will become
excellent when she knows the rôle by heart. From the scenic point of view I
can say nothing positive, not having seen her in costume. But, unless I am
greatly mistaken, you will find her perfectly satisfactory.'
    Verdi came to Paris for the première, on 18 April, 1894, of the French
translation by Boito and Paul Solanges. In addition to Maurel and Grandjean, the cast included Edmond Clémont (Fenton), Gabriel-Valentin Soula-
croix (Ford), Landouzy (Nanetta), Marie Delna (Quickly), Esther Chevalier
(Meg). The Conductor was Danbé.
    This letter was written in French.]

Thank you for your gracious letter. I saw Maurel yesterday, and he
repeated to me what you had already written.
    It is very, very kind of you, but you have forgotten one quite tiny
detail. You have forgotten that I am eighty years old!! At this age one
needs tranquillity and rest, and, though I feel relatively well, I can
no longer stand the work or the fatigue or the annoyances which are
an inevitable part of theatre life. I know what you will say on that point,
but I have been acquainted with the theatre for a long time (unfortunately), and I know what to expect. For the rest, I can only repeat
to you what I said to Maurel: 'If my health, my strength and my eighty
years allow it, I shall come to Paris'.
    Meanwhile, pay great attention to the rôle of Alice. First of all, of
course, it needs a beautiful and very agile voice, but, most important,

it needs an actress of personality, with a little of the devil in her. The rôle of Alice is not developed as much as that of Falstaff, but it's as important from the stage point of view. It's Alice who leads all the intrigues of the comedy.

Please accept, my dear M. Carvalho, my warmest compliments, and my wish that both you and I shall have good luck with *Falstaff*.


[287]

*To Riccardo Gandolfi*                                    *Montecatini, 5 July, 1894*

[Gandolfi was the librarian of the Florence Musical Institute. The Institute later became the present Conservatorio di Musica, whose library contains some rare works of the fifteenth and seventeenth centuries, and a great deal of German as well as Italian music. Gandolfi published a volume, *Biblioteca del Real Istituto Musicale di Firenze* in 1901.

Vincenzo Galilei (1520–1591), who was born and who died in Florence, was the father of the astronomer, Galileo Galilei. He composed madrigals and instrumental music, wrote theoretical works, and was also famous in his lifetime as a lutenist. *Il Conte Ugolino* is a cantata for solo voice, to words from Dante's *Divine Comedy*. Galilei is known to have sung it himself to viol accompaniment.

Verdi's request to examine Galilei's composition gave rise to rumours that he and Boito were planning an opera on Count Ugolino.]


Forgive me for troubling you, maestro, but could you please tell me if, at the Florence Musical Institute, or in the library, you have *Il Conte Ugolino* by Vincenzo Galilei? If you have, could I be allowed to see it? Would it be possible to have a copy made (at my expense, of course) which I could send back to you if the regulations of the Institute required it?

Please reply to me at Montecatini. Again, my apologies for troubling you.


[288]

*To the Director of the Deutsche Verlags-Anstalt, Stuttgart*
                                                    *Sant'Agata, 21 June, 1895*

[Verdi wrote this letter in French.]

Never, never shall I write my memoirs!

It's good enough that the musical world has put up with my notes for so long a time. I shall never condemn it to read my prose.

I thank you for the kind compliments in your letter, and for the offer you have made me, and ask you to accept, sir, my sincere compliments.


[289]

*To Camille Bellaigue*                  *Milan, 2 May, 1898*

[Camille Bellaigue (1858–1930) was a French music critic, whose *Verdi* was published in Paris in 1912. He had sent the composer a copy of his book, *Portraits et silhouettes de musiciens*.]

Dear Bellaigue,

I am late in replying because I wanted to read your book, *Les Musiciens* with the utmost attention. It is very beautiful, deeply thought out, and masterfully expressed. I shall talk to you only about music, simply music, and I join you in applauding the three giants, Palestrina, Bach, Beethoven. When I think of the miserably sparse melody and harmony of our times, Palestrina seems a miracle to me.

Everyone thinks as you do about Gluck, yet I can't help feeling that, despite his powerful dramatic sense, he was not very much superior to the best of his time, and musically inferior to Handel.

The silhouettes of Chopin, Schubert, Saint-Saens etc. etc. are most beautiful, and the St Cecilia is particularly splendid and elevated.

About Rossini and Bellini you say many things which may be true, but I confess I cannot help thinking that *Il barbiere di Siviglia*, with its abundance of real musical ideas, its comic verve and its truthful declamation, is the most beautiful *opera buffa* in existence. I admire *Tell* as you do, but how many extremely lofty and sublime things one finds in many other of his operas. Bellini is poor, it's true, in instrumentation and harmony, but rich in feeling and in his own individual melancholy. Even in his lesser-known operas, such as *La straniera* and *Il pirata*, there are long, long, long melodies, like nothing that was ever written before him. And what truth and power in declamation there is, in, for example, the duet before Pollione and Norma! And what nobility of thought in the first phrase in the introduction to *Norma*, followed a few bars later by another phrase,

badly orchestrated, yet no one has written anything more beautiful or celestial.

Take note, my dear Bellaigue, that I do not mean to pass judgments (Heaven forbid)! I am merely giving you my impressions.

You speak with great indulgence of *Otello* and *Falstaff*! The composer does not complain, and Giuseppe Verdi presses your hand in gratitude, and thanks you.

Please convey my respects and greetings to your very kind and gracious wife, and believe me your sincere friend.


[290]


*To Countess Giuseppina Negroni-Prati*          *Montecatini, 23 July, 1898*

For a good many days I've intended to reply to your most beautiful, very dear and very sad letter, but I really would not have been able to say anything more cheerful! . . .

Life is sorrow! When we are young, we are ignorant of life, and the beguilments of its movements, its distractions, its excesses fascinate us, so that we accept the little ups and downs without being aware of living. Now we are conscious of life, we feel it, and its sorrow oppresses and crushes us. What shall we do? Nothing. Just live, sick, tired, disillusioned until. . . .


[291]


*To Countess Giuseppina Negroni-Prati*          *Sant'Agata, 16 August, 1900*

[King Umberto was assassinated at Monza on 29 July, 1900. The Queen wrote a prayer which was printed in the newspapers:

O Lord, he sought to do good in this world. He felt rancour towards none. He always forgave those who acted evilly against him. He sacrificed his life to duty and to the good of his country. Till his last breath he struggled to fulfil his task. For his red blood which flowed from three wounds, for the good and just works he performed, merciful and just Lord, take him into your arms and grant him his eternal reward.

Some months before his death, King Umberto wished to offer Verdi the highest royal decoration, the Collare dell' Annunziata. To Verdi this was as bad as being Marquis of Busseto, an honour he had refused seven years earlier (see letter 276), and he refused. Curiously, at the same time he appears not to have demurred when the Austrian Emperor Franz Josef, who held Verdi in high personal regard, conferred upon him the highest Austrian honour for intellectual attainment.

The Countess Negroni-Prati wrote to Verdi, suggesting that he set the Queen's prayer to music. Despite his reply, the 87-year-old composer did, in fact, begin to sketch a few bars of a setting.]

Dear Signora,

I was so upset by the terrible tragedy of a few days ago, that I could not bring myself to answer your letter immediately.

As for what you propose, it was already my desire to do this, but I am rather ill, and it's impossible for me to take up any task.

In its pure simplicity, the Queen's prayer reads as though it was written by one of the early fathers of the church. Inspired by her deep religious feeling, she has found words of such truth and, as it were, primal feeling, that it would be impossible to equal them in music, which would appear affected and inflated. We should have to go back three centuries to Palestrina.

[292]

*To Professor Gerardo Laurini, Salerno*          *Sant'Agata, 18 August, 1900*

[Professor Laurini had also written to Verdi about the Queen's Prayer (see letter 291), enclosing his own rhymed verse version of the prayer, in the hope that Verdi would set it to music.]

Sir,

My age, my health and my doctors all forbid me to undertake even the smallest task. I should also add that I would not have set a rhymed version of this prayer to music. In the original prose of the Queen there is more sincerity, more spontaneity and a primal feeling which the verses would naturally lack.

[293]

*To Victor Sauchon*                                   *Milan, 17 January, 1901*

[Sauchon was an officer of the Societé des Auteurs et Compositeurs Dramatiques.

   This, the original of which is in French, is probably the last letter Verdi
wrote. He died ten days later, on 27 January, 1901.]


My dear M. Sauchon,

   I have received the cheque for 2691.80 lire for my composer's royalties up to the end of the year 1900. Please accept my thanks and my
compliments.

                              G. Verdi

# Personalia

Brief biographical notes of people mentioned in the letters. Notes on the recipients of letters will be found to accompany the first letter to each recipient.

*Marietta Alboni* (1823–1894) was taught the contralto rôles in the Rossini operas by the composer himself. Her voice is said to have been a rich, deep contralto of two octaves from g below middle c. Alboni once sang the baritone rôle of Carlo V in Verdi's *Ernani* in London, when the part was found to be too difficult for the baritone engaged.

*Marianna Barbieri-Nini* (1820–1887), soprano, created the rôle of Lady Macbeth in 1847, although Sophie Loewe was Verdi's first choice. Barbieri-Nini also sang in the première of *I due Foscari* (1844) and was the Gulnara in the first performances of *Il corsaro* in 1848.

*Luigia Bendazzi* (1833–1901), soprano, created the rôle of Maria in *Simon Boccanegra* at the Teatro Fenice, Venice, on March 12, 1857.

*Anna Bishop* (1810–1884), English soprano, was the wife of Sir Henry Bishop. She had an extremely colourful career much of which was spent travelling all over the world. She appeared in Naples in Verdi's *I due Foscari*, though earlier Donizetti had rejected her with, 'No, for Christ's sake, not la Bishop! Are you pulling my leg?'

*Virginia Boccabadati* (1828–1922), soprano, was one of three sisters who were all singers. Their mother was a well-known mezzo-soprano, Luigia Boccabadati.

*Giuseppina Brambilla*, contralto, was one of five sisters, all of whom were distinguished singers. The eldest, Marietta Brambilla, contralto, was perhaps the most famous of the five. Teresa Brambilla was Verdi's first Gilda.

*Giuseppe Capponi* (1832–1889) was the tenor in the first performances of Verdi's Requiem in 1874.

*Filippo Coletti* (1811–1894), baritone, sang the rôle of Gusmano at the première of *Alzira*. He also created the leading baritone rôle in *I masnadieri* (London, 1847). In 1880, he published a book, 'La scuola di canto in Italia'.

*Giuseppe Fancelli* (1833–1886), tenor, sang Radames in the Milan première of *Aida*. Verdi then wrote of him, 'Fancelli—beautiful voice but nothing else' (in a letter to Arrivabene. Alberti: *Verdi Intimo*).

*Jean-Baptiste Faure* (1830–1914), the distinguished French baritone, sang at the Paris Opéra for over fifteen years, during which time he created the rôle of Rodrigo in Verdi's *Don Carlos* in 1867. He published two volumes of songs, and two books on singing.

*Fedele Fenaroli* (1730–1818), composer, was a pupil of Durante and Porpora, and taught for several years at the Santa Maria Conservatorium in Naples. He wrote at least two operas as well as a large number of sacred compositions.

*Gaetano Ferri* (1816–1881), baritone, was thought to be a fine Carlo in *Ernani*, but the only Verdi rôles he created were secondary ones: Marcovaldo in *La battaglia di Legnano* (1849) and Briano in *Aroldo* (1857).

*Gaetano Fraschini* (1815–1887) was one of the most admired tenors of his time. He sang in the first performance of *Alzira*, and created other Verdi rôles, in *Il corsaro*, *La battaglia di Legnano*, *Stiffelio*, and *Un ballo in maschera*. Verdi was keen to have him for *I masnadieri* in London in 1847 but, though he sang in the company at Her Majesty's Theatre in that season, the tenor lead in *I masnadieri* was sung by Italo Gardoni.

*Erminia Frezzolini* (1818–1884), soprano, created the rôles of Giselda in *I Lombardi* (Milan, 1843) and Giovanna in *Giovanna d'Arco* (Milan, February 1845).

*Carlo Guasco*, tenor, sang in the first performances of *I Lombardi* (1843), *Ernani* (1844), and *Attila* (1846). Of his Ernani on the first night, Verdi wrote: 'Guasco had no voice at all, and was so hoarse that it was frightening.' (Letter 4.)

*Jenny Lind*, soprano, 'the Swedish nightingale', was born in Stockholm in 1820, and died in Malvern in 1887. She made her début in Stockholm in 1838 as Agathe in Weber's *Der Freischütz*, and later studied with Manuel Garcia in Paris. Her first appearance in London was in 1847 with Benjamin Lumley's company at Her Majesty's Theatre in Meyerbeer's *Robert le Diable*. Later in the same London season she appeared in Verdi's *I masnadieri*. Two years later, Jenny Lind retired from the operatic stage and continued her career purely as a concert singer.

*Sophie Loewe*, soprano, was born in Oldenburg in 1816, and studied singing in Vienna, where she made her début at the early age of sixteen in Donizetti's *Otto mesi in due ore*. Later, she created a furore in Berlin as Isabella in Meyerbeer's *Robert le Diable* and Amina in Bellini's *La sonnambula*. In London in 1841 she was successful in Bellini's *La straniera* at Covent Garden. She created the rôle of Elvira in *Ernani* in 1844. Upon her marriage to Prince Lichtenstein in 1848, she retired from the stage. She died in 1866.

*Marcellina Lotti de la Santa* (1831–1901), soprano, sang Mina in the première of *Aroldo* in 1857.

*Francesco Lucca* (1802–1872), worked for some years for Ricordi as a music-engraver, before founding his own music publishing firm with his wife Giovanna.

*Maria Malibran* (1808–1836), daughter of Manuel Garcia, was one of the most famous singers of the nineteenth century. Although her voice was classified as mezzo, she sang such soprano rôles as Amina in *La sonnambula* and Leonora in *Fidelio*.

*Henri Meilhac* and *Ludovic Halévy*, authors of *Froufrou*, were boulevard dramatists and librettists. They wrote 21 libretti for Offenbach, *Carmen* for Bizet, and *Manon* for Massenet. Halévy was the son of the composer, Léon Halévy.

*Saverio Mercadante* (1795–1870) composed about sixty operas, among them *Il giuramento* which is still occasionally revived. Verdi was to some extent influenced by him. From 1840 until his death, Mercadante was Director of the Naples Conservatorium.

*Bartolomeo Merelli* (1793–1879) was for a time the impresario of La Scala, with interests in Vienna and elsewhere. He accepted Verdi's *Oberto* for La Scala in 1839, and also staged his three following operas.

*Henrietta Meric-Lalande* (1798–1867), French soprano, was a pupil of Garcia. Chorley wrote of her that her voice 'had contracted a habit of trembling, in those days a novelty (would it had always remained so!)'.

*Raffaele Mirate* (1815–1885), tenor, was the first Duke in *Rigoletto* in 1851.

*Giuseppe Montanelli* (1813–1862) was a professor of law who became a patriotic fighter. In 1857 he helped Verdi by re-writing several of Piave's verses for *Simon Boccanegra*. In 1859, Montanelli returned to Italy from his exile in Paris in order to fight in the ranks of Garibaldi's Alpine Brigade against the Austrians.

*Emanuele Muzio* (1821–1890) was Verdi's pupil and amanuensis. The son of a village cobbler in Zibello near Busseto, he had, like Verdi, been helped and encouraged by Antonio Barezzi. He remained Verdi's friend and staunch disciple for life. He composed operas, and achieved a certain success as a conductor. In 1861, he conducted *Un ballo in maschera* in Boston.

Before he died (see Letter 259) in Paris, in a hospital with no friend beside him, Muzio left a will in which Verdi's letters to him are mentioned: 'It is my *absolute wish* that all of them be burned, because I do not wish them to become objects of gift or, in time, of commerce, traded for profit for their autographs.'

*Nicolini* (1834–1898), was a French tenor, who, after making his début under his real name of Ernest Nicolas, went to Italy, and sang as Nicolini. In London, he frequently partnered Adelina Patti, whom he married in 1886.

*Charles Nuitter* (1828–1899) was a French librettist and writer on music. In collaboration, usually with A. Beaumont, he wrote a large number of libretti, including several for Offenbach. He also translated many opera libretti from German and Italian. In 1865, he became archivist of the Opéra. Nuitter and Beaumont were the librettists of the revised French version of Verdi's *Macbeth*.

*Adelina Patti* (1843–1919), soprano, was born in Madrid, but came from an Italian musical family. She made her operatic début as Lucia in Donizetti's *Lucia di Lammermoor* in New York in 1859, before she was seventeen. Two years later, she appeared in Bellini's *La sonnambula* at Covent Garden, to great acclaim. Rosina in *Il barbiere di Siviglia* was one of her most popular rôles, for which Rossini re-arranged much of the music for her voice and range. Her last public appearance was at the Albert Hall, London, in 1914, when she was nearly seventy-two.

*Maria Piccolomini* (1834–1899) was the soprano Verdi wanted for Cordelia in his proposed *Lear* in 1858.

*Antonio Poggi* (1808–1875), created the tenor rôle of Carlo in *Giovanna d'Arco*, at La Scala in 1845.

*Józef Poniatowski* (1816–1873), Polish singer and composer, was the great-nephew of Stanislaus Augustus, King of Poland. He studied composition under Ceccherini, and wrote a number of operas which were produced in Italy and Paris. After the 1848 revolution, he lived in Paris as the plenipotentiary of the Grand Duke of Tuscany, who made him Prince of Monterotondo. After Sedan, he followed his friend Napoleon III to England, where he died. His opera *Gelmina*, written for Patti, was produced at Covent Garden in 1872.

*Adelaide Ristori* (1821–1906) Italy's great actress of the nineteenth century, was the greatest rival of the Swiss Jewess, Rachel (1821–58).

*Pietro Romani* (1791–1877), musical director of the Teatro della Pergola, Florence, when *Macbeth* had its première in 1847, was also a composer of operas and ballet music. For the Florence performances of Rossini's *Il barbiere di Siviglia* in 1816, he wrote a bass aria, 'Manca un foglia', to replace Rossini's 'A un dottor della mia sorte' which the singer found too difficult. Romani's aria is still occasionally heard in performances of Rossini's opera.

*Giorgio Ronconi*, baritone (1810–1890), was the first Nabucco at La Scala in 1842. He sang at Covent Garden nearly every season for twenty years, and was greatly admired as Rigoletto. He continued to sing until 1874.

*Giovanni Battista Rubini* (1795–1854), Italian tenor, was famous for his Bellini roles. During the composition of *Il pirata*, Rubini stayed with Bellini, trying out the tenor passages as they were composed.

*Marie-Constance Sass* (1838–1907), Belgian soprano, sang at the Paris Opéra for ten years from 1860. In 1867, she created there the rôle of Elizabeth in Verdi's *Don Carlos*.

*Maria Spezia*, soprano, was the Violetta of the second Venice production of *La traviata* in May 1854.

*Teresa Stolz* (1834–1902), Czechoslovakian soprano, was the first Aida in Italy in 1872, and sang in the first performances of Verdi's Requiem in 1874. In February 1869 she sang Leonora in the revised *Forza del destino* in Milan.

*Eugenia Tadolini* (b. 1809), soprano, created the title rôle in Verdi's *Alzira* in Naples in 1845.

*Antonio Tamburini* (1800–1876), baritone, was renowned for the beauty and agility of his voice. He is said once to have astonished the prima donna in Mercadante's *Elisa e Claudio*, and to have frightened her off the stage, by singing her rôle as well as his own, duets and all.

*Felice Varesi* (1813–1889) was one of the leading baritones of his day. He created the title rôles in *Macbeth* (1847) and *Rigoletto* (1851). He was also the first Germont père in *La traviata*, but is said to have given a merely perfunctory performance on the first night of that opera in 1853.

*Auguste Vianesi* (1837–1908), Italian conductor, completed his musical education in Paris. He conducted in New York, Moscow, St Petersburg, and London where he was in charge of the Italian operas at Covent Garden for twelve years. He eventually became chief conductor at the Paris Opéra.

# Index

(The numbers refer to pages)

# List of Recipients

(The numbers refer to letters)